Robert Charles Leslie

Old Seas Wings, Ways, and Words, in the Days of Oak and Hemp

Robert Charles Leslie

Old Seas Wings, Ways, and Words, in the Days of Oak and Hemp

ISBN/EAN: 9783337035303

Printed in Europe, USA, Canada, Australia, Japan

Cover: Foto ©ninafisch / pixelio.de

More available books at **www.hansebooks.com**

OLD SEA WINGS, WAYS, AND WORDS.

OLD SEA WINGS, WAYS, AND WORDS,

IN THE DAYS OF OAK AND HEMP.

BY

ROBERT C. LESLIE.

WITH 135 ILLUSTRATIONS BY THE AUTHOR.

LONDON: CHAPMAN AND HALL, Limited.

1890.

PREFACE.

It was in December, 1884, that I received the following kind words of encouragement from Mr. Ruskin, about some sketches and notes upon old ships, boats, sails, and rigging:—

"My dear Leslie,

"I never saw anything half so delightful or useful as these compared sails so easily explained. Do set yourself at this with all your mind and time on this plan. It will be the most refreshing thing to me to take it up with you I could possibly have.

"Ever your grateful,

"J. Ruskin."

Since then, I have been collecting material, and working in this same direction; and in 1887 I sent an illustrated article to Messrs. Harper Brothers, which appeared in the August number of their magazine for that year.

I have to thank Messrs. Harper for allowing this article to be incorporated with the present work. Most of it has however been entirely rewritten and rearranged, with much additional matter. In treating a subject of such vast dimensions as the build and rig of the ships and boats of the past, I have found it quite impossible to do so in a modern, exhaustive, or even in a systematic way; so that, to use a family motto, I have merely tried to "grip fast" or hold on to those few facts which, during many years devoted to the study of marine stores, I have chanced to fall in with, in reading, painting, or travelling, or from observation and experience afloat, or when at work among practical boat-builders in the boat-yard, building, repairing, or fitting out my own boats.

Writing upon such a technical subject it has been impossible to avoid using much of the old-sea language; but in doing so I have, whenever I could, tried to point out how such terms originated, and their connection with similar ones in use on shore.

ROBERT C. LESLIE.

CONTENTS

CHAPTER I.

INTRODUCTORY.

PAGE

Life afloat among the ancients, and in the Middle Ages, probably not so far behind that of shore life as we are apt to think—Want of reliable records of sea-life and shipping of the past—The sea, and those that go upon it, more conservative than the land and landsmen—The life of the old shipman more distinct from that of life ashore than to-day—Old sea-going craft a floating part of their country more than now, etc.—Steel spars and wire rigging, and their effect upon the modern seaman—"The sweet little cherub," etc., no longer wanted 1

CHAPTER II.

SEA WINGS—THE SQUARE AND LUG SAILS OF THE NORTHMEN, ETC.

Difficulty of finding anything satisfactorily explained in an Encyclopædia about sails—Spencer's definition of a sail—An early form of sea wing—The flying-proah—The Chinese junk—Squaresails, courses, or "pacfi"—A maincourse and details—The bowline—Lugsails, Deal boats, etc.—A Norwegian squaresail—The bilandre and Yorkshire billyboy 11

CHAPTER III.

THE GIBBOUS OR TRUE SAIL-WING OF THE SOUTH.

Leading edge and after leech of a sail-wing—"Cut of his jib:" a good old maxim—Lifting power of jib—Gybing—Transition rig—The ketch, origin of the term—The bomb-ketch,

French and English—The old lateen-mizzen—"Bagpipe the mizzen"—Crojacks and spankers—Origin of forward rake of foremast—Bowsprits, spritsail-yards, and topmasts; value of them and the spritsail in action, boarding, etc.—The origin of the jack staff 26

CHAPTER IV.

THE FULL-RIGGED SHIP.

Old three-masters—The polacca—A Genoese carrack—The lateen-yard—The strength of the pine—Mast-building—The old French chasse-marée—Beer Head boats—Beaching them—Clench and carvel work—Brixham trawlers—Clench boat-building—The "Portaferry frigate"—Origin of the term "On the stocks"—Boat-building by machinery—Boats for Arab shooting, or for ascending or shooting the Nile cataracts 40

CHAPTER V.

LONG AND SHORT SAIL-PINIONS.

Nile boat and the Dutch eel-schuyt—Clipped sail-wings—Lugsails of the Adriatic—Hudson River sloop—Lazy-lines and squalls on the Hudson—Rochelle cutter—Her net—Stone trawl-heads—Rochester bawley-boat—The old king's cutter—Her dimensions, spars, etc.—Modern racing yacht—Limit of lead and leverage—The *America* and Squire Weld—American yachts and pilot-boats—Fit of their canvas—The *Henrietta*—Tidal seas and English yachts—The centre-board—The inventor of it—The *Lady Nelson* centre-board store-ship—Rudders below keel in Venetian craft and Yorkshire cobles 54

CHAPTER VI.

WHERRY-BUILT BOATS.

Probably of Norse origin—The Portsmouth and Ryde wherry—The old bumboat, etc.—Norfolk wherry—Yoke steering gear, etc—Spritsails—The London barge—Her rig, leeboards, and sail-rudder—Antiquity of the Thames barge—A thirteenth-century ship 74

CHAPTER VII.

"UP TO THE SEA," ETC.

Dutch fishing-boats at Scheveningen — Italian lake - craft: their rudders, and those of Rhine boats—The "timoneer" — Rig and sail of lake-craft, "robands," etc.: their low bow—The Arab dhow—St. Paul's ship—Slavers, etc.—A Baltimore clipper—The ten-gun brigs—Distinction between the true brig, or brigantine, and snow—The English experimental brig, *Flying-fish*—The end of British naval sailing seamanship—H.M.S. steam-frigate *Firebrand* ... 87

CHAPTER VIII.

ORIGIN OF THE CUTTER.

The only safe way of learning to-day much about the rig of ancient shipping—Southern origin of the cutter-rig—The Brighton hoggy—The old Itchen Ferry rig—Advantages of the cutter-rig—American cutters, etc.—The modern yawl —The true yawl or dandy—Drawbacks to the fore-and-aft rig, with the exception of the lateen-rig and French lugger, for sea-going ships 104

CHAPTER IX.

UNDER SAIL AND OAR.

An eighteenth-century galley—Arrangement of her benches and oars for development of man-power—Comparison between it and modern horse-power of nineteenth-century war-ship—The carrosse, or captain's cabin, origin of the "coach" of our old ships—Rig of a galley described—A suggestion—Decorations, etc.—The galley's offspring, the eighteenth-century galley-built corvette—Mode of attack by galley, the origin of the importance attached by our old seamen of always getting and retaining the weather gauge of an enemy—A sixteenth-century sea-fight, etc. 114

CHAPTER X.

FIGURE-HEADS.

"Old Friends"—Figure-heads ashore, on and off duty—Heads of "Fighting *Téméraire*" and *Victory*—The *Téméraire* at Trafalgar, and towed to her last berth—Turner's accuracy in certain details in this picture—The anatomy of a sea-going ship's beak-head, etc.—An early type of true stem—The upright American axe-bow—The old frigate bow, some advantages and drawbacks of it—Bowsprit gammoning—A naval figure-head out of place—From the eye of the Chinese junk to the highly developed human eighteenth-century figure-head, etc. 131

CHAPTER XI.

FIGURE-HEADS (*continued*).

Strange head of New Zealand war-canoe—How did it get there?—The old rampant lion-head—"The lion's whelps"—"The sweep of the lion"—A Frenchman's description of and objection to—A Yankee skipper's objection—An equestrian figure-head, and its connection with the fate of Charles I.—The *Sovereign of the Seas*—Her knight-heads, apostles, and cat-heads—Career and fate of this ship—A later equestrian head, the *Royal George*—Why she was lost—Coloured figure-heads of old war-ships—A figure-head laid up in ordinary—Figure-heads and their removable limbs in action—The modern steamer's geographical head—The respectable nineteenth-century merchantman's head—A very humble little lady-head—A revival of her in other forms among yachts, etc.—Figure-head in repose 146

CHAPTER XII.

OLD SEA-LIGHTS.

The sea-chandelier — Great size of early poop-lanterns, and reason for it—Importance of the ship-chandler and art of candle-making to old seamen—Night-signal at Battle of the Nile—Rodney's night-action off St. Vincent, and naval manœuvres in 1781—Code of old naval night-signals—How St. George's Channel was lighted a hundred and forty years back—Between-decks and below in the cock-pit during a night-action, etc. 164

CHAPTER XIII.

THE OLD SHIP-FARM.

A luxurious voyage about the Cape in 1682—A New York packet-ship's long-boat forty years ago—The old sea-cow—Stock not always home-fed at sea—Great value of the pig as sea-farm stock, and superiority of ship-fed pork—The goat and his appetite on board ship—Naval model sea-farm—Poultry bred at sea—A crowing hen—Root crops in the lower hold, and other crops in the jolly-boat 176

CHAPTER XIV.

OLD GROUND-TACKLE.

From hemp and sails to chain and steam—A lost art—Keeping a clear hawse—Size and weight of old hemp cables—The old wooden-stocked anchor—Some advantages of it—A ship's "manger," and what she disposed of in it—A foul anchor—Two round turns in the hawse—Consequent troubles—"The bitter end"—Anchoring under sail and steam—Big and little ships as roadsters—Dragging, etc.—Proceedings on board Lord Anson's ship, *Centurion*, anchored off the island of Tinian—Wind against tide—Pooped by her long-boat—Drives to sea with three cables hanging in her hawse, etc. 184

CHAPTER XV.

EARLY NAVIGATORS AND THEIR NAUTICAL INSTRUMENTS.

An early training college for young gentlemen at Wapping New Stairs—The whole art of navigation as taught there by Joshua Kelly, mariner—Domestic navigation—A Dutch picture of sea-bottom—Five ways of finding the longitude—A sand clock—Its chimes—Making eight bells—"Flogging the clock" or glass—One that was never flogged, painted for us by Mr. Hogarth—A good rule for all master-mariners—The old binnacle—Captain Cook's compass—Davis's quadrant—The cross-staff—A star clock—A frigate's day's work at sea in 1742—The traverse-board ... 200

CHAPTER XVI.

THE BLACK X LINER.

Security of the Atlantic passage between Bristol and New York 150 years back—An extinct skipper and his ship—A popular and lucky captain—His precautions against fire—Useful passengers, mercenary seamen, and ungrateful owners—A steerage passage—Sleeping and cooking arrangements, etc. 216

CHAPTER XVII.

FROM THE ST. KATHARINE DOCKS TO THE DOWNS FIFTY YEARS AGO.

Definition of a packet—The dock quay on sailing day—Those who live by seeing ships out of dock—Temperance ships—Christian knowledge and crime—Their diffusion and emigration—Latter-day Saint and ship-chandler—Sound and motion—"Any more for the shore?"—Too late—In tow—Brought up in the Lower Hope—A very quiet night—Under way again—Topsails *versus* steam—The pride of the morning—Feeling the way over the flats—A freshening breeze—Ready about—To windward through the Gull Stream into the Downs 230

CHAPTER XVIII.

THE PILOT.

A Channel letter-box—A man found at sea—Pleasant flavour of the land about him—The pilot's hat—Sad Old-World prejudices of a through-and-out Trinity pilot—A pilot's fare and lot not all cakes and ale—Aversion of pilot to long walks and short naps—Blind faith of passengers in him—The pilot as a man of business on the Stock Exchange, etc.—Examiners examined—Weakness and mannerism of elderly pilots—Foreign pilots—A French and Yankee one—Modern pilot's risks and work—The old rule of the road at sea—Pleasures of the starboard tack—Sailing in convoy, etc. 244

CHAPTER XIX.

THE WINGLESS WAR-SHIP OF THE FUTURE, AND THOSE IN CHARGE OF HER.

A seaman's workshop—His tools, etc.—The old definition of seamanship—Soldiers and sailors compared as firemen—Sea-legs required for work upon a modern mastless war-ship—An old one, and how she behaved—How France will always command a good and constant supply of ready-made sailor-men—The naval officer of the future as a protection of our sailing merchantmen—"Lame ducks," or broken-down steamships under canvas—Stokers and firemen as a boat's crew—A prize-master in the hands of his prisoners 256

CHAPTER XX.

AN ALPHABETICALLY-ARRANGED LIST OF SEA-TERMS, SOME OF WHICH, THOUGH OBSOLETE AS TO THEIR MEANING AFLOAT, ARE STILL USED ASHORE 267

LIST OF ILLUSTRATIONS.

	PAGE
Front Door, or Entry Port, of 18th-Century Ship	5
Poor Jack	9
Sea-urchin's Ship	10
Flying Proah (Friendly Islands)	12
Chinese Junk	14
Lateen-foresail, with Sheet forward	16
Windward Side of Ship's Mainsail	16
Lee Side of Ship's Mainsail	17
Scotch Skiff, whole Sail, Macaroni Lug	17
Scotch Skiff, Sail reefed, Macaroni Lug	18
Deal Galley-punt	21
Norwegian Coaster	23
Flemish Bilandre	24
Yorkshire Billy-boy	25
Bird's Wing	27
Jib cut for making	28
Transition Rig between Lateen and Square Sails	30
Man-of-war Ketch	31
French Bomb-ketch laid Head to Wind, under Mizzen-topsail	32
Old Frigate, with Lateen-mizzen	33
Mizzen "bagpiped"	34
Bowsprit and Spritsail on a Wind	36
Spritsail-topmast, 16th and 17th Centuries	37
Boarding-axe	39
Squaresails, 18th and 17th Centuries	41
Staysails, 18th and 17th Centuries	41

LIST OF ILLUSTRATIONS.

	PAGE
Lines and Timbers of French Corvette	42
French Corvette, 18th Century	43
Polacca-rigged Bark	44
Genoese Carrack, or Carrick	44
Section at Deck of made Mast, and Mast showing Hoops and Rope Wooldings	45
Norman Chasse-marée	46
Beer Head Fishing-boat	47
Boat-builder's Old Hammer	50
First Stage of Clench-built Boat, *on Stocks*	52
Dahabeeyah of the Nile	55
Channel Island Boat	56
Coaster of North Adriatic	57
Dutch Sloop	58
Hudson River Sloop	59
Rochelle Trawler (West France)	60
Rochester Bawley-boat	62
Old King's Cutters	64
King's Cutter on the Stocks	66
Yacht *Henrietta*	69
Venetian Craft, with Rudder going below Line of Keel	72
Old Portsmouth Wherry	76
Norfolk Wherry	78
Topsail Thames Barge	82
Barge, with Sail reduced by Brails, or Sixty Tons of Bricks, in a Squall	83
Some 14th-Century Ships (as usually drawn for us)	85
Scheveningen Boat	88
Italian Lake-craft (Como)	91
Rhine Barge Rudder and Tiller, also Rudder of Boat on Lake Constance	92
Side-slung Rudder on Lake Isao	92
Arab Dhow	94
Piratical Chinese Junk	95
Smuggling Junk	96
Baltimore Clipper or Slaver	97
True Brig of 1780	100

LIST OF ILLUSTRATIONS.

	PAGE
H.M. Brig *Flying-fish*	101
H.M. Steam-frigate *Firebrand*	102
Lateener, with Sail "abidot"	106
Brighton Hoggy	106
Old Itchen Ferry Boat	108
Dandy-rig	111
18th and 17th Century War-galley	115
Half-deck Plan of Galley, showing Arrangement of Benches; also Stern View, and Two Half-sections	116
Oar of Galley	117
Galley's Shroud, with Toggle Connections between it and Deadeye	121
Galley-built Corvette	126
Armed Xebec, Spanish or Arab, of 18th and 17th Centuries	127
Xebec with Sails "en Oreilles de Lievre" (Hare's Ears, or Goose-winged)	130
"Old Friends." From a Drawing by H. Stacy Marks, R.A.	132
Head of "Fighting *Téméraire*" (Turner's), a 98-gun Ship	134
Head of *Victory*	135
Head of 18th and 17th Century War-galley, with Half-deck Plan of the Same	137
Head of Greek War-galley (Old Coin)	138
Bow of 18th-Century Line-of-battle Ship on the Stocks, before the addition of the Beak-head	139
Decoration on Stem of Ram-bowed Ironclad	139
Early Egyptian Boat, with Lotus *Stem* at either End	140
Figure-head of H.M.S. *Warrior*	143
Figure-head of *Jupiter* (French 28-gun Ship)	144
Head of New Zealand War-canoe	147
One of the Lion's Whelps	148
Lion-head, 18th Century, French	149
English Frigate-head, 18th Century	150
Sovereign of the Seas, 1637. From a Drawing by the elder Vandervelde	152
Head of *Royal George*, 1756	155
Trafalgar, 190 Guns. Lord Nelson housed	158
Figure-heads in Action	160

LIST OF ILLUSTRATIONS.

	PAGE
A 19th-Century Ruler of the Waves	161
Figure-head of Collier Brig	162
Figure-head in Repose (Tom Tug)	163
Arrangement of 17th-Century Poop-lanterns	165
Night-signal Lanterns, Battle of the Nile	167
An Old Lighthouse	172
Light-rooms and Magazine	174
Deck Farm-buildings, etc., on board New York Packet, 1840	178
Frigate's Cable-tier, etc.	186
Old Wooden-stocked Anchors lying in State	187
Brig riding in the Downs	193
Centurion riding in Gale off the Island of Tinian	197
Master-mariner Costume of 1740	201
Old Sea-clock	205
Old Binnacle	208
Captain Cook's Compass	209
Figure with Davis's Quadrant	210
Cross-staff, and Manner of Using	210
Ring-dial, or Astrolabe	212
The Nocturnal	212
Traverse-board	215
Black X Line of Packet at Sea	219
Steerage Cooking-galley	225
Ship in Tow of Thames Tug	236
Light Colliers dropping down with Last of Ebb	237
Heaving the Lead	241
French Pilot-boat	253
Dutch Sailor on his Narrow-backed Horse	258
Skiff of Duck-pond	266
An Adze, or Addice	268
Anchor and Parts	269
Carved Belfry	274
Bowline-knot	278
Capstan, with Bars, etc.	281
A Carrick-bend	281
Cartridge-box	282
The "Coach"	284

	PAGE
Ship's Stern, Counter, etc. (Vandervelde)	287
A Dogger	289
Pole-mast, Top, and Garlands	295
Outside of Old Top-gallant Forecastle	297
Ship scudding under Goose-winged Foresail	298
Palm, or Sailor's Thimble	310
Sheep-shank Knot	317

OLD SEA WINGS, WAYS, AND WORDS.

CHAPTER I.

INTRODUCTORY.

Life afloat among the ancients, and in the Middle Ages, probably not so far behind that of shore life as we are apt to think—Want of reliable records of sea-life and shipping of the past—The sea, and those that go upon it, more conservative than the land and landsmen—The life of the old shipman more distinct from that of life ashore than to-day—Old sea-going craft a floating part of their country more than now, etc.—Steel spars and wire rigging, and their effect upon the modern seaman—" The sweet little cherub," etc., no longer wanted.

The nautical antiquary has very little in the shape of ruin (restored or otherwise) to help him in the study of the sea-castles, homes, and ways of the men whose business was upon the great waters of old; and we know to-day rather more about the structure of some pre-Adamite oyster, or of the wings of an extinct lizard, than we do of the build of hull, or cut of sail, of those ships of Tarshish and others spoken of in the Bible, but which seem to have been making regular over-sea voyages even before the days of King Solomon.

Modern life afloat is too full of bustle and anxiety to afford our sailors time to think about or study the ways and craft of the seamen of the past; while landsmen are often wanting in that technical knowledge which alone enables any one to describe clearly the details and meaning of the very few ancient marine stores he may fall in with.

This is always found to be the case on seeking for real information or instruction in books or pictures on these subjects, which are the work of men not actually connected with the sea. And probably it is owing to this that we know so little of, and so greatly underrate, the seamanship of the men by whom, and seaworthiness of the craft in which, the commerce of the world was carried on long before the fifteenth century;[*] and that it is historically rather the fashion to think that the arts of naval architecture, navigation, and seamanship leapt into comparative perfection toward the close of that time.

---

[*] We know that the Anglo-Saxon King Athelstan, soon after he was crowned, in the year 925, decreed "that every merchant who made three voyages to the Mediterranean on his own account, should be raised to honour and enjoy the privileges of a gentleman." And it is quite impossible, supposing these to have been mere coasting voyages—which for many reasons is not likely—that men undertook them in craft so utterly unshipshape as those which, even to-day, are pictorially accepted by landsmen when describing the seafaring ways of a far later date.

Now the more carefully, by the help of such light as we have left, we examine the actual progress made in these arts since then, or up to the latter part of the eighteenth century, the more certain does it appear that sea-life in the Middle Ages, and before them, could not have been as far behind that of life ashore as we are apt to think it was.

Before the introduction of steam, and iron shipbuilding, nothing connected with the great conservative sea or its service moved in leaps or bounds; and the evolution of a sea-going ship, even of the Elizabethan period, with all her complication of masts, sails, and tackling, must have required a longer time for its development than has elapsed since the days of the Armada.

We have, as I hope to show, many craft yet with us, even in England, which are still able, spite of steam, etc., to hold their own and fulfil their original purpose * under sail, which have altered little in build or rig for the last three or four hundred years. And it is only fair to infer that vessels so well contrived

---

* Since writing this, I chanced to travel from Paris to Boulogne with an English practical engineer, who, speaking of the delay and difficulties he had met with in getting certain heavy exhibits conveyed from London to the Paris Exhibition, said, "The fact is, if I had loaded them all on board a Thames sailing-barge, they would have reached Paris, not only at a cheaper rate, but in three or four days' less time!"—April, 1889.

as these did not arrive at something very like perfecttion in a day. The fact is that all those having real business upon the sea learn to distrust innovation; the phrase, "Move with the times," has almost as little meaning for them as it has for the sea itself; and with her enemy always round her, a ship must and will ever retain much of the character of an old feudal castle, and, so far as the sea is concerned, stand or fall subject to the same laws as it did; for though we may have oiled for a few minutes the crest of a modern head-sea wave into some barbaric form of smoothness, we have never, so far, been able to improve one of them off the face of the sea.

My chief object, however, in the following pages, is not so much to speculate about prehistoric shipping and its seamen, as to try to record, or hold on to, some of the forms, rigs, and ways of shipping recently passed away, or which, though still remaining among us, are rapidly doing so. Before the days of steam and iron ships, or less than fifty years ago, life at sea was far more distinct, as a way or manner of life, from that of the "*landman*" than it is now; and unless a man chance to be the skipper and part owner of a Yorkshire billy-boy, or a Dutch galliot, it is not easy for even a master-mariner of to-day to realize how much more a ship was the home of the old seafaring man, to be loved and lived in, than she is to-day, when voyages that were reckoned in months and years, are

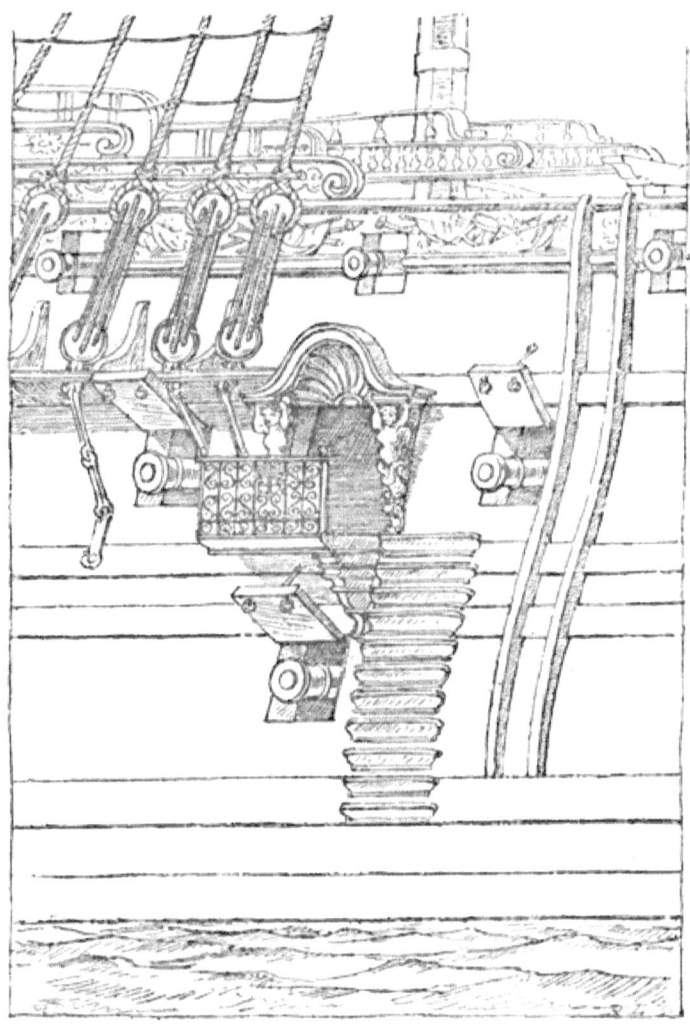

Front door, or entry port, of eighteenth-century ship.

measured in days and hours. Nothing speaks of this home-like love of his ship more than the affectionate decoration given to every little detail of their craft by the sixteenth, seventeenth, and eighteenth century sailors. Iron or steel hulls do not certainly lend themselves to much external ornament, but with a view perhaps of softening the miseries of the modern short ocean voyage, or of catching the eye of a passenger, the inside decorations of some of our steamers, as to polish and upholstery, may vie perhaps with that of the seventeenth and eighteenth century ship. We know, however, from old pictures, and a few models, something of the outside look of ships of the sixteenth and seventeenth century, and though these give nothing to guide us as to internal fittings, yet, looking at them and the richly decorated homes of landsmen of the same period, it is safe to infer that the cabins of their ships were not wanting either in ornament or comfort. The very word "state-room," still given to that limited form of comfort and sleeping arrangement for three or four persons on board a modern steamship, is an old one, like the word "saloon," "salon," or "dining-room," on board ship, and in their Spanish sense both words were probably used on board the great galleons of the Armada, etc.

In many old Spanish inns, or fondas, all the sleeping-apartments open upon a long salon, lighted only at either end; and the first idea this arrangement suggests is that of some old ship's saloon, with its row of stateroom doors on each side, the low pitch, and heavy beams crossing the ceiling, adding greatly to this ship-cabin look of these Spanish inn saloons; while the rooms opening into them are veritable state-rooms, furnished not merely as sleeping-rooms, but as the state-rooms of our older passenger-ships were, as comfortable and pleasantly decorated sitting-rooms. For it must be borne in mind that in the days of the old East Indiamen, passengers, like the ships, were in no hurry. Men did not actually live longer then, but they had more time; and a voyage was not looked upon as so much misery to be endured, or time to be got through, but as another form of life, to be enjoyed and made as pleasant as possible while it lasted. The ship was a bit of Old England afloat, where the passenger rented for so many months a well-lighted, roomy, unfurnished apartment, which, according to his taste and means, he fitted up for the voyage with numberless comforts and sea stores that none but a yachtsman would think of cumbering himself with at sea to-day; and, reading narratives of these old long sea-voyages, one is constantly coming across expressions of regret by passengers when they "took leave" of the good ship that for so many months had been their floating home.

These fine old passenger sailing-ships were, like a

man-of-war, entirely dismantled at the end of each homeward voyage, and underwent a complete overhaul and refit before starting again on an outward one. Passengers usually sold their state-room furniture by auction on board the ship upon her arrival in port.

Steam has not, happily, so far entirely banished the use of sails on board sea-going ships. But the introduction of steel spars and wire rope has so greatly changed the work, not only of fitting out but of keeping a ship's gear in repair at sea, that a modern rigger, working among iron masts and yards, supported by steel-wire shrouds and stays, with much of the running rigging of chain, has far more of the smith or engine-room artificer about him than of the old seaman rigger; while, the greater part of such work being now done in port, by gangs of experts from on shore, it follows that few of the hands, even on board a large clipper sailing-ship, especially Englishmen, are now able even to turn in a deadeye, strop a block, or point a rope, in the old "ship-shape Bristol fashion."

Some of this old "seamanship," as it was called, still remains among our coasters, fishermen, and yachtsmen, as it does among the Swedes and Norwegian seamen; though even with them wire rigging is fast taking the place of hemp in their smart little pine-built brigantines and barques. Our young naval officers and blue-jackets have also still to go through a course of instruction in such work; but, like schoolboys' Latin, it is nearly all forgotten a few years after leaving the training-ship, for want of practice. But as masts and sails are condemned as useless incumbrances upon our fighting-ships, so must sail-drill, the use of the marling-spike and palm, soon become things of the

Poor Jack.

past, and a time arrive when "the sweet little cherub that sat up aloft, and kept a watch o'er poor Jack," will find no resting-place above the iron hull of a warship.

Maybe, however, or let us hope, that the greatly improved class of seamen gunners, engine-room artificers, and stokers, by whom the navy of the coming century is to be manned, will be as much better able to take care of themselves and ships afloat without him as they certainly do now of themselves ashore, compared with the Tom Bowlings, Pipes, and Hatchways of the last century.

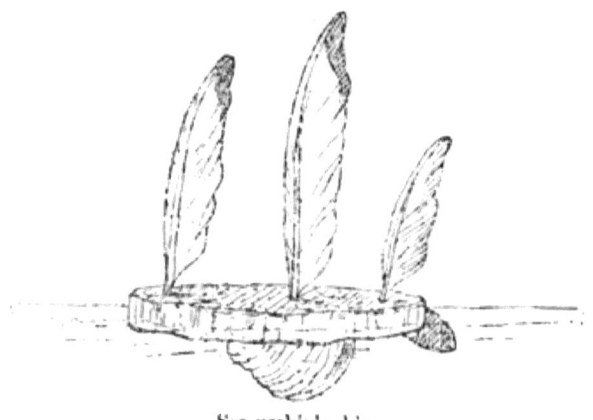

Sea-urchin's ship.

CHAPTER II.

SEA WINGS—THE SQUARE AND LUG SAILS OF THE NORTHMEN, ETC.

Difficulty of finding anything satisfactorily explained in an Encyclopædia about sails—Spencer's definition of a sail—An early form of sea wing—The flying-proah—The Chinese junk—Squaresails, courses, or "pacfi"—A main course and details—The bowline—Lugsails, Deal boats, etc.—A Norwegian squaresail—The bilandre and Yorkshire billy-boy.

UNDER the article "Sail," in my Encyclopædia, I am told that "the principal problem connected with the motion of vessels under sail on the water has for its object the determination of the resistance between the velocities of the wind and of the vessel, and its solution consists in finding algebraic expressions for those pressures, and making them equal to one another," etc. The mystery of the way of a ship under sail having been practically solved by seamen ages before modern algebraic formula were invented, I am not surprised to find in the next sentence that, even with such help, "many practical difficulties present themselves in investigating that relation." When unable to find anything worth knowing about a word in my Encyclopædia, I turn to an old "Johnson's Dictionary," being sure of finding something there—however little that something may be—which I can understand. One of the meanings given there to the word "sail" is "wing," Spencer being referred to as the authority.*

Flying-proah—Friendly Islands.

I fancy the first pinacchio, or wing of the kind, must have been like this found among the natives of

---

* While writing this, I received from Mr. Ruskin a wonderful model, four feet in length, of the primary quill of a kestrel hawk's wing; by striking the air with which "one learnt," he said, "practically more about, and realized better, the actual propulsive force of a wing, or of a well-set fore-and-aft sail, than in any other way;" for, in waving it even slowly through the air, this model feather seemed to lift, or, as a sailor would say, "take charge" of your whole arm and hand. The model (made by Mr. W. E. Dawes, naturalist, etc., of Denmark Hill) is itself quite a work of art, beautifully painted, so as to give the colour, as well as the sword-blade-like form and rigidity, combined with lightness, of the original feather.

the Friendly Islands by the Dutchman Tasman, when, unluckily for them, he first sailed their way in 1643.

This is a far more homely form of proah than that described, and so much admired, by Captain Woodes Rogers, in 1710, that he carried one to London, "thinking it might be worth fitting up there as a curiosity on the canal in St. James's Park;" and of which a second account, with drawings, appeared in "Anson's Voyage," thirty years afterwards. But though less perfect as a sailing-machine, this Friendly Island proah is most interesting from the way the yard is supported by a mast raking forward, like the "trinchetto," or foremast, of an Italian felucca. The fine race of sea-loving men of these islands are, I believe, all of Malay origin; and as the lateen-sail is the sail of the Indian Ocean, it would seem to have travelled east into the Pacific through the Malay Islanders, and probably west toward the Mediterranean up the Red Sea, *via* the Arab dhow. Among the more northern Japanese and Chinese, longer masts and the shorter yarded lugsails are found; and there may be some connection between the words "lorcha" and "lugger." There is no doubt, however, that with her ribbed, dragon-like sails, heavy rudder, or rather exaggerated form of steering oar, held in place and controlled by many "rudder bands," her strange windlass projecting outside her stem (cathead and windlass in one), this junk of China is one of the oldest links left between the over-sea ship of the past and present.*

It is rather the custom to underrate Chinese naval architecture; but it is a mistake to look upon all their

Chinese junk.

vessels as unweatherly craft, or dull sailers; and though many of the great junks, built or designed for a

* In the year 1690, speaking of certain barks used by the Chinese for passing dangerous rapids among rocks, Le Compt the Jesuit says, "they divide them into five or six apartments, separated by good partitions, so that when they touch at any place upon a point of rock, only one part of the boat is full, whilst the others remain dry, and give time to stop the hole."

particular trade, in which they make use of the regular monsoons, are not of much account except in a fair wind, those whose duty has been to cruise in Chinese waters know well enough that they often meet there piratical junks, smugglers, and fishing-boats, which, like the Arab dhow, in a good breeze can—or could a few years ago—keep their distance from some of her Majesty's steam gun-boats.

Roughly speaking, sails are all either squares or triangles. The oldest form of squaresails are those now called courses, or running sails. Originally there were but two of these, the main and fore course, known among old French seamen as "le grand et le petite pacfi." It may be noted here that the lower corners of these two sails, the sheet and tack clews—that is, the corners to which the ropes called tacks and sheets are attached—practically change in name as they change in position each time a ship goes about.

With four-sided lugsails this is not the case, nor with the square topsails above the courses, nor with any of the triangular sails, unless the sheet-clew of a lateen-foresail may be called the tack-clew when brought forward in running before the wind.

The two sketches of a maincourse, with some leading ropes, show how this change from sheet to tack is practically carried out; each corner or clew being divided among three blocks—the sheet, tack, and clewline blocks.

Compared with the courses, topsails are of recent

Lateen-foresail, with sheet forward.

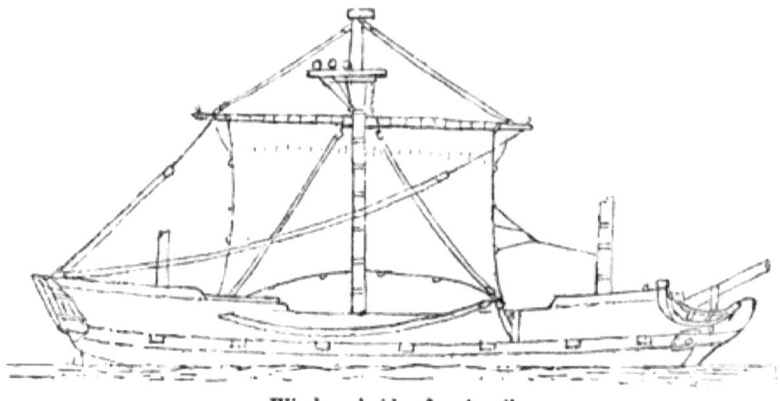

Windward side of mainsail.

date, and when square, both clews, whether used to windward or leeward, always remain topsail sheet-clews; from which it appears likely that the original form of maincourse was set and used as a lugsail, a sail which varied in shape from nearly square, to one

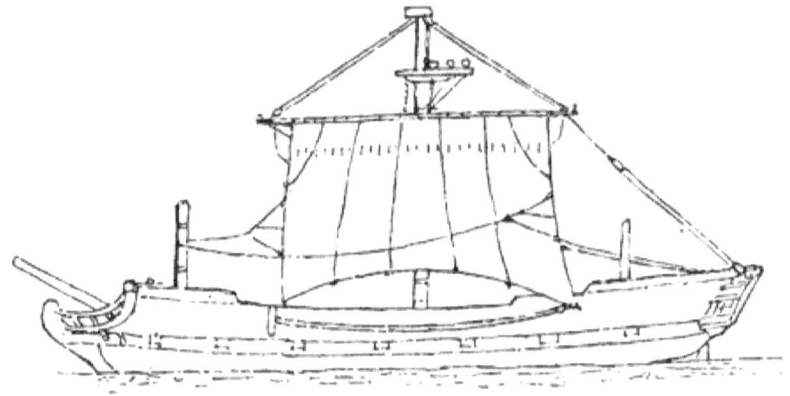

Lee side of mainsail.

which, when close reefed, is almost a lateen-sail. Some lugs, in fact, are called by English sailors

Scotch skiff, whole sail, macaroni lug.

"macaroni lugs." Perhaps, however, the name was given to this sail in contempt, as easier to handle than the other lugsails, and so suited to a macaroni or blockhead; this rig is also known as a French or standing lug, and among us as the balanced lug.

Besides the tacks and sheets, the windward view of a mainsail shows the clewlines, and the lee one the buntlines and leech, or sidelines; by the combined action of which the sail is hauled up to the yard, and the wind "spilled," as sailors say, or squeezed out of

Scotch skiff, sail reefed, macaroni lug.

it ready for furling. Like a lateen-sail, a course is always hauled or clewed up to its yard, which is now never lowered before this is done, as topsail-yards are; and, when furled, the position of the buntlines and clewlines, upon opposite sides, gives the form of the sail best known to landsmen and steamboat sailors, with the triangular ends of the clews and their blocks pendant, with the ropes of sheet and tack on either side the great mass, or bunt of the sail. In the seventeenth century, squaresails were not furled or "farthel'd" in this way, or, as it was termed, "in the body or bunt," unless the ship was in port.

Other ropes used for controlling a squaresail and its yard, are the braces, lifts, and bowlines. These last are for tautening the windward, or leading edge, or weather leech, when the sail is used near the wind; hence the term "on a bowline," for a ship close hauled. In an old fifteenth-century sea-song, which occurs in "The Stacions of Rome and the Pylgrym's Sea Voyage," published by the Early English Text Society, the bowline is spoken of thus—

> "Hale the bowelyne! now vere the sheet!
> Cook, make redy at noon our mete;
> Our pylgryms have no lust to ete;
> I pray God give hem rest!"

This bowline was no doubt originally made fast to the actual stem or bow, as it is now in the Norwegian skiff, and some other boats; and though the knot called a bowline may have been used to connect the span or bridle on the edge of the sail with the bowline, it probably took its name from being the knot used for the loop at the loose, or sliding end, of a bowstring.

All these names and details about the gear of a mainsail are pretty much with us to-day as they were in the time of Queen Elizabeth; how much older, it is hard to say. But in one thing the modern mainsail, bent to its iron yard, differs from that of a hundred years ago, which is that the yard is now permanently slung by a chain from the top, and pivots upon an iron gooseneck in front of the mast, always remaining aloft; while from entries in the logs of old ships, and pictures, it is certain that it was quite common with them to "lower ye main yard on deck," or "a portlast," or "portoise," terms synonymous with gunwale. "To ride a portlast," meaning with the lower yards on the gunwale, and topmasts struck in a gale; and the old seamen had a vast assemblage of slings, jears, etc., for this business, besides rolling tackles and trusses, to confine the yard to the mast in a seaway. While owing to the ease with which, if shot away, all this rope gear could be repaired at sea, this way of slinging lower yards was retained in the Royal Navy long after it was out of date in the merchant service.

As I said before, the sail of northern races was and is a squaresail, either slung simply like a ship's mainsail by the middle, or a very square-headed lug, like those used by the Deal men in their "galley-punts." These boats sail very near the wind, and are out in all weathers. They seldom reef, but shift both sail and mast according to the force of the wind. Like many powerful sails, this shape of lug requires great skill and care in handling (I had nearly said a knowledge of algebra), for it has to be lowered and hoisted each tack. This is done so smartly that the sail is down and hoisted again on the other side of the mast while the boat shoots up in the wind, and before she has lost her headway. They are long, deep boats, and carry much ballast, and, like their namesakes, the old

Deal galley-punt.

galleys, row as well as sail fast. Though rigged in the same way, the Deal galley is a longer, lighter, and narrower build of boat than the "galley-punt," and is mostly used under oars in calms or light winds.

The "galley-punt" is, in fact, the sea-going galley of Deal, and is a connecting-link between the galley and the three-masted Deal luggers and "cats" of twenty or thirty tons, in which heavy anchors and cables are, or were, taken off to vessels in want of them in the Downs. Steam and chain cables have, however, greatly spoiled this once important business of the Deal boatmen; and the "galley-punt" is now the boat chiefly used there for tending vessels, taking off or landing pilots, etc. In one of these the boatmen will charge a steamer passing at nearly full speed. The big sail is dropped in an instant, and the boat being protected by a large permanent fender forward, and others amidships, the monster is grappled with a short boathook to which a strong warp is lashed. A turn of this taken round a stout bollard, fitted in the boat like that in a whale-boat, enables the men, as they tow foaming through the water alongside the steamer, to hold on or ease away as required. As these boats are entirely undecked, one of the crew of five or six is, in bad weather, constantly at work with the pump.

Among other northern square-sailed boats are the "keels," used in the Tyne to carry coals for loading colliers, and which are not unlike the large one-masted square-sailed coasters of Norway.

The lower half of the sail of this Norwegian vessel is made up of bands or "bonnets," laced together across the sail, which are easily taken off and stowed away, thus avoiding the heavy roll of canvas, which, if reefed, would, after the first reef was taken in, be difficult to handle, especially when wet in a seaway. The sketch is from a photograph, and shows one of these old type of vessels before a light wind, with a small square topsail set upon the polehead of her single lofty spar. In many respects the rig of this

Norwegian coaster.

Norwegian coaster is very like that of some of the larger boats upon the Italian lakes, and was, no doubt, the rig of what was known as the Vikings' ship, described in another place.

In the Bay of Cancale, Normandy, large square-rigged fishing-boats are used, of thirty tons and over; and are locally known as "carres," an old rig probably left among these people by their Norse ancestors.

Another type of old French square-rigged coaster is the "bilandre," which, except that she wants the

Flemish bilandre.

gaff-mainsail or trysail, reminds one of a Yorkshire billy-boy—a vessel which, like the Thames sailing-barge, survives among us in all her original colours and form—the largest clinker-built craft in England, or perhaps in Europe. These old Dutch-looking vessels usually hail from Goole, and are built with their flat sides to fit certain canal locks, just as the Dutch galliot is; while the mast is stepped above deck, into what sailors call a "tabernacle," or strong trunk, built up through the deck from the keelson, so that the whole mass of spar and rigging can be lowered, like a barge's, by the forestay for passing bridges.

The billy-boy carries a large cargo, and is often manned and officered by her owner, his wife and

Yorkshire billy-boy.

family only. Nothing about her of importance has been changed for centuries; yet, wonderful to say, like the galliot, spite of steam, she still holds her own commercially, especially for the carriage of grain and other things requiring a tight, dry hold.

CHAPTER III.

THE GIBBOUS OR TRUE SAIL-WING OF THE SOUTH.

Leading edge and after leech of a sail-wing—" Cut of his jib: " a good old maxim—Lifting power of jib—Gybing—Transition rig—The ketch: origin of the term—The bomb-ketch, French and English—The old lateen-mizzen—" Bagpipe the mizzen "—Crojacks and spankers—Origin of forward rake of foremast—Bowsprits, spritsail-yards, and top-masts; value of them and the spritsail in action, boarding, etc.—The origin of the jackstaff.

LEAVING for a while these northern squaresails, with their bowlines, braces, clewlines, buntlines, tacks, and sheets, and turning to the triangles, jibs, staysails, and gibbous wings of the Latin and Southern races, the first thing that strikes one about these sails is that, like a bird's wing, the great need for all effective sail-power used to windward is a rigid leading edge, or " weather leech," obtained in squaresails only by the forward drag of the bowline; but in all the true lateen-sails by the yard or bone of the sail-wing itself; in staysails by the rigidity of the mast supporting stay; and in jibs by a stout roping kept taut in modern vessels by the use of chain halyards. Before the introduction of chain for this purpose, a cutter's jib was, like the first string of a violin, constantly getting out of tune, or in want of setting up.

Another point in all good sails is that the after edge, or leech, when held in place by the rope called the sheet, should be as nearly upright or vertical as possible; this edge is always parallel to the seams of the sail, and, like the after edge of a wing, unconfined by anything more than a hem or lightest of rope binding, save where a reef-band requires extra strength. A cloth at this after edge of a jib, or fore and aft mainsail, is at times seen shaking, while the rest of the canvas is as still as though frozen; and though this is a fault in the sail, it is better that the wind should pass it freely so, than be girt in or held by it.

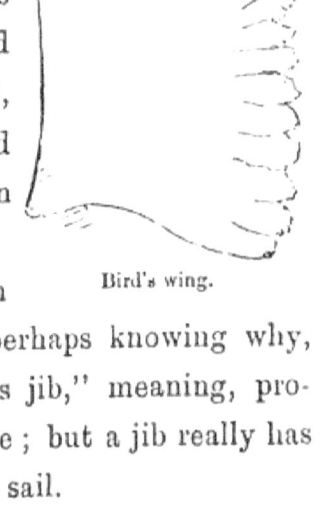

Bird's wing.

There is an old saying, often used too by landsmen without perhaps knowing why, "I knew him by the cut of his jib," meaning, probably, his nose, or leading feature; but a jib really has more cut about it than any other sail.

Here are the cloths of one, showing how it is cut a little convex upon the leading edge, and the right position of the sheet corner or clew with respect to this convexity, without which the leading edge or luff

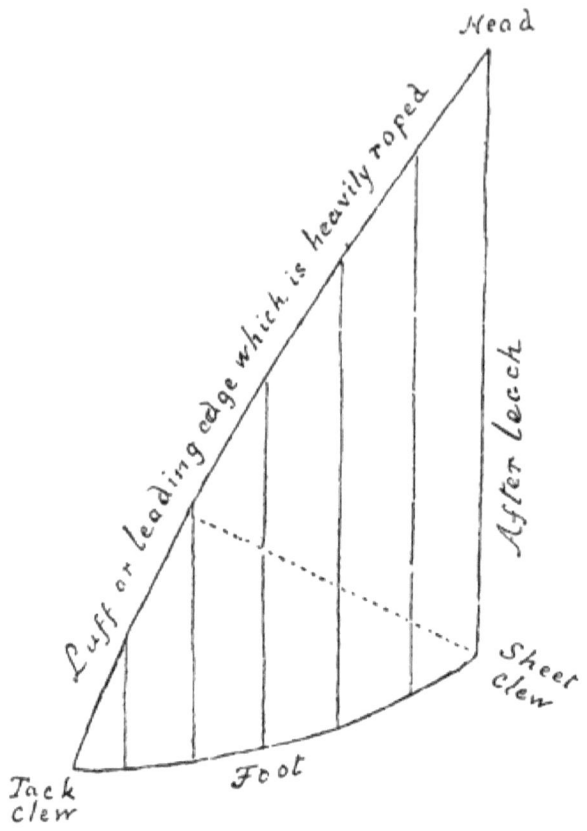

Jib cut for making.

of the jib would be concave instead of straight when roped and hoisted. Though few practical sailmakers know much of algebraic formula, they all have their fixed rules handed down from old time for cutting out sails; and, wind and water being entirely conservative elements, they seldom go far wrong. Among these rules is that of working by thirds: that is, when at a loss as to the best proportion for one thing toward another, to take a third. A boat always takes a third of the fish caught in her; the yard of a lugsail is slung a third of its length from the fore end; the convex part of a jib is at one-third of the luff, measured from the lower forward corner or tack; and the sheet-clew should be exactly opposite this point. Among seafaring people, a pious adherence to this ancient mystery saves much troublesome calculation, and when our shipbuilders thought a third a good proportion of beam to length, a fair amount of stability and handiness was insured to ships. Sailors speak of a sail as either lifting or pressing, quite independently of its propelling force, or power of driving a vessel ahead. Now all the jibs, and many staysails, are lifting sails, which do their work with the least tendency to force a vessel's lee side down. They are also, especially in boats or small vessels, safe sails to gybe, or veer round under before the wind; hence perhaps the term "gybe." The angle at which the weather edge of a jib stands, and the position of the sheet, has much to do with this lifting quality; for a cutter's foresail, though triangular, is not a lifting sail. The sail which, next to a jib, has most of this lifting power is no doubt the lateen (latin?) sail of the south, particularly as set upon the trinchetto or foremast of a felucca; and the splendid lifting, wing-like power of this sail may have led to its retention as a head-sail in the curious combination of rigs given here, the "barque" or "barca" of the Mediterranean.

In many respects the rig of an old French man-of-

Transition rig between lateen and square sails.

war ketch, with her staysail and two jibs in place of the foremast, and great lateen-sail, is an improvement on the rig of this "barca," the staysail and jibs being lighter to handle, though in a seaway the long bowsprit would be an objection; and with the wind a trifle free, the single spread of canvas of the lateen-sail would give more speed.

Giving Shakespeare as his authority, Johnson says the word "ketch" means a heavy ship; from the Italian *caicchio*, a barrel. The rig has become almost obsolete, for the Jersey dandy-rigged vessels now known by that name are fore-and-afters, while the original ketch was square rigged upon the mainmast, and carried a square

Man-of-war ketch.

mizzen-topsail. The name was originally *quaiche*, in French—spelt by the Bretons *keich*—in Spanish, *queche*, the Spaniard calling a French chasse-marée *queche-marea*. In Dutch it becomes *kaag*, the *g* being a guttural; Swedish, *koog*. The word also greatly resembles the Icelandic *kayack*, and the Turkish *caique*; while the Scotch *quaich* is perhaps of similar origin.

The French were the first to make use of this rig for mortar-vessels, or bomb-ketches, in which the mizzen-topsail was used when possible as shown here, to regulate the position of the vessel, when, all her forward rigging being cleared away except the main-

French bomb-ketch laid head to wind, under mizzen-topsail.

stay, which was of chain, to resist the burning powder, she lay head on to an enemy or fort. English bomb-vessels were usually three-masted, and delivered their fire from the side, thus exposing a larger mark to the enemy; but as the range of a shell at that time much exceeded that of any gun, this was not thought a disadvantage. The strength of timber, or scantling, of one of these old bomb-vessels equalled that of a fifty-gun ship. The French bomb-ketch carried two mortars, upon a massive timber bedding forward of the mainmast.

Another curious combination and retention of the

Old frigate, with lateen-mizzen.

lateen-sail with the square rig was the old lateen-mizzen and its yard, which, until 1670, and many years later, was always a complete triangle. Subsequently, the fore part of the sail disappeared, but the end of the lateen-yard kept its place until the beginning of the nineteenth century—found useful, perhaps, in balancing or keeping up the lofty peak. The fore and aft sail, which has superseded it, is still known as the spanker, or driver. This was originally, however, a much larger form of the old lateen-mizzen set upon the same yard, the foot being extended by a boom considerably over the ship's stern, while the head was extended by a jack-yard hoisted to the mizzen-peak, a

Mizzen "bagpiped."

sail which, in Drake's time, must have been both a "spanker and driver," as it swelled out above the old ship's lofty poops, the fore part of the long yard running down at a suitable angle with the sheer of the hull. It was the shape which the lateen-mizzen took when laid aback, with the sheet hauled up to the mizzen-shrouds, which gave rise to the old sea-term, "Bagpipe the mizzen."

This lateen mizzen-yard, about the year 1800, became a gaff; but the lower yard upon the mizzen-mast, which should have succeeded to the title, never did so, but remained a crojack, or crossjack-yard (*la vergue sèch*, the barren yard of the French), and rarely had a sail upon it, until some fifty years ago, when a Yankee captain set what he called a crojack, or mizzen-course, upon it. But old English skippers only shook their heads when they saw one, and knew the ship ten miles off for a d——d Yankee.

A clipper ship of to-day carries so many masts, and so many kinds of yards upon them, that they have almost lost their identity, and, like the streets in an American city, have numbers instead of names; so that a man may be ordered aloft upon No. 8 yard, fifth mast, etc.

In all old lateeners the "trinchetto," or foremast, rakes forward quite as much as in the Malay proah (see page 12), and for the same reason, namely, that in this way it supports the yard and sail so as to give it the lifting quality of a jib. This forward rake of the foremast is found also in most of the early types of lugger; but long after ships ceased to be luggers, and the necessity for this rake was past, a trace of it remained, a sort of fashion among old-world skippers, who were never satisfied with the look of their ship unless her fore-topgallant-mast looked down almost upon her figure-head. The old bowsprit, or "bolt-sprit" (sprit sometimes kept in place by a bolt), was almost a fourth mast, reminding one much in its original form of the trinchetto of a felucca; and the spritsails carried below

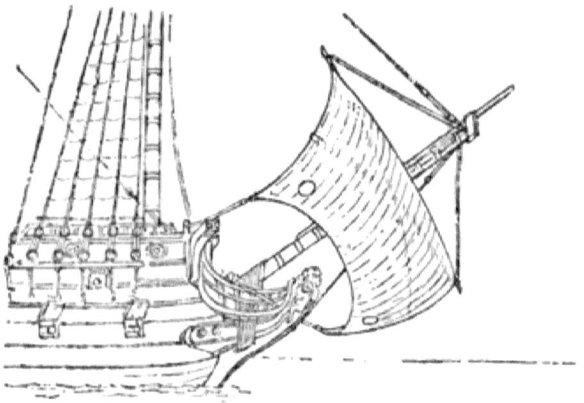

Bowsprit and spritsail on a wind.

it were greatly valued by our old seamen as a means of retaining command over a ship by veering her round under them before the wind, in case of losing their foremast by shot or tempest.

These two squaresails were not only used when going free, or before the wind, but on a wind, or with the wind abeam, by topping up the yard; while the reef-points were placed diagonally, so that, when reefed, the part of the sail nearest the sea was narrower than the upper part, and the lower sail, or spritsail proper, had holes in each corner to allow any water caught by the sail to run out of it, as the ship plunged, instead of splitting it (in French, " les yeux de la civadidre ").

Spritsails, and spritsail-topsails, were certainly sometimes carried by ships of the early part of the present century; after which the fixed, or standing

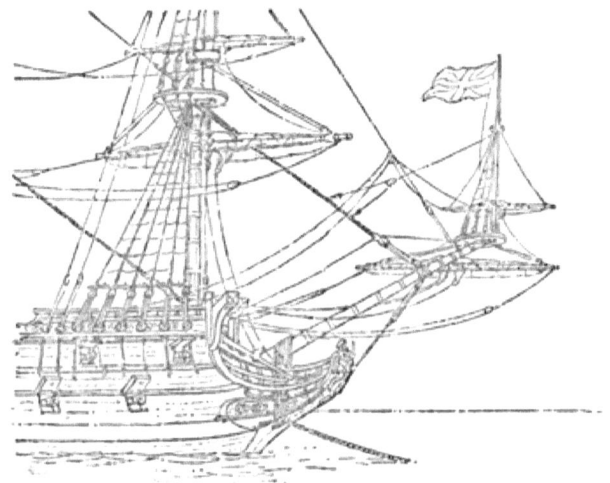

Spritsail-topmast, sixteenth and seventeenth centuries.

part of the bowsprit, was much reduced, the jibboom increasing in length, and taking the place of the long outer end of this important spar, which in ships of the fifteenth, sixteenth, and seventeenth centuries ranked almost as a fourth mast, being fitted at the end with a regular round-top, from which rose that strange little spar, the "spritsail-topmast," supported like the other three topmasts by shrouds set up with deadeyes and lanyards from this spritsail-top. This mast not only had a squaresail, the spritsail-topsail, set upon it, but terminated in a pole-head or jackstaff, upon which the flag known as "the jack," afterwards the Union jack, was hoisted.

One cannot help being struck at the old seaman-like audacity of this candlestick-like form of mast and round-top carried at the end of these long, old-fashioned bowsprits; particularly when one considers that the principal support, not only of the ship's foremast, but, through it, of her main-topmast, was the forestay, which was secured to the bowsprit. This bowsprit-top must, however, have been of use, not only as a splendid look-out place in thick weather, but as a coigne of vantage for a small body of resolute men to assemble upon just before running an enemy on board, and from which to drop upon her deck, after first clearing it by a flight of arrows, or musket-balls, or with the contents of a "stink-pot." For some years after this top and mast disappeared, the spritsail-topsail was retained, set beyond the spritsail upon the jibboom, which in the eighteenth century, with the flying-jibboom, superseded this old spritsail-topmast.

The fashion, however, of setting a small naval Union jack upon a short staff, stepped upon the cap at the end of the bowsprit, is still retained in our rigged ironclads and gunboats, a rudimentary form of this curious old mast.

The spritsail yard or yards of a ship boarding another were always braced fore and aft, as in this position they not only allowed of closer contact between the ships, but, what was of more importance, formed a good gangway for the boarders after the enemy was grappled. In attacking very lofty ships, use was often made of the pole or boarding axe; the points of several being driven one above the other into the planking of the vessel attacked, so as to form temporary scaling-ladders for the boarders.

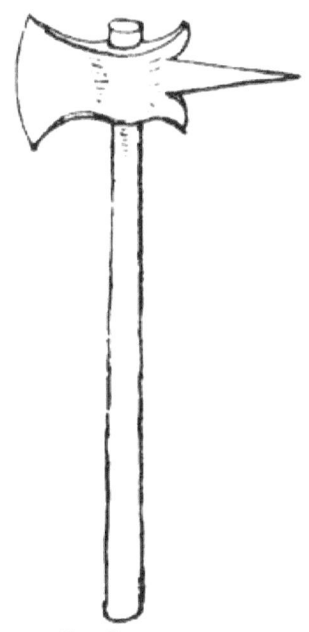

Boarding-axe.

CHAPTER IV.

THE FULL-RIGGED SHIP.

Old three-masters—The polacca—A Genoese carrack—The lateen-yard—The strength of the pine—Mast-building—The old French chasse-marée—Beer Head boats—Beaching them—Clench and carvel work—Brixham trawlers—Clench boat-building—The "Portaferry frigate"—Origin of the term "On the stocks"—Boat-building by machinery—Boats for Arab shooting, or for ascending or shooting the Nile cataracts.

UNTIL the last forty years, or when, owing to the great increase in the size of ships, the use of double topsail-yards and the division of topsails into upper and lower became almost a necessity in our rather short-handed merchant navy, the square-sails, staysails, and jibs of a full-rigged ship were, sail for sail, pretty much as shown in the next two diagrams, which go back nearly two hundred years.

There were thirty sails all told (note the number, three tens). It was under these sails that England's line-of-battle was formed, and her ships handled, by men like Benbow, Anson, Rodney, Howe, Hawke, Jervis, Nelson, and Collingwood; while of English cruising frigates and sloops we could say then, what we hardly can to-day, namely, that nothing afloat could overtake or get away from them. This was especially the case with frigates taken from the

Squaresails, eighteenth and seventeenth centuries.

French, or built upon the lines of captured French vessels. I therefore give a drawing to scale of the principal sails and gear of one of these old French

Staysails, eighteenth and seventeenth centuries.

corvettes, as a good type of fast cruiser, sea-keeper, and privateer, of 1780.

With her tall three-storied masts, tops, and crosstrees, the rig of this corvette is a long step from the simple three-masted xebecs, feluccas, and luggers; but the square-rigged polacca, or pole-rig, still seen in Mediterranean ports, forms a link in the chain.

In general arrangement of sail, the polacca (see page 44) is not unlike the old Genoese and other carracks, which in the sixteenth century brought the

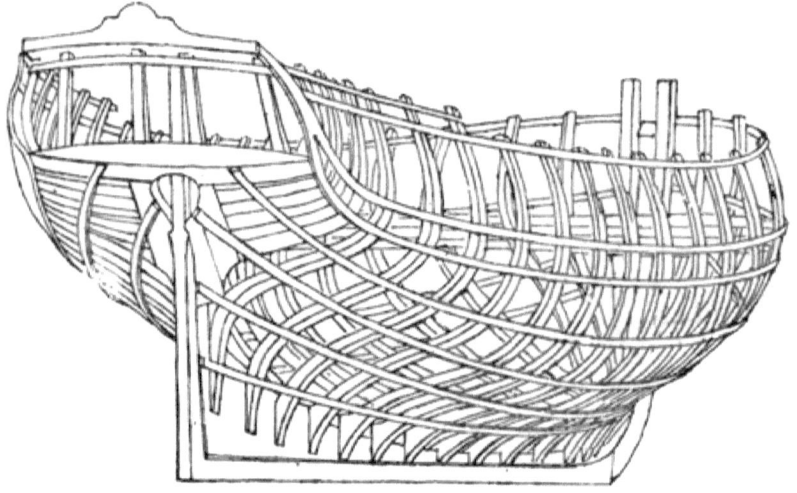

Lines and timbers of French corvette.

wines and silks of the south to the south hams of England—ships with long pole-masts of a date when large pines were plentiful.

As the lateen-yard tapers toward either end, it is always made of two spars, grown as nearly as possible of the proper size, which are fished or scarfed together, and this is done because the strength of a pine stick lies chiefly in the outside circles of the wood next

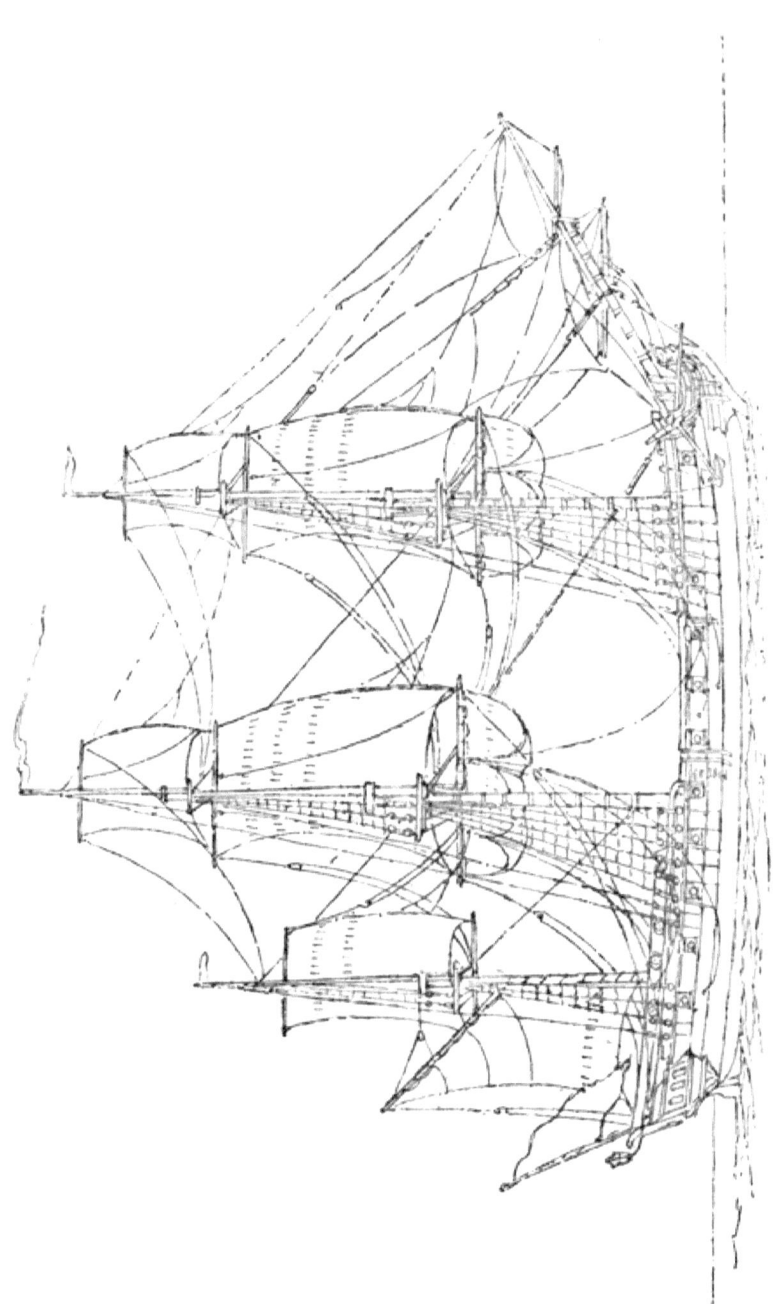

French corvette, eighteenth century.

the bark. But the polacca's masts are usually in one piece, the natural form and size of the forest pine.*

Polacca-rigged bark.

Genoese carrack, or carrick.

* In 1592 a Portuguese carrack was taken by Sir John Barrough, of 1600 tons, 165 ft. long over all by 47 ft. beam. Her mainmast, which was 121 ft. long, was 3 ft. 8 in. in diameter at the deck, and her mainyard 106 ft. long.—Charnock, vol. ii. p. 11.

As ships grew larger, and good spars became scarcer, the art of mast-making grew in importance, until it reached perfection in the mainmast of a line-of-battle ship, built up of many pieces, hooped and woolded or bound together.

Nearly all big ships' masts and yards are now tubes of iron or steel.

As one of these richly laden, richly carved carracks came rolling up Channel, a good look-out was no doubt kept from her round-tops for a very different type of pole-masted ship—the heavily built, well-manned Norman chasse-marée—a vessel which is with us to-day, pretty much as she must have been in the twelfth century—her bluff lofty bow rising sharply as though to face a sea, rather than for passage before the wind in fine weather, and with some trace of the lateen rig about her, in the heavily fished yards, high-peaked sails, and foremast close to her stem.

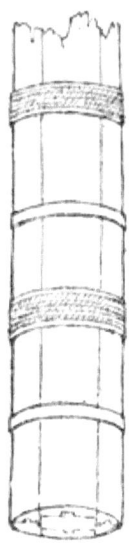
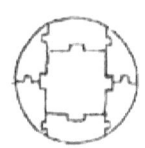

Section at deck of made mast, and mast showing hoops and rope wooldings.

Like the mainsail of the Norwegian coaster, this vessel's foresail is fitted with a deep bonnet-piece, laced to the foot of the sail, which has only one or two reef-bands in it. In rough weather the mainsail is usually stowed altogether, and the boat worked under this reduced foresail, with a storm-mizzen and jib. In light winds a maintopsail is set upon the long pole-head of the mainmast, bearing about the same proportion to the mainsail itself as the topsail set by the Norway coaster does to her mainsail.

Every day these old Norman luggers become scarcer

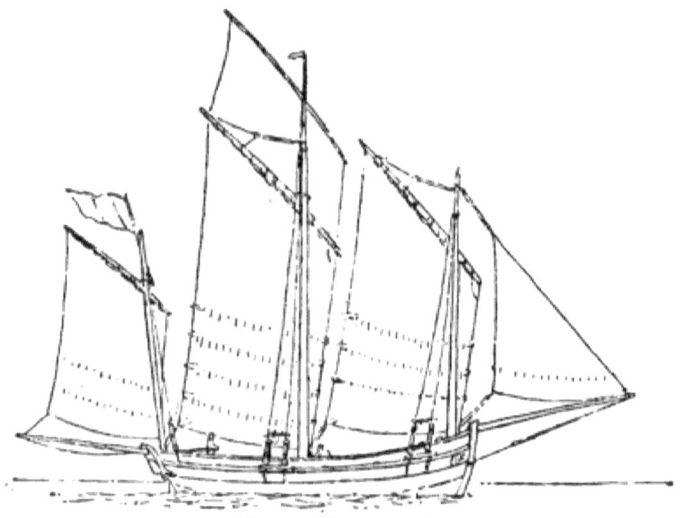

Norman chasse-marée.

—replaced by the handier ketch, or rather dandy rig— and the ponderous hull of one may be now often seen, roughly refitted as a ketch, her mainmast having been done away with, her foremast moved further aft, and her mizzen stepped a little forward.

These vessels bring across Channel to us large cargoes of onions, potatoes, etc., earning enough in this way to afford to return home in ballast, consisting usually of the roughest kind of heavy town refuse, such as old brickbats, etc. But then it must be remembered that her Breton crew are not above harnessing themselves to a truck, and hawking much of their cargo round the country for miles; and I have actually seen a horse and cart brought by them on their lugger's deck from France for this purpose, or to save the expense of hiring in England.

Beer Head fishing-boat.

This rig was much used by the French privateersmen and smugglers of the seventeenth century; and when at her best, with fifteen or thirty men to handle her, it required a smart vessel to overtake, or escape from, a chasse-marée in a breeze.

Nearly opposite the ports these vessels hail from, upon the English coast, a little fleet of some eight or ten fishing-boats are nestled together under Beer Head, which, though very much smaller, are also a true type of early ship, not unlike the chasse-marée; they are fast weatherly boats, but from the character of the sails and manner of setting them, require both care and skill in handling.

Indeed, with their high peak, long yards, and main tack, or forward lower corner of the mainsail, hooked to windward of the mast, the Beer-man's sails have more of the lateen character about them than most other professional lugsails; while the curve given to the leading edge by a small spar, something like a clothes-prop, called "the foregirt," and used instead of a bowline to twig out the weather edge both of the mainsail and foresail, also adds greatly to this lateen look when seen from a distance. These Beer boats carry no bowsprit or jib, the great foresail, the tack of which goes to an iron bumpkin, taking the place of a jib, as it does in most lateen-rigged boats; while this bumpkin is probably the origin of the spar of the same name, by which the fore tack of square-rigged vessels was extended; though in the Beer boat the bumpkin stands rather in the place of, or answers one of the purposes, of the "flech" or permanent projection beyond the stem of the Mediterranean lateeners, to which the fore tack of their foresails is also made fast. The Beer boats are rather sharp-bottomed and entirely undecked; they are used for trawling, drift-net, and line-fishing, and in landing, when the tide is up, they are sheered nearly broadside on to the steep wall of beach at Beer, against which they are pressed and held upright, when there is a sea on, by the sails, which are laid aback, some of their big stone ballast being shifted at the same time into the lee bilge, until the crew have had time to toss overboard the rest of it, after which the boat is hauled up to her capstan above high-water mark; the time chosen for these landings being, if possible, upon a falling tide, so that the boat may soon be left by the sea. Like nearly all our smaller English fishing-boats, the Beer boat is clench or clinker built. It is noteworthy that of "carvel" or smooth-built English fishing-boats, the Brixham trawlers were among the first. These cutters have much in common with certain French fishing-cutters described in another place. As far back as the time of the Armada, the Brixham trawler was mentioned as a fast vessel, suitable for carrying news, etc.; while it was the Brixham men who, about fifty years ago, first taught the North Sea fishermen deep-sea trawling, which I suspect they in turn learnt from the French. Still, all our older English cutters were clench, or, as it was sometimes called, cutter built, a mode of construction evidently left among us by the Norsemen; and as showing the size of this kind of vessel with us years ago, I may mention that when living at Sidmouth, about six miles from Beer, I had a boat-builder working with me who used a hammer that had been in his family for three generations at least, and which in his grandfather's time had driven the nails of a clench-built *ship* of a hundred tons.

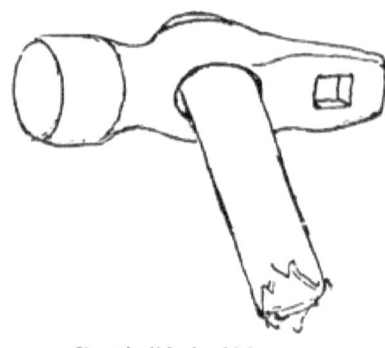
Boat-builder's old hammer.

This ancient tool weighed about four pounds, and had a hole in the tail rather over half an inch square for pushing on the washers, or "roves," and breaking off the ends of the iron nails before riveting them; somewhat such a hammer as the Vikings must have used in building their galleys.

In confirmation of William Connant, the Sidmouth boat-builder's story, there is, or was, in the library of the Dean and Chapter of Canterbury, a manuscript record of how, in 1347, "Sydmouth" supplied Edward III., for his "South fleet," "three shipps and fifty-two marriners;" which would give about seventeen men to each "shipp": while the small tonnage of square-rigged vessels of even the seventeenth and eighteenth centuries is shown by the following extract from the *Naval Chronicle* of July, 1802, which tells us that "a vessel lately arrived at Whitehaven from Strangford, which is known to have been coasting, chiefly in St. George's Channel, for a hundred and thirty years. She is called the *Three Sisters*—Donnan, master—but is better known as the Portaferry frigate; she is *thirty-six* tons burthen, and rigged at present as a brigantine; but is reported to have been formerly *ship-rigged*. It is certain that she was employed at the siege of Londonderry in 1689, and was successful on an emergency in supplying the garrison with provisions. This venerable piece of naval architecture, which, from the great improvements made in the last century, is now viewed as a curiosity, is allowed, we are told, the privilege of using any of the public docks at Liverpool free of port charges, in consequence of her having been the first vessel that entered the old dock."

As I said before, most English boats are clench-built, and this seems to hold good with many other northern types of boat, while nearly all the boats of France, Italy, and Spain, however small, are carvel-built. This would not be surprising if England's boats were the only ones that landed or were kept upon open beaches. But this is not the case, as one constantly sees numbers of carvel-built boats, of a very old type, hauled up daily, high and dry, upon the open shores of the Mediterranean and elsewhere.

Still, clench work is undoubtedly better adapted for this sort of rough usage, being both lighter and stronger than carvel work; the lapped outer skin giving to the boat almost as much strength as the ribs, which are most of them bent by boiling or steaming, and are fitted into the boat after she is planked up. So that, as plank by plank the form of the boat unfolds from the keel upwards, her model depends almost entirely upon the builder's eye, instead of on moulds or lines

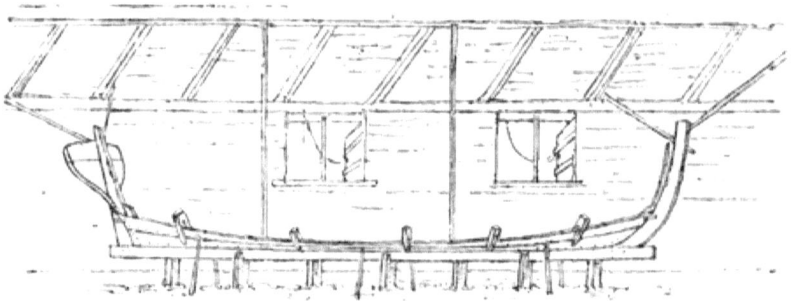

First stage of clench-built boat, *on stocks*.

laid off upon paper, or upon the mould-loft floor beforehand. Indeed, experienced clench boat-builders can finish the planking of a boat without putting a single mould or pattern into her to work by.

In carvel work, on the other hand, every frame or rib is cut out from a pattern, and sometimes none are set up in place upon the keel until all are ready. It was with a view chiefly to this carvel kind of boatbuilding, that about twenty-five years back some

Americans started a company in London for boat-building by machinery; but it came to nothing, as it was found that most English customers required the old-fashioned, tough, basket-like clench-built boat, which could be planked, ribbed, and riveted together by hand as fast as in any other way. And so, owing to insular prejudices, etc., this company wound itself up; and whenever a lot of light strong boats, to go Arab shooting in, are wanted in a hurry, orders have to be sent to boat-builders all round our coasts, which is not as it should be in a progressive country.*

* The whole of the above chapter was written in 1885, long before M. Du Chaillu's interesting book was heard of; but I am bound to say that everything connected with English boatmanship and boat-building goes to show the distinctly Viking character of our work as compared with that of French, Spanish, and Italian fishermen.

CHAPTER V.

LONG AND SHORT SAIL-PINIONS.

Nile boat and the Dutch eel-schuyt—Clipped sail-wings—Lugsails of the Adriatic—Hudson River sloop—Lazy-lines and squalls on the Hudson—Rochelle cutter—Her net—Stone trawl-heads—Rochester bawley boat—The old king's cutter—Her dimensions, spars, etc.—Modern racing yacht—Limit of lead and leverage—The *America* and Squire Weld—American yachts and pilot-boats—Fit of their canvas—The *Henrietta*—Tidal seas and English yachts—The centre-board—The inventor of it—The *Lady Nelson* centre-board store-ship—Rudders below keel in Venetian craft and Yorkshire cobles.

HAVING, in the digression on boat-building in the last chapter, drifted as far south as the Nile and its dahabeeyahs, their long, lofty pinions, suited for catching and holding every breath of air above a river-bank, remind me that I have not dwelt enough upon the great value of a high-peaked sail, especially in latitudes favoured with steady winds and weather. Indeed, wherever sails of this kind are common, it will be found, I think, that steady dependable winds are the rule. Want of observation, or knowledge of this, was one reason that the progress of our first, and let us hope, our last, military boat expedition up the Nile, was so slow; for in it our boats were furnished with sail-power of a character and size for use in half a gale of wind in English waters, in place of lofty-peaked sails, capable of propelling them before the wind against the stream of a great tropical river.

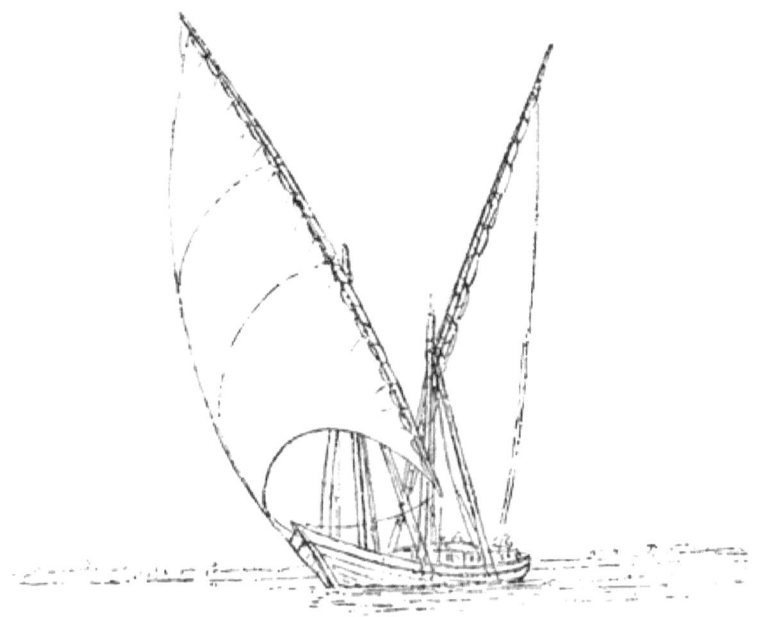

Dahabeeyah of the Nile.

It is true that from first to last this expedition, though much aided in its execution by our blue-jackets, was a soldier's scheme; while it was thought, no doubt, that higher peaked, or larger sails, might have cost us a few lives, and, so that no risks might be run, boats were sent to contend against the Nile stream with pinions clipped almost as short as the stumpy guillemot wing of a Dutch eel-boat—a wing or sail better adapted for beating dead to windward than for making the most of a fair wind. Without, however, going as far north as Holland, instances of the reduction in length of yard and sail-pinion, to suit prevailing weather, etc., may be found in certain craft of the northern ports of the stormy Adriatic, where most of the coasters and fishing-boats

Channel Island boat.

are of the clipped lateen, or almost lugger type; and these two boats, one an ordinary Jersey fishing-boat, and the other a vessel belonging to the little port of Rimini, have really more in common than with a two-masted lateener.

These luggers of the Adriatic are fine models, with handsome elliptical sterns, rather of the wherry type, having the rudder all outside. They rise well forward, with a springy sheer, and rather swan-like bow, more elegant, but reminding one greatly of the big Norman lugger. Nothing, in fact, can speak plainer of hard winds, and short heavy seas, than the build and sails of these boats. The cautious Dutchman in his schuyt is, however, the only shipman quite content to almost entirely give up the advantage of a peak to his sail; choosing for pattern the wing of a diver rather than

Coaster of North Adriatic.

that of a tern or swallow. This may be for want of sea-room when working under sail among buildings, or up the streets of his towns, where it is very desirable to keep a vessel as nearly upright as possible that she may not interfere with roofs or windows; while this form of sail and mast is easily handled or lowered and hoisted again by the skipper and his wife and family.

Though upon a larger scale, and with more hoist,

this short-peaked Dutch-cut sail was evidently the origin of the sail used on board the old Hudson River sloops and schooners, which, before the introduction of steam, and, indeed, for years afterwards, carried all the heavy merchandise between New York, Albany, Troy, and other places upon that river. Here a short

Dutch sloop.

peak was found advantageous when sailing among mountains and steep hills, between the funnel-like gaps of which heavy flaws of wind constantly come down upon this river with tremendous force; squalls which were usually met or "negotiated" by the crew of one or two men in these big sloops, by luffing, or heading up to them, and letting go the main and short-peak halyards, which were in one, when the sail came down at once upon the boom, confined to it between what were called "lazy-lines," which passed on either side the sail from the boom to the mast-head, somewhat in the fashion of a number of double topping-lifts.

Hudson River sloop.

In spite of this arrangement of sail, etc., these big sloops and schooners sometimes came to grief, and it was not uncommon, upon that part of the Hudson near West Point among the "Highlands," for a brick or other deep-laden sloop to vanish in one of these whirling puffs of wind, and leave nothing beyond a man's hat to show where she had floated a moment before. With a beam wind upon the smooth water of the Hudson, these large sloops sailed very fast, and, most of them being fitted with centre-

Rochelle trawler (West France).

boards, were as handy in turning to windward as an ordinary una-boat; they were, in fact, the origin of the present large American centre-board yachts and pleasure-boats.

With the tall mast so far forward, the sloop-rig is

certainly better suited for smooth water than for work in a seaway; and both Englishmen and Frenchmen, in their cutters and luggers, and Italians, Spaniards, and Arabs, in their lateeners and dhows, have always retained as much of the valuable peak and upright after-leech or edge in their sails as possible. Among French cutters this is well seen in an old form of them still found at Rochelle.

This vessel, which carries an enormous square-headed topsail, is pole-masted; and the great size and low position of the jaws of her gaff remind one very much of a Thames barge's sprit. She is an exaggerated type of other cutters of some northern French ports, while the old Brixham trawler had many points in common with her.

It may be noted here that the trawl-net of Rochelle is simply an oblong or nearly square bag, which, though furnished with the usual side "pockets," has no opening like our longer trawl-nets at the lower end or cod of the trawl; also that, in place of iron trawl-heads, or runners at the ends of the beam, they use two large stones, about the size and shape of an American cheese, which are bored edgeways, or through their diameter, and are thus linked by short chains to the ends of the trawl-beam—literally stone "trawl-heads."

The "Rochester bawley-boat" and the Lee

shrimper, with their short masts, long gaffs, and topmasts, are another type of fishing-vessels in which the long peak and perpendicular after edge of the mainsail is remarkable.

Rochester bawley-boat.

These boats are without a boom, and though low amidships, and bluff-looking about the bow above water, they are fast and handy for work among the dangerous sandy flats and narrow channels at the mouth of the Thames; while, owing to the shortness of their lower masts, they are, when the topsail is off them and the topmast down, like a Rochelle cutter without her topsail, at once under snug canvas.

A very different and now quite extinct form of early cutter is the old English packet, revenue cruiser, and despatch-boat of Nelson's day. Her rig is that of the old Margate hoy, the Leith sloop, and English Channel packet-boat, that Turner has shown us "coming in," in his "Calais Pier."

His Majesty William III.'s cutter, *Youngfrau*, described by Marryatt in "Snarleyyow," must have been one of this class of vessels, "which in 1699," he tells us, "protected the revenue against the importation of alamodes and lutestrings."

These old cutters were generally clench-built up to the deck, and the topmast was stepped abaft the masthead. How it stood the strain of the great square topsail is a mystery. In all old ships the mast-heads and heels, or doublings, were shorter than they are now, and topmasts must have been always lowered in bad weather, or lost. Sir Cloudesley Shovel, writing in 1690, speaks of "the heads of our lower masts as too short, which occasions our loss of many topmasts." As this early English cutter was one of the most heavily sparred and fastest vessels of her time, and had a reputation for speed even among French eighteenth-

century ship-builders, I give here the principal dimensions of one, with the length of her spars, etc., taken from an old French work on shipping, in which we are told "that some vessels of this class were built for the naval port of Brest."

Dimensions of Hull.

	ft.	in.
Length from stem to stern-post	50	0
Rake of stem	1	10
Rake of stern-post	1	4
Midship beam	21	0
Length of floor timbers amidship	10	8
Rise of floor amidship	1	5
Height of wing-transom*	10	2

Spars.

	Length.		Diameter.	Head.	
	ft.	in.	in.	ft.	in.
Mainmast	71	6	17	6	6
Bowsprit	49	0	15		
Boom	49	0	12	End	
Gaff	24	0	7½	1	5
Topmast	26	0	6½	5	6
Mainyard	39	0	7½	3	3
Topsail-yard	29	0	6½	3	3
Topgallant-yard	24	0	6	2	2
Studding-sail boom	21	0	6		

---

* "Wing-transom." This term in naval architecture is, I think, derived from the name of the long projecting sides of the counter, or overhanging stern platform, common to all galleys, xebecs, and feluccas of the Mediterranean, and which, probably from their resemblance to the closed ends of a sea-bird's wings at rest upon the water, were known as "les ailes de galere;" the wing-transom being the transom or cross beam which supported and connected these wings with the stern-post.

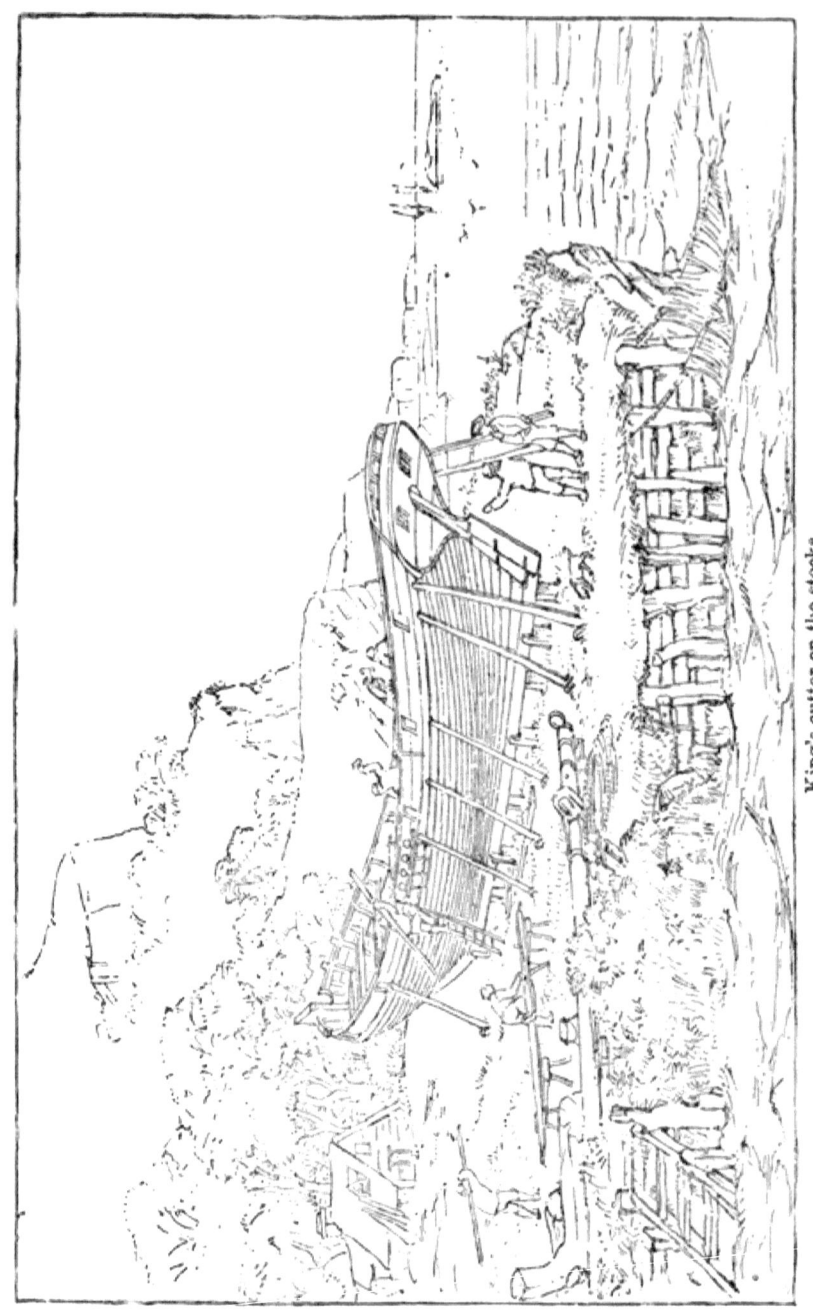

King's cutter on the stocks.

This studding-sail boom was an addition to the main boom, run out to extend the sheet of a studding-sail, or "ringtail," set abaft the mainsail in light winds. According to a very fine old rigged model of one in the Naval Museum at the Hague, these cutters carried a jib-topsail, and both lower and topmast studding-sails, set much as they are (or were) in square-rigged ships. This ancient lower studding-sail was probably the origin of the spinnaker in our modern racing cutter.

There is one feature which the English cutter of to-day shares with that much older type of fast vessel, the Arab dhow, namely, a deep heel, or great draught of water aft, in proportion to her forward draught. This feature has always been retained in our cutters; indeed, in the modern racing cutter, this cutting away of forward depth of keel has of late been carried farther than in any other vessel—the Arab dhow, I think, excepted. But many of our recent racing yachts, with their deep leaden keels, are in model little more than an axe blade on edge, going through the water, without rising to a sea, with the force of a heavy fly-wheel of some eighty tons weight.

It was formerly said of horse-racing that it improved the breed of English horses, and of yacht-racing that it led to improvements in naval architecture. Of late this has certainly not been the case with either sport; for our racers are good for nothing else, while even if, in these days of steam, any improvement were wanted in sailing-vessels, it could hardly be looked for among our yachts, up to a certain size, especially since the introduction of outside lead ballast and sliding keels. I say "up to a certain size," because there is a point at which excessive draught of water, and the strain upon spars and canvas, resulting from an unlimited amount of stability, acts as a check upon the use of lead and leverage; so that very large sailing-yachts must still be built with some kind of ship-shape form about them.

In more than one of our recent larger racing yachts, the after corner, or clew of the mainsail, though made up of eight thicknesses of new canvas, has proved too weak to stand the strain of her mainsheet in a breeze.

Some years ago (1851?), when the New York pilot-boat (for she was nothing more), the *America*, came to England and beat our best yachts, there was one man, Mr. Weld, of Lulworth Castle, a first-rate amateur yacht-builder and sailor, who seemed to understand the situation, and who soon made alterations in his yacht, the *Alarm*, which enabled her to meet the new-comer. My old friend, Mr. John Nichols, was Mr. Weld's racing skipper, and chancing one day to see some draughts of old French eighteenth-century war-ships, said, "Why, here is exactly the *Alarm's* middle section! Squire Weld must have seen this book." I mention this merely to show how far advanced naval architecture was in France a hundred years back; for few men have a better eye for a really

Yacht *Henrietta*.

fine sailing model than Captain John Nichols, one of the longest-headed yachtsmen in Southampton. But to give the yachts and their wings their due, especially the American yachts, I believe it would be hard to find a finer instance of really efficient fore and aft sail-power, with every inch doing its work, than is shown in this portrait of the schooner *Henrietta*, winner from two other American schooners of a race from New York to Cowes Roads, the distance being *sailed in fourteen days.*

The speed and power of working to windward of these American schooners was greatly helped by the wonderful fit and cut of their sails, for which all the New York river craft and coasters were remarkable; and I believe that New York sailmakers owe this knack of making sails set flat to their Dutch and Swedish ancestors, every stitch of whose canvas was, and is, always cut and set to the greatest advantage. This yacht, *Henrietta,* like the *America,* was simply a glorified New York pilot-boat, a class of schooner built expressly for speed and cruising in all weathers in the Atlantic. Our Liverpool pilot-boats, which work in St. George's Channel, are not unlike these New York boats, but built to meet shorter tidal waves, etc.

It is, I think, owing very much to the entirely different character of wave met with upon American and English yacht racecourses, that our yachts have been so unsuccessful when competing with American vessels in their own waters.

Any one who has had experience with a full-bodied beamy vessel in working to windward in a breeze, with a strong English tide under her, will understand this. Such a boat, even with a fine bow, must rise to each steep wall of water, and has nearly all the life knocked out of her, so far as headway goes; whereas a longer, deeper vessel, though wet enough, will hold her way clean through these short steep seas, in place of tossing up her bows at them. It is in this sort of tidal sea that a yacht of the *Irex* type would lead the way, though in smooth water, or over longer and truer-running Atlantic seas, she might be beaten by an American flatter-floored sloop-rigged yacht, especially when fitted with a sliding keel.

Though Captain Shanks, of our navy, was the inventor of the central movable keel nearly a hundred years ago, when it was tried in the revenue cutter *Trial*, it is to the Americans that we are indebted for the centre-board boat, a skimming-dish form of naval architecture which has produced a large crop of second-rate amateur boat-sailers; in fact, though in an English tide-rip these boats are about the wettest and most uncomfortable of small craft, they are so handy in smooth shallow waters that they may be called the landlubber's boat. There is a record, however, in the *Naval Chronicle*, vol. viii. p. 76, "of a voyage made by a Lieutenant Grant, to and from Australia in the *Lady Nelson* store-ship of sixty tons, which was fitted with three sliding keels on Captain Shanks's plan. Lieutenant Grant reported well of this vessel, as particularly adapted for purposes of discovery. This was in 1801, and she was the first English ship that passed the strait between New Holland and Van Diemen's Land."

In most of the craft which work both at sea and among the shallow lagoons round Venice, the rudder is so arranged that its action upon the boat in deep water is almost that of a centre-board—the form of

Venetian craft, with rudder going below line of keel.

hull and position of the after canvas making this action coincide nearly with the centre of effort of the boat's sails. These deep curved rudders, which are very like, and act much in the same way as, the rudder of a Yorkshire coble, are hung with great care, and fitted with a purchase or tackle for hoisting clear of the ground in shoal-water; and the lagoon-sailor, who perhaps often owed his safety in bygone times to the small draught of his vessel, still keeps all the splendid iron-work about them not only well oiled, but even brightly polished; while the rudder-heads are lovingly enriched with carving and pictures of the Virgin or of some patron saint.

CHAPTER VI.

WHERRY-BUILT BOATS.

Probably of Norse origin—The Portsmouth and Ryde wherry—The old bumboat, etc.—Norfolk wherry—Yoke steering gear, etc.—Spritsails—The London barge—Her rig, lee-boards, and sail-rudder—Antiquity of the Thames barge—A thirteenth-century ship.

THERE is a distinct connection between the words "wherry," a light passage-boat, and "ferry," the passage; Shakespeare using the word "ferry" for the boat itself. The term "wherry-built," as used by boat-builders, means a boat without a wing-transom, the ends of all the after planks terminating in the stern-post, just as the bow planks do in the stem. The true wherry, as an open boat, has no gunwale, and, if decked, no top rail to her bulwarks; the side timbers being all carried up through the water-ways, as high as, or in some cases a trifle above, the top strake.

This fashion of building appears to be of Norse or Viking origin; most of the lighter Norwegian skiffs and boats being so built. Wherries are generally clench-built, with comparatively light timbers rather far apart, which may have led to this mode of constructing the bulwarks or upper works without gunwales, of vessels chiefly employed in peaceful trade, upon inland waters.

The "trim-built wherry" of the old London Thames waterman is now, I think, almost an extinct craft, though, with its long overhanging stern, very like that of a Turkish caique, it was one of the pleasantest of water-coaches to step in or out of, at low water or half tide, from some old-fashioned shelving Thames hard. These boats were, however, without wings, and used only under "sculls" or "oars," according to the means or time at the disposal of those hiring them.

The square-sterned, dandy-rigged skiff of the Lower Thames waterman—another class of boat which, like the wherry, is built without a gunwale—still remains among us; and though now rarely patronized by the "quality" below London Bridge, she may often be seen plying among shipping at Gravesend, or even as far seaward as the Downs.

First among the true wherries come those of Portsmouth and Ryde; and for all-round good qualities few open boats to-day excel these old sea-cabs, which, before the days of steam, worked the ferry in all weathers between the main and the Isle of Wight.

Steam has shortened this passage, but it has not cheapened it; for the poet Gray, in a letter dated Southampton, 1764, describes the charms of a voyage from there to West Cowes, made in two hours, for the small sum of sixpence!

The smaller class of these Portsmouth wherries still hold their own, and ply for hire from the common

Old Portsmouth wherry.

hards of Portsmouth and Southampton—the same old bumboats that in Nelson's time tended our fleets winter and summer out among the punishing tide-rips of Spithead. Their masts being short, when the long sprit is down, and the mainsail brailed in, with the foresail and mizzen all within board, the wherry is at once under storm canvas; while, without her sprit, the low mast of a wherry made her extremely handy when going alongside an old-fashioned line-of-battle ship, below all the projecting boats, booms, davits, etc.

Besides sailing well, a wherry rows splendidly, and, built of oak and copper-fastened, is nearly imperishable, descending from generation to generation of watermen; and though I have lived for years among them, I never remember seeing an entirely new wherry, or one that was thought past repair or work. Certain boats of this kind did not always confine their operations to tending our fleet at Spithead, but now and then took a trip across Channel after a small cargo of spirits, etc. And some thirty years ago quite a small open wherry, which still plies for hire under the sporting name of the *Johnny Broome*, was intercepted on a stormy morning some miles outside the Needles by a revenue cruiser, before her crew of two men had time to get rid of her little cargo of tubs. Indeed, it is said that, owing to fatigue and the coarseness of the weather, these bold smugglers were not altogether sorry to be picked up, even by a revenue cutter.

The model of the wherry is very like that of another fine sea-boat, the Scotch herring-skiff, one of which chancing somehow to wander south among the Southampton watermen, was at once recognized by them, and, rigged as a wherry, was found to sail as well as the best of these boats of her length. Though called wherries, the low, beamy, roomy-cabined craft of the Norfolk broads are evidently built with a

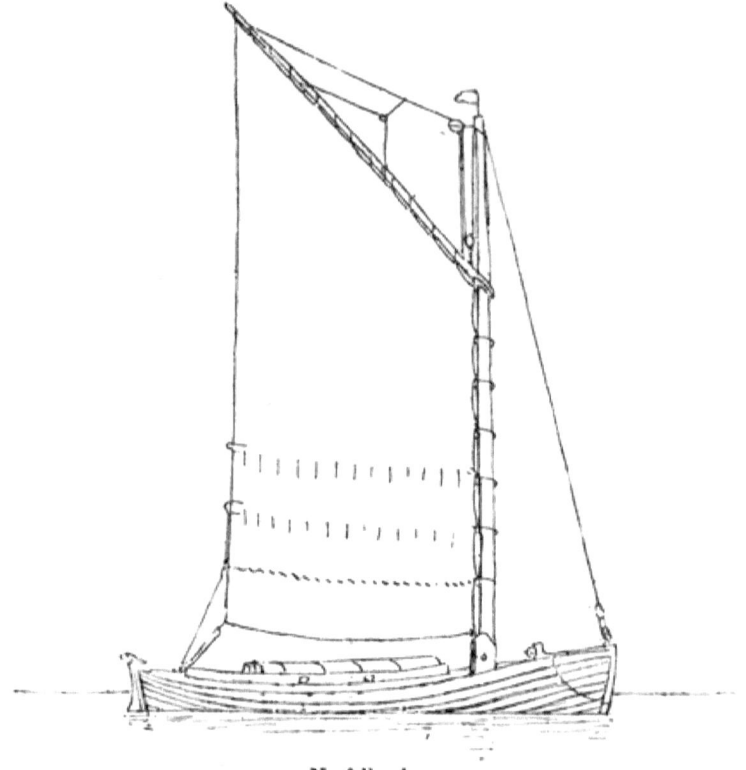

Norfolk wherry.

view to smooth-water navigation; while their long-pinioned, high-peaked single sail looks almost as though it may have once been a lateen, or lateen-cut lug, which is indeed a favourite sail among small yachts and pleasure-boats upon these " broads."

Some of the Norfolk wherries measure thirty or forty tons, and in all of them the heavy mast is pivoted in a kind of tabernacle, and so weighted at the heel below with iron or lead as to be easily lowered and raised, like a river-steamer's funnel, in passing a bridge.

Spite of the conservative power of salt water among boats and men, purity of breed, or type of build and rig, is not nearly so persistent to-day as it was formerly; and I regret to have to record that even the waterman of the "nineteenth century" is not entirely free from the restless love of change of the times; his old wherry being often seen now with a longer mast and gaffsail, in place of the good old-fashioned spritsail; while owing perhaps to bad times and low fares, together with the expensive build of a true wherry, her place is often filled to-day by some mongrel kind of craft, usually an old ship or steamer's boat, bought for a mere song, and rigged as a ketch, but with little else about her to remind one of the true Portsmouth wherry. Before leaving these boats, the fact that they are almost always steered with a yoke and lines instead of a tiller, must not be overlooked; though the original yoke of the wherry was in reality only a tiller or wooden bar, thrust through a hole in her rudder-head at a right angle to the line of the boat's keel.

This arrangement is found in many other boats with outside rudder-heads, particularly in Norway, where, in place of yoke-lines, this transverse tiller in the smaller skiffs is worked by a single long rod or staff jointed to one end of the tiller, the other end of the staff reaching well forward into the boat, where the rudder is moved to port or starboard by a forward pull or a backward thrust of this rod.

This plan does not interfere, any more than yoke-lines do, with the mizzen of a boat, or with an after load of passengers; while the action of the rigid staff gives the steersman a quicker and truer sense of the position of his rudder in a seaway than yoke-lines ever do. There is, perhaps, some connection between this old Norse method of steering and the obsolete sea-term "whipstaff," a piece of wood fastened to the helm or tiller, held by those steering a vessel before steering-wheels came into use.

A spritsail, as fitted and used to gain a lofty peak with a short mast, is essentially an English or Northern sail; for though the Turks have a vessel which carries a sprit, it is used in her to extend the head of a kind of squaresail abaft the mast, the peak of which is no higher than the mast-head.

Like the wherry, the Thames sailing-barge, in all her details and bright colours, dates back for centuries, and is even to-day a very flourishing old-world craft indeed, which, spite of steam-lighters, tugs, etc., is still found economically well adapted for the carriage, not only of heavy goods like bricks and machinery, but of lofty deck-loads of hay and straw; while her very light draught makes her one of the handiest of vessels for the winding navigation of the Thames, both above and below London, and enables her to work her way close inshore, and thus take advantage of every tidal eddy in plying to windward against tide, or, as an old pilot would say, "to hug a bight and shun a p'int," when doing so. And this, with the splendid set of her perfectly wind-tight sails, dressed with fish-oil and ochre, and her power of holding way as she shoots up in the wind in going about, makes it hard for even a fast-sailing boat to beat one. The sprit of a London barge is certainly the longest and heaviest spar of its kind, and is supported in the middle by a stout tackle from the mast-head; while, owing to the fixed position of the head of a spritsail, it cannot be reduced by reefing beyond the single row of reef-points, tied up at times to allow a load of straw to be carried below the sail.

This is one drawback to these large spritsails, which, instead of being reefed as the wind freshens, are gathered in toward the mast, foot by foot, by a

G

number of brails. There are two distinct classes of these sailing-barges—one, known as the dumpy, without a topmast; the other as a topsail-barge, which, like the Rochester bawley, carries a topmast as long, or

Topsail Thames barge.

longer, than her lower mast. The topsail-barge also carries a jib and bowsprit; but this bowsprit is so arranged that when not wanted in working among a crowd of shipping, or at anchor, it can easily be triced up on end out of the way; while, for passing bridges, the barge's short-mast and long-sprit are lowered together aft on deck, or to any required angle, by means of her windlass and a huge fourfold block-purchase at the end of the forestay.

The lee-boards, upon which a barge's handiness and power of holding way to windward so much depend, are also fitted with blocks and chain-tackle falls, which, like those in a Dutch schuyt, lead aft,

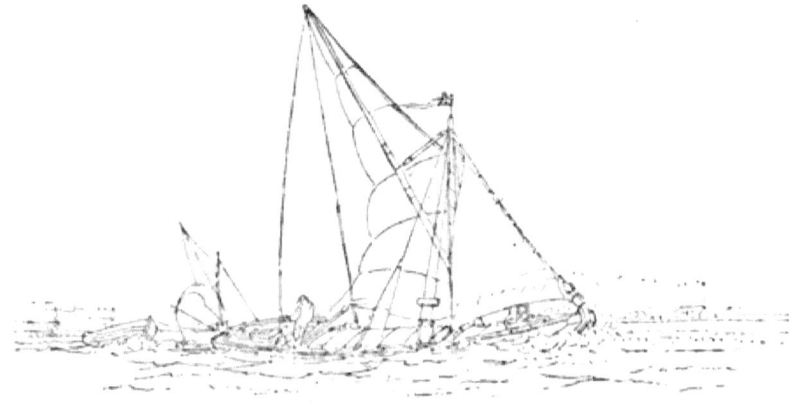

Barge, with sail reduced by brails, or sixty tons of bricks, in a squall.

close to the steersman's hand, who can thus raise or lower them as wanted.* When light, the barge's stability depends entirely upon her flat bottom, and should the weather edge, or "chine," of it be once lifted out of water she stands a good chance of capsizing.

* A deep-sea sailor, having shipped on board a London barge, was greatly at a loss to understand her skipper's command, "Hoist up the weather lee-board."

A pair of long stout peak or sprit "vangs," as the ropes and tackles which prevent a barge's sprit from sagging away to leeward are called, are also a leading feature of this rig, and, when sailing on a wind, the weather one is always as taut as a bar. The lofty peak of a lateener's yard is also furnished with vangs, or "l'oste," which lead aft, and act upon it in the same way that these ropes do upon a barge's sprit. A barge's tiny mizzen-mast is the only mast of the kind, I believe, actually stepped upon a rudder-head; and with its sheet made fast to the after end of the broad rudder, the little sail is really **a second rudder in the** air, acting in unison with the one below it in the water.

I can never see one of these great sailing-barges, in an upper reach of the Thames or Medway, without feeling admiration and respect for the ingenuity which contrived a vessel that, with a draught of some three feet, can, handled by two men, carry sixty or eighty tons of bricks or coal to where she lies, far up among the fresh-water weeds and lilies, with all that tangle of rope, mast, and brown sail now flat upon her deck, yet so easily raised or lowered * as she passed a bridge ;

---

* A topsail-barge will charge a bridge like that of Rochester with topmast on end, and lower it and mainmast, holding her way through the bridge, and hoisting sail again after passing it before losing way.

and with scarce any freeboard and hold of the water, yet able with her great lee-boards to hold a fine wind, or turn in her length, and make long voyages round stormy headlands almost out of sight of land.

In truth, if much of the shipping of the Middle Ages was as well found and fitted for its work as this London barge, of which we have authentic records in pictures of the time of Elizabeth, naval architecture

Some fourteenth-century ships (as usually drawn for us).

could not have been far behind that of the land. And yet one is constantly asked to accept, as a portrait of a fourteenth century sea-going ship, some such quaint old decorative picture of her as the above, or even the heraldic device, which poses as a ship, in the arms of the city of Paris.

As I have tried to show, nothing connected with seafaring matters, or men, before the introduction of steam, ever moved in a rapid or striding way, and it is most unlikely that ships leaped, so to speak, from these old nondescript manuscript or heraldic craft, to ships like the Genoese carrack and others of the fifteenth century. Southern seamen, it is true, were very likely in advance of the Normans as to size and decoration in their vessels; but I suspect that we need not go farther back than the present single square-sailed coaster of Norway for a true picture of the smaller square-rigged thirteenth-century ship.

CHAPTER VII.

"UP TO THE SEA," ETC.

Dutch fishing-boats at Scheveningen — Italian lake-craft: their rudders, and those of Rhine boats — The "timoneer" — Rig and sail of lake-craft, "robands," etc.: their low bow — The Arab dhow — St. Paul's ship — Slavers, etc. — A Baltimore clipper — The ten-gun brigs — Distinction between the true brig, or brigantine, and snow — The English experimental brig, *Flying-fish* — The end of British naval sailing seamanship — H.M.S. steam-frigate *Firebrand*.

A LEE shore, the dread of most sailors, is the only port of many Dutch fishermen; and a fleet of Scheveningen boats putting to sea after much heaving and hauling upon warps from anchors ashore and seaward, and then working out under canvas, with a flowing tide among the breakers, is a sight not easily forgotten.

The boats all lie upright, like a flock of surf ducks, the broad central keel resting upon the sand, while their floating bodies just lift them off the ground with each roll of the sea. This central keel is slightly curved or "cambered," so that even before the boat is really clear of the sand, which becomes very loose as the tide flows, she is easily slewed, or turned head to wind and sea, by capstan power on board her. Unlike most beach boats, the Scheveningen boats are seldom, except for repairs, or when out of commission, hauled up high and dry—if one can use such a term in a land where people oftener go up than "down to the sea in ships"—the usual plan being to merely

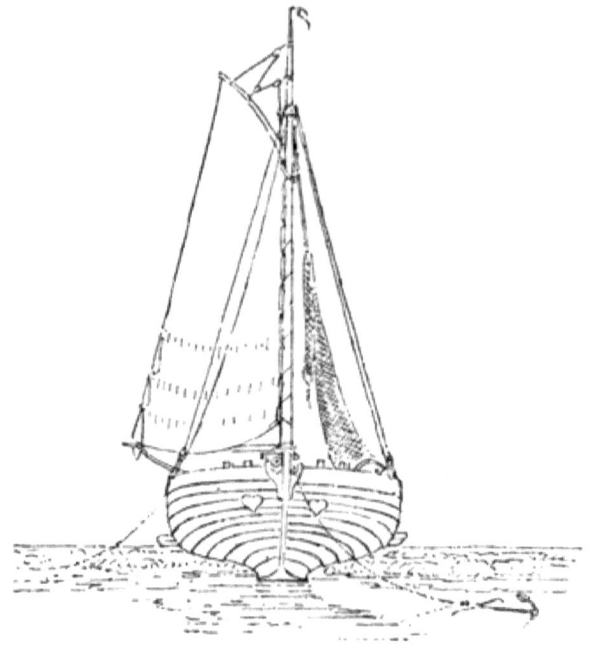

Scheveningen boat.

run them in upon the flat shore with an ebbing tide, and then, with an anchor to seaward, to let them bump until the tide leaves them, when the catch of fish is hoisted out, and the nets cleaned and repaired ready for use again, when the boat puts to sea upon the next flood.

These boats, which are sloop-rigged, and just twice as long as they are broad, carry from eight to ten men. They are clench-built of inch oak plank, fastened with iron nails, but pegged to the inside timbers with oaken "tree-nails." Unless it be a London omnibus, it is hard to conceive of anything put together by man, stronger for its weight than one of these Dutch fishing-boats; and the fit and bend of plank round their very bluff bows or breasts is fine manly work.

The external stem is merely an abutment for the ends of these planks, which are nailed to a very broad inner stem or "apron," in which also, where it rises on either side the stem, is cut a score or crutch on the port side for the bowsprit, and upon the starboard for the hawse-pipe to rest in; the bowsprit being kept in place above by a movable iron strap. They are all decked boats, with low bulwarks planked to timber ends, which (there being no top-rail or gunwale) project above the bulwarks as in many of our old-fashioned wherry-built craft. When new, the Scheveningen boats are bright and golden with pine varnish; but, beyond here and there a patch of brown tar, the older boats are left bare, so that it is easy to trace every fibre of the oak in their grey, weather-stained planks; though, strange to say, one rarely sees a sign of rust about the large iron nail-heads. Some of the nails and rivets found in remains of the Viking ships are of the exact size and pattern of the nails used in these boats. Beyond some device like a big heart, or a swan, painted upon each side of the bluff bow, with sometimes a touch of red, green, or yellow about the hawse-pipe, they are without decoration. Their sails are, however, dressed, like those of a Thames barge, with fish-oil and red or yellow ochre. Like most Dutch small craft, they are of course provided with lee-boards, though, owing to their central keel, they can make fair way to windward even before the water is deep enough to allow a lee-board to be effectively used. Altogether, the Dutch coasting-craft, built to withstand and contend against the combined forces of wind, wave, *and sand*, and dependent solely upon strength of timbers, planks, and fastenings, to do so, are second only to their dikes as proofs of the power of this amphibious race over their best servant and worst enemy, the North Sea.

In rig, the large trading-boat of Lakes Como and Maggiore distinctly reminds one of the big, single-masted, square-sailed Norwegian coaster, mentioned at the end of the last chapter; while, owing to being almost entirely cut off from the world's broad highway, floating as they do upon water six hundred feet above it, these lake-boats, and all details about them, no doubt remain with us to-day as a very early type of sailing-craft. In them the rudder, for instance, retains its original form of steering oar, or rudder and tiller in one, slung loosely to the top of the stern-post.

A curious early modification of this form of rudder is found in certain boats and barges on the Rhine, boats which, though closely resembling those upon the Italian lakes, are, in navigating this river, brought into

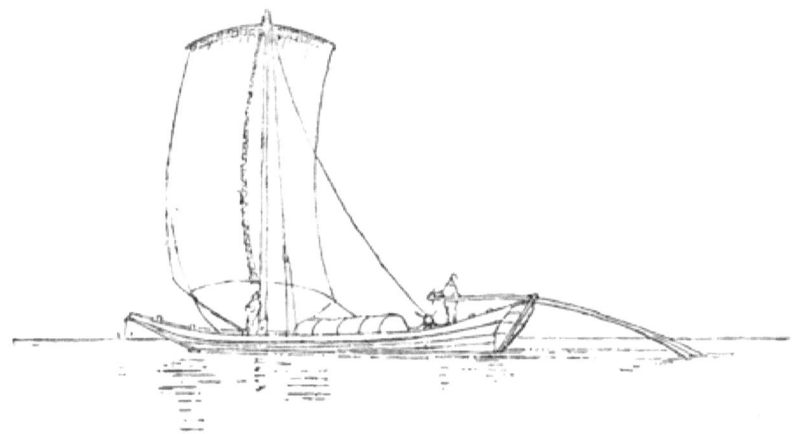

Italian lake-craft (Como).

direct communication with sea-going craft. In such boats, though the tiller still extends aft beyond the stern-post, the rudder itself has a distinct head and "main-piece," hung by pintals and gudgeons, or hinged to the stern-post, unless, as in some quite small craft, it is held in place by simply passing through the overhang or counter of the boat's stern.

The enormous rudder required by boats navigating

the Rhine and Rhone is due to the strength of their current, which makes it impossible to steer a boat down stream upon them without a very powerful rudder and long tiller. The Italian word "timone," the helm or tiller of a ship, means also the pole of a carriage

Rhine barge rudder and tiller, also rudder of boat on Lake Constance.

and the beam of a plough, and the old sea-term, "timoneer," or steersman, is of course derived from this word; which is also used by the Italians in this sense, to distinguish the wheelers, or horses harnessed to the pole of a carriage upon which the steering of

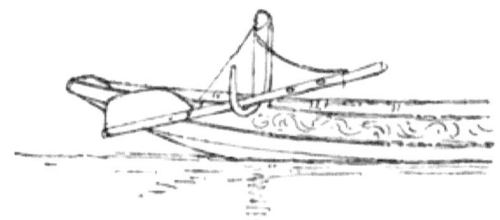

Side-slung rudder on Lake Isao.

it depends, from the leaders. The following lines, in Falconer's "Shipwreck," show how this word was used in his time:—

"'Starboard again!' the watchful pilot cries.
'Starboard!' the obedient timoneer replies."

The Italians and Spaniards have, in fact, no word which actually expresses the rudder as distinct from its tiller; the old word "rother," so spelt by us as late as 1678, and "tiller," or "helm," being of Teutonic origin; while the sea-term, "helm's a-lee"—used in tacking ship, and meaning that the rudder itself is to windward —when the tiller is put down, or over to leeward, would be nonsense, if one word stood for both rudder and tiller, or helm.

In these primitive lake-boats we have also a very early form of squaresail, slung so that it can be dropped instantly if struck by a gust from between the mountains, and which, like most sails used for inland navigation, has a great hoist, and is very square aloft. This sail is divided down the centre, the two parts, when hoisted, being held together by a lacing, which is cast loose before it is lowered, and allows the great sail to be easily gathered in aft in two parts; the long mast itself being so arranged that it can also be rapidly lowered forward—not aft—when the boat is running before a hard mountain storm. The manner in which these sails are attached to their yard throws a light upon the old word "robands," the name of the short tiers formerly used to secure a squaresail to its yard.

In these boats the sail hangs from the yard upon a series of bands, or loops, made in the head of the sail, through which the yard passes—a handy plan, no doubt, upon inland waters, where a sail left permanently bent would prove a strong temptation to the first poor peasant landsman that might board a boat in the absence of her owner; that sacred feeling about robbing a vessel of her tackling rarely extending far above high salt-water mark. Like most very early types, these lake-boats, large and small, are much higher aft than forward, having a look about them of the coot, seagull, and several other water birds, in the way they sit upon the waves. The Arab dhow, with her

Arab dhow.

well-arranged splendid sail-power and lines of hull, which really agree very much with the "wave-line" theory, fussed over and said to have been first discovered by ship-builders about forty years back, is another instance of this sharp low form of hull forward and lofty poop.

Like the Chinese, the Arab himself of to-day, and all his belongings, is the Arab of a thousand years ago; and I suspect that in one of these dhows we see pretty much the ship, though not so large, in which St. Paul was wrecked—a vessel which, with her low bow and lofty stern, might ride best, as he describes, in a gale, with four anchors, stern to sea and bow toward the shore, ready for the final rush landward when the wished-for day broke. There is especial mention that in St. Paul's ship the rudder was either triced up, or very

Piratical Chinese junk.

carefully secured, as it would need to be in riding thus; for they "loosed the rudder-bands, and hoisted up the mainsail to the wind," before, "falling into a place where two seas met, they ran the ship aground; and the fore part stuck fast, and remained unmoveable, but the hinder part was broken with the violence of the waves." Which evidently points also to a very light draught forward, such as we find in the Arab dhow and other old-world craft of present times.

In the piratical and smuggling craft of China, which have much in common with the Arab dhow, we have, I believe, good representative types of the naval architecture and sail-power among the barbarians, as we sometimes call them, of Northern Asia, dating back for centuries. These are all fast, weatherly craft,

Smuggling junk.

quite unlike the heavy trading junk, built to sail only before a fair monsoon.

In many of them it is curious to observe how the fighting men's shields are ranged along outside the top-rail, just as they were in the old war-galley of the Mediterranean, the Viking ships, and those of other European races.

Practically, these junks are all luggers, and the

good qualities of the bamboo-ribbed sail-wings of the "heathen Chinee" has of late led to their imitation and use among some of our smaller yachts upon English waters.

Fifty years ago, the slave and fruit trades produced a number of very fast schooners, brigs, and brigantines; and, with her long, low hull, and tall, raking masts,

Baltimore clipper or slaver.

the Baltimore clipper was probably the fastest of these. In the year 1841 the writer visited that port, when more than one vessel actually intended for the slave-trade might still be seen there on the stocks.

The first thing that struck one about these schooners was their great beam on deck, and the flare-out of the top sides and bulwark forward; the bow as seen from above being very broad and full in a line across the cat-heads, but with a stem or cutwater raking aft quickly below into lines of entrance, which ran straight back at once into the wedge-like underwater body of the hull. It was this form of hull that gave a slaver so little "head-room" between decks, or above the platform below which all the water and provisions for her living cargo was stowed. These clippers were also remarkable for the small amount of what shipwrights call "dead wood" below water; that is, of solid timber about the cutwater forward, and run and stern-post aft. Besides these schooners, one saw at that time plenty of slaves sunning themselves on the wharves of this old southern port, or lying asleep in the shade of shanties, alongside of which, perhaps, lay the actual ship in which some of them had endured all the horrors of the middle passage over the Atlantic.

The look, however, of these lazy, fat, jolly niggers did not impress one with a very vivid idea of the cruelty or tyranny of the Baltimore slave-owner.

Indeed, it was only after repeated assurance of the fact, that one could realize that these comfortable-looking fellows were slaves, or the personal property of any one but themselves.

The builders of the Baltimore clippers were, many of them no doubt, descendants of the old shipwrights who, about the end of the seventeenth century, learnt their trade in building piratical small craft, which, in the hands of the buccaneers, were the dread of all other traders to the West Indies, until an expedition was sent from England, commanded by that most accomplished of privateersmen, Woodes Rogers, to extirpate them. It was undoubtedly the slave-trade, and the speed of the vessels employed in it, that a few years before the introduction of steam stirred the Admiralty to build a number of gun-brigs, designed especially for speed in light winds. Of the first series of these—the ten-gun brigs—several were never heard of again after leaving port, having, it is supposed, either capsized, like the *Eurydice*, under sail, or foundered at sea in bad weather, after having shipped more water on deck than the vessel was able, owing to the height of her bulwarks and insufficient means of exit for it, to clear herself of. In fact, these brigs were so constructed that they were little better than open boats, with the disadvantage that those in charge of them looked upon them as decked vessels. Though these vessels were all called brigs, they would a few years before have been known as snows. The term "brig," which is not given in Johnson, 1760, is really a modern contraction of the older word "brigantine," or "brigandine," from "brigand," a robber; "brigantine" being originally a general name for any fast vessel used by corsairs or pirates. The original brig, or brigantine, though she carried a square maintopsail and topgallant-sail, never had a square mainsail below it, like that carried by the snow.

The old brig's mainmast was in fact rigged exactly

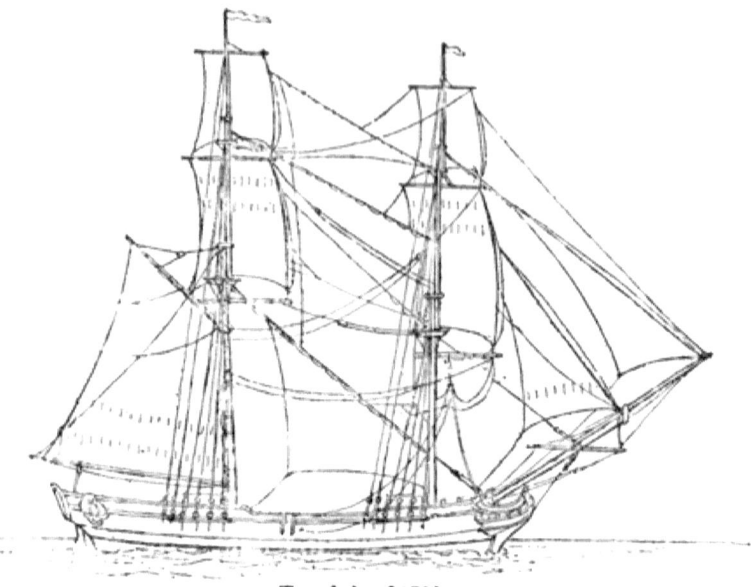

True brig of 1780.

like a ship's mizzen-mast, and, like that mast, had originally a lateen-mainsail and yard upon it; and this was, no doubt, one reason that after this form of sail became obsolete, a squaresail was not set upon what was really the brig's crojack-yard. When this was afterwards done in the rig we call a brig—then called a snow—the fore and aft sail upon the mainmast, or spanker, was always bent to hoops which ran upon a small spar or jack-mast just abaft the mainmast; an arrangement which enabled this sail to be carried without interfering with the old seaman's practice of lowering his mainyard a-port-last in bad weather.

I close this chapter with a portrait of the *Flying-*

H.M. brig *Flying-fish*.

fish of twelve guns, one of the smartest of the vessels known as the experimental brigs. She was designed by Sir William Symonds, then director of naval construction to the Admiralty.

It will be seen in her that, with the more modern way of slinging lower-yards, the small additional mast, abaft the mainmast, sometimes called a trysail-mast is absent. I have heard it said by old naval men that the great square mainsail of these vessels was often found a very pressing and difficult sail, even for a man-of-war's crew, to handle in a squall; and this being so may have led to the omission of it among the older class of small trading-brigs, particularly in the coal trade.

H.M. steam-frigate *Firebrand*.

The modern rig, often spoken of as a brigantine, has no square-yard upon her mainmast, which is in fact schooner-rigged. These vessels were first known as hermaphrodite brigs.

In the twelve-gun brigs, frigates, and sailing line-of-battle ships of Sir William Symonds's time, the English Navy may be said to have reached its highest point in all matters pertaining to old-fashioned seamanship, and the handling of fleets under canvas only. And how the conservative naval mind then clung to its old sea wings, is seen by a reference to the portrait of one of our first steam-frigates, the *Firebrand*, on p. 102.

CHAPTER VIII.

ORIGIN OF THE CUTTER.

The only safe way of learning to-day much about the rig of ancient shipping—Southern origin of the cutter-rig—The Brighton hoggy—The old Itchen Ferry rig—Advantages of the cutter-rig—American cutters, etc.—The modern yawl—The true yawl or dandy—Drawbacks to the fore-and-aft rig, with the exception of the lateen-rig and French lugger, for sea-going ships.

THERE are few records of sails and rigging of value earlier than the fifteenth century; while we are chiefly indebted for even the little we do know of such matters before then to the work of nuns and monks, who could have had very little practical knowledge of a ship or her tackling, and at best were able only to give us feeble impressions of vessels as they saw them. It is not surprising, then, seeing the hash often made of such subjects by modern land-artists,* that from their work we get but a faint notion of the ships even of Norman times. If we go back to Roman, Greek, or

---

* Written before the introduction of instantaneous dry-plate photography, which enables any painstaking landsman now to draw a modern vessel correctly under sail.

Egyptian art, the case is much the same; for, though we can from it form a fair idea of the look of these people, and their land dwellings, we have little record, beyond certain conventional odds and ends of beaks, and tails, or poops, upon coins, of the look, or tackling, of the ships they sailed and fought in. A thousand years hence, when our own ships shall have all returned to oxide of iron, and the photos of them faded away, what notion would be obtained of a four-hundred-foot ocean steamer, or even of an *Inflexible*, from a contracted image of her on a penny-piece?

It is for this reason that I think it likely that to-day we may be able to form a better idea of the character and model of a Viking galley, by carefully studying the construction of certain present types of Scotch fishing-boats, or of an old Portsmouth wherry, than from any pictures, or by even looking at the unearthed bones of the ship herself.

Again, a modern single-masted lateener, seen, as they often are in fine weather, working short tacks to windward, with the fore part of her sail in the position known as "abidot," or aback, when compared with the rig of the old Brighton hog-boat, or "hoggy," seems to suggest at once how it may have occurred to some ancient sailmaker to cut a lateen-sail in the line of the mast, and give the fore part of the sail a sheet of its own, and the after part, which would become a balanced lug, a stout roping down

Lateener, with sail "abidot."

the leading edge; while this would be followed soon by an arrangement of hoops on the fore end of the

Brighton hoggy.

yard, so that the now detached foresail could be lowered in a squall, and the boat at once be relieved to the extent of a reef in her mainsail. With her high-peaked boomless mainsail, the outline of the mainsail and foresail together, of this old Brighton fishing-boat, is, like that of the same two sails in a London barge, almost exactly the outline of a single lateen-sail.

The rig of the "hoggy" is certainly an old one among the men of the south hams of England. She is not a true cutter, or even a sloop, as she carries a cutter's running-bowsprit. But a distinct feature of this boat was that the tack of her foresail and forestay went to a curious stout oak or ashen bumpkin, which in section was flat, rather than square or round, and, curving downwards and projecting some four feet beyond her stem, was wide enough for a man to stand upon, and not unlike a rudimentary form of the beak, or "flech," of a lateener. The cut or shape of her jib, which was nearly an equilateral triangle, also resembled that of many lateeners.

Some of these hoggys had a lug-mizzen, and, like the Scheveningen boats, were nearly half as wide as they were long; hence, perhaps, their name of "hoggy." They were flat floored, and, being fitted with two strong bilge-keels, lay upright upon the hard sand, as the Dutch boats do among the low breakers of a flat shore. It is noteworthy that the rig of the original Itchen Ferry shrimpers was almost the same as that of the one-masted Brighton hoggy; but they were smaller boats, and in them the bumpkin was of iron, and not longer than that of a Beer lugger. Most of these handy little craft now have a boom-mainsail; they are broad in beam and heavily ballasted, and, as single-handed boats in tidal waters, are not easily surpassed by anything of their

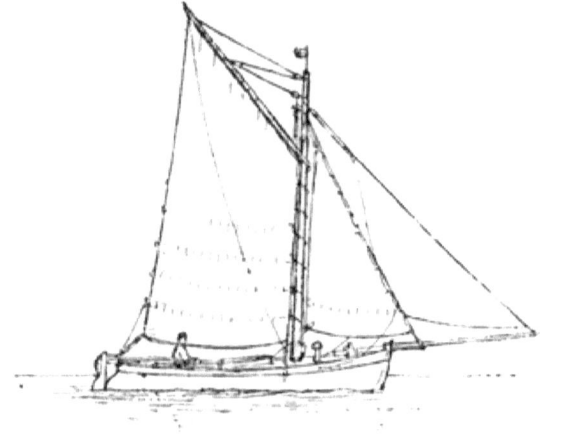

Old Itchen Ferry boat.

size afloat. I have owned one, and sailed among them for more than twenty years, but never knew one come to grief, or leave a widow and orphans, as so often happens with other small fishing-boats of northern ports. Poetical writers about the sea are fond of dwelling upon the Viking, and his influence upon English naval history. But though the *personnel* of England's navy no doubt owed much to these hardy northern boatmen (for they were little more), all our earliest and more important material improvements in naval construction came from southern and eastern nations; and when cannon really begun to supersede older weapons in Henry VIII.'s time, he at once called in the assistance of Italian shipwrights, to help him build that fleet of small ships, destined, under his successors, after repelling Spain's attack upon our coasts, to make England mistress of the seas.

The fact is, these hardy Norsemen were almost as far behind the architects of the south in matters naval as their wooden structures on land were, compared with the fortified cities, castles, and dwellings of the inhabitants of Italy, Greece, or Spain, who were, indeed, the earliest civilized rulers of the waves.

I have tried to show that that most effective rig to windward, the cutter, has much really in common with the one great triangular sail-wing of the south. The first cutters we hear of in England hailed from Brixham, and are mentioned as early as the time of Elizabeth, when a Brixham cutter was despatched by Drake to carry news of his first successes to London, and bring him back more powder; while, as I said before, it was the Brixham men who, in their fast cutter-rigged smacks, first introduced the deep-sea beam trawl-net among our northern fishermen.

That the cutter is the most effective fore-and-aft rig known is clearly proved, I think, by the fact that it is the rig now adopted even by American yachtsmen to defend the American cup under all conditions of wind and weather.* For, in spite of the American term "sloop," all their latest-built yachts for this business, such as *Volunteer*, etc., are practically cutters. Even the modern yawl of the aristocratic yachtsman is really only a clipped cutter with a sort of half-bred flagstaff of a mizzen stuck on the end of a very long counter, to enable her (if a racer) to claim the time allowance given to yawls; or to allow the owner and his lady guests an upright table for their champagne-bottles and lunch, as the big ship jogs along under it and her head canvas, with a soldier's wind, up and down South-

---

* An instructive and striking instance of the power of a well-handled fore-and-after to face bad weather, were the late attempts (February, 1890), crowned at last with success, of the Crookhaven pilot-cutter *Self-Reliance*, manned by a volunteer crew, to go to the relief of the starving light-keepers on the Fastnet Rock, after all efforts to do so by the *Halcyon steam* tender, appointed for this work, had failed. After this it will be surprising if the Trinity Board or Admiralty do not build one or more well-modelled, stout cutters of fifty tons, which, properly fitted with some *outside* lead, and gear of a reliable quality to match it, would, where there was a small harbour to start from, prove more capable of making their way in a gale to a given point, and keeping the sea when there, than any steam tender or even lifeboat; while, if used for nothing else, such vessels would prove handier and less expensive for police work in bad weather among our North Sea smacksmen than a modern steam gunboat.

ampton Water (which undoubtedly she would do quite as well without it).

That this class of mizzen has little other use is clear from the fact that, in bad weather at sea, it is generally the first sail stowed, and when a close-reefed mainsail cannot be carried, that a trysail is as often the real storm canvas of one of these yawls as it is of a big cutter. The honest mizzen, carried well forward of the rudder-head and tiller by so many small

Fig. 66.—Dandy-rig.

traders and fishermen, now known as ketches, but really dandy-rigged, is a very different kind of sail, which enables such vessels to be handled with fewer men than any cutter, and, like a wherry, to be snugged down at once in a hard wind under a mizzen and foresail. Considering the advantages of this rig, it is surprising that it is so rarely adopted by sea-going yachtsmen.

It may be asked by landsmen why, if a cutter, and the two-masted cutter-rig the schooner, is the most effective rig to windward, is it that most of the sea-keeping sailing-craft of the world are, and have been, nearly always square-rigged vessels? The answer is that in actual passage-making, upon long ocean voyages, it is seldom that a vessel has to depend for any time upon her power of turning dead to windward; but rather upon a great spread of canvas, which can be carried in a heavy sea with the wind abeam, or a little abaft the beam.

Again, in all boom-sailed fore-and-aft rigs, the difficulty of handling and steadying a large boom or booms in a seaway increases rapidly with the size of the vessel, and becomes so great when rolling heavily in a gale, that they have to be secured amidships, with the sail dependent upon them stowed, and replaced by a boomless trysail, or some form of sail bent to a square-yard for running under; while even the sheet of a trysail in really bad weather often proves difficult to handle. (The writer has seen the crew of an eight-hundred-ton ship unable to get the sheet of her main-trysail or "spencer" aft until the quarter-deck capstan was rigged, and the sheet-tackle fall taken to it to be hove in.) In rolling along before a gale, or with one on the quarter, a fore-and-after's boom is, like a ship's lower studding-sail boom, constantly in danger of being caught by a sea; with the additional risk of the sea breaking into the sail, and either bursting it or dismasting the vessel. This is an especial danger when, American fashion, the mainsail is laced along the foot to the boom, as it is now in most of our racing yachts.

The only fore-and-aft sail for large vessels in a seaway not subject to these drawbacks was and is the old boomless lateen-sail of the Mediterranean, or some modification of it like the great balanced lugsails of an old French chasse-marée. But both these rigs, owing to the great weight and length of their yards, require a strong crew to handle them in proportion to the size of the vessel, so that as ships increased in size, after the introduction of movable topmasts, the square-rig rapidly superseded the lateen in all but comparatively small craft engaged in the coasting-trade. One advantage of the lateen-sail over that of other fore-and-aft sails is that, like those of a square-rigged ship, it is reduced by reefing aloft to the yard; while, in the large French luggers, the weight and stress of a bag of reefed sail at the foot is avoided by the use of bonnets or bonnet-pieces laced to the lower edge of the sail, and easily detached by simply casting this lacing adrift.

CHAPTER IX.

UNDER SAIL AND OAR.

An eighteenth-century galley — Arrangement of her benches and oars for development of man-power—Comparison between it and modern horse-power of nineteenth-century war-ship—The carrosse, or captain's cabin, origin of the "coach" of our old ships—Rig of a galley described—A suggestion—Decorations, etc. —The galley's offspring, the eighteenth-century galley-built corvette—Mode of attack by galley, the origin of the importance attached by our old seamen of always getting and retaining the weather-gauge of an enemy—A sixteenth-century sea-fight, etc.

Up to the end of the eighteenth century lateen-rigged galleys of considerable size, rowed with from twenty-six to thirty oars on a side, were common enough in the Mediterranean ports; and, as we have really authentic records and models of these direct descendants of the war-ship or galley of the Greeks, Romans, and Middle Ages, I give here a figure of one of the later types of them, with some details of her fittings and rig, as described by Lescallier, who wrote just before the galley was laid aside in the French Navy, superseded more or less by the galley-built corvette and frigate.

A galley of the first rank, like that given in the

IN THE DAYS OF OAK AND HEMP. 115

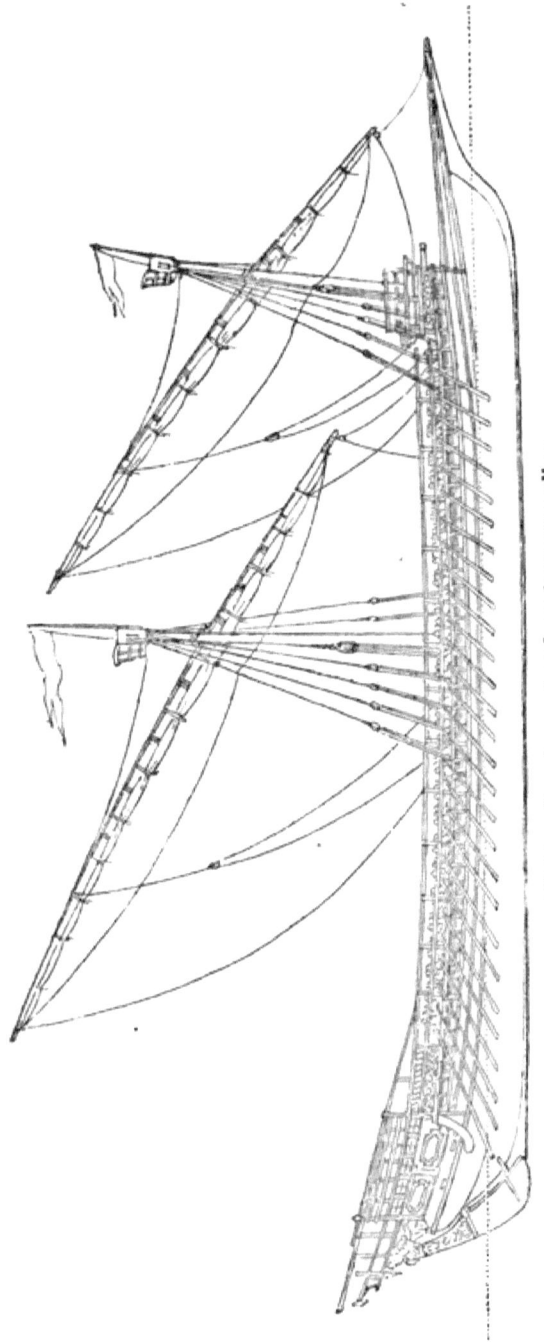

Eighteenth and seventeenth century war-galley.

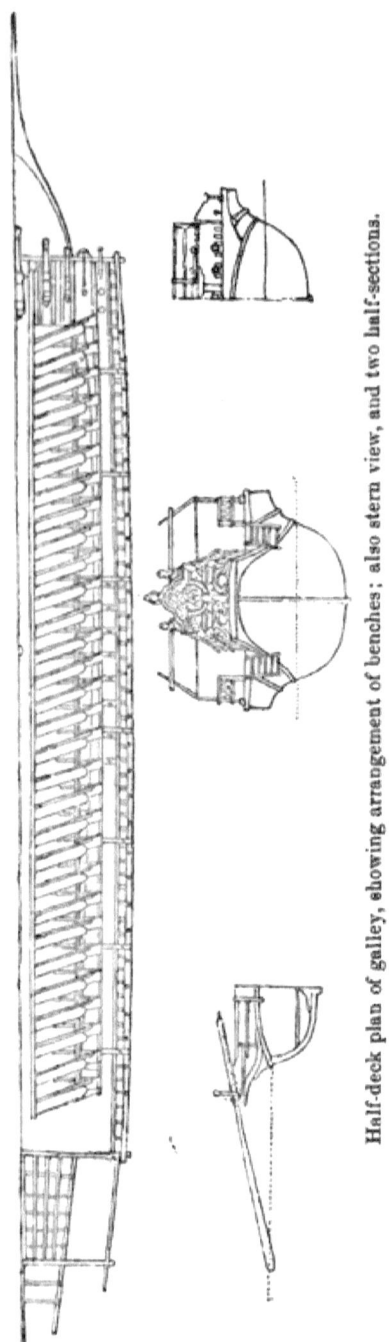

Half-deck plan of galley, showing arrangement of benches; also stern view, and two half-sections.

figure, was 166 feet long, with a beam of from 32 to 35 feet, and rowed thirty oars on a side, which worked against thole-pins, ranged upon a rail projecting above and beyond the deck, which rail was supported by a number of vertical knee-timbers, or brackets, called "bacalas," or "corps-de-lattes," just as the oars of an Italian lake-boat are supported to-day; the lower arms of these projecting knees being bolted to the deck or covering-board of the galley. The benches for the rowers were arranged obliquely upon the deck, as shown in the half-deck plan, which gives those upon the starboard side.

It is evident that, had the thwarts of the galley

not been arranged in this manner, the men who worked the inner end of the oar would have had to leave their seat each time it was carried forward to catch the water. These long, heavy oars were never pulled far through the water after catching it, as those of a modern racing-eight are; but, after a short, strong tug, were at once carried forward for another stroke. This style of working a long, heavy oar or sweep may be seen by any one who watches the way a Thames lighterman, or a pair of them, use a long sweep; while a short, strong pull or tug is the style of stroke of a boat's crew in the Turkish Navy to-day.

Between the benches for rowers, in the centre of the galley, was a passage known as the "coursier," or waist, at the fore end of which, upon a platform, cut off from it by a sliding door, a twenty-four-pounder was mounted, with two smaller guns, about eight-pounders, on either side of it, all five pointing forward, as bow-chasers.

The oars of a galley, which were about 44 feet

Oar of galley.

long, were handled by means of a cleat, or "main-tenant," nailed to the great loom of the oar. The number of men to each oar varied from five to six or seven, one or more of the best being always told off to the actual handle at the end of the oar. Where the oar worked upon the rail against the thole-pin, it was strengthened and protected by smooth, flat pieces of wood nailed to it, as well as by a rope woolding. It will be seen, by reference to the cut, that this part of the oar ("la galaverne") had also an arrangement to keep it from slipping outwards, very like the leather collar or button upon a modern fresh-water oar.

Allowing six men to each oar, we get a total of 360 man-power in one of these great galleys. In these days of steam (and labour-saving engines?), we always speak of the horse-power of a ship. But is not all this horse-power, nominal or phenomenal, of an Atlantic liner, or modern war-ship, with her enormous crew of begrimed stokers, firemen, and shovellers, or coal-trimmers, sweating day and night before her furnaces, or down in her stifling bunkers, really as dependent upon actual man-power as the ancient galley was?

And is the life of such men a great improvement * upon that of a galley-slave, who, at any rate, worked in pure air and sunshine? While, with a fair, or beam-wind, the galley's splendid sail-wings must have often

---

* During the Naval Manœuvres, 1889, the usual temperature in the engine-room of H.M.S. *Nymphe* was 112°, while in her bunkers 180° was recorded; but this must have been higher than usual, as at that *temperature* we are told that "the coal became ignited!"

given her *man-power* long spells of entire rest. That the life of a galley-slave was not altogether as hard as is sometimes imagined, is partly shown by the fact that there were always men on board the galleys who had shipped voluntarily for this work of tugging at the oar, for pay as well as their keep. These men, as volunteers, of course took rank above the ordinary galley-slave; who, in spite of his being a convicted felon, was not, I suspect, much worse off, or worse treated, than many of the pressed landsmen in our navy of that date were.

But, to return to the galley and her fittings, the captain's cabin aft was always under a kind of tilted canopy, like the cover of a waggon, known as the " carrosse," or coach, from which we no doubt got the name of that apartment under the poop of our old men-of-war and East Indiamen, called the " coach," in which originally there stood an old-fashioned four-post bed for the captain or admiral's use.

Immediately in front of the captain's cabin— between it and the benches for the galley-slaves—was a square open space or platform known as " l'espalier " (probably from the French "*espar*," a spar, whence, perhaps, the term " spar-deck," or light upper-deck— used by the crew in handling the spars and sails of a ship). This spar-deck in the galley was bounded on either side by ornamental balustrades and seats, and was fitted with two gangways and short accommodation-ladders. These eighteenth-century galleys were much used as vessels of state, or for the conveyance of great people bound upon short voyages in fine weather; and though usually they were steered by a long tiller, the end of which extended as far forward as the middle of the captain's cabin, it was customary in them, and other pink, or "lute sterned" vessels like them, to place the steersman sometimes upon a bench abaft the rudder, called the "bancassi," from which, in order not to incommode those in the carrosse, he worked a tiller projecting aft in the reverse way of the ordinary one. This tiller was most likely handled with some kind of yoke-lines.

Directly under the coach or carrosse was a decked cabin, "le gavori," lighted by windows in the side of the galley. Forward, beyond the rowers' benches, raised some feet above them and the deck, stood a platform or forecastle, known as "la rambade." This deck was useful as a shelter for the five bow-chase guns, and to the seamen working the foresail, etc. It was also furnished in the sixteenth century, as shown by the model in the Arsenal at Venice, with a pair of very cleverly contrived mitrailleuse, each composed of twenty revolving barrels worked by hand, and pointing aft, so as to rake the *man-power* of the galley in case any of it showed signs of insubordination. The prow of all the galleys ended in a long beak or "flech" beyond the stem of the vessel, very like the "rostrum" of an antique galley. This flech is a feature in most of the vessels and boats belonging to South Italian ports, and even to-day the small fishing-boats of Catania, in Sicily, are armed with these long beaks, carried out to a very sharp point, shod with iron. The galley had two masts—"arbre de mestri," the mainmast, and "arbre de trinquet," the foremast, with, at times, a mizzen. These masts were short, with a "calcet," or square head or block, mortised to receive the sheaves

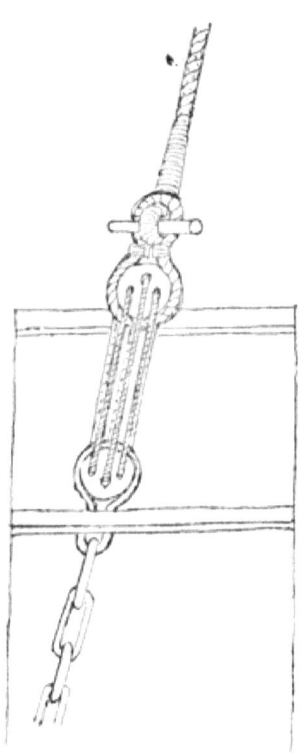

Galley's shroud, with toggle connections between it and deadeye.

over which ran the jeers and other ropes for hoisting the yards. The masts had no stays, and the "sarti," or shrouds, of a galley differed from those of other vessels in having the deadeyes coupled to them by stout wooden toggles, so that the lee-rigging could be cast adrift to allow the great yard free play on either tack in jibing, or when running before the wind. The masts could also be lowered flat on deck, if required.

Abaft the calcet, or head of the mast, was the top. The word "antenne," the yards of a modern galley, is the same word used for the yards of the old Roman galley, the sails and rig of which no doubt differed little from those of these eighteenth-century galleys.[*] These galleys were always superbly decorated, and a glance at the stern-view of one, with its carving and

---

[*] One cannot help feeling that the simple sail-power of these eighteenth-century galleys should not entirely be lost sight of, even by modern naval architects, or that some well-contrived form of the lateen-sail might prove of use in many of our smaller war-ships intended for other work than that of mere harbour defence. We have, in the ram-bow, reverted to an antique type of war-vessel which, like a modern steamer, was able for attack or retreat without the use of sails. But one has only to think of one of these great galleys, caught in a short gale and heavy sea, to see the wisdom of not leaving her entirely dependent upon her oars, or without some form of sail and mast, if only to steady the hull as it rolled in the trough of the sea; but with help of which she must have often succeeded in clearing a rock-bound lee shore, and gaining a port, or the shelter of the nearest island. When a lateen-sail is furled, and its long yard secured low down, or on deck, in a fore and aft position, this rig, with its short stumpy mast or masts, offers less resistance in steaming to windward than any other; while, when wanted upon any emergency, the strong crew of a man-of-war would quickly re-hoist the yard, and loose this most effective sail to the wind. The stout head of a lateen-mast, with its top, or crow's-nest, abaft it, is also admirably adapted for a look-out, or signalling-station, or one in which protection might be given to riflemen, or a small machine-gun.

gilded ornamentation in low relief, shows, I think, the real origin of the lofty poop, with its overhanging stern and quarter-galleries, of the larger ships and galleons of the sixteenth and seventeenth centuries. Most of the flags and banners of a galley were of crimson damask or silk, embroidered in gold; even the covering of the carrosse, or captain's cabin, and the awning over the little deck aft was of the same material.

They continued to be used by the Turks, the Pope, the Venetian Republic,* and the Maltese and Spaniards for some time after they were laid aside in the French Navy. Drawing little water, they were able to sail close under the land, and, under sail, or oars in a calm, were effective for harassing or cutting out other vessels, especially the pirates of the Barbary coasts. But, like the duration of a calm, their superiority over heavier sea-going vessels was often of short duration.

* In a letter to Sir Robert Mansell, dated Venice, 1621, James Howell tells us how "he was lately to see the Arsenal here, one of the worthiest things of Christendom : they say there are as many Gallies and Galleasses of all sorts belonging to St. Mark, either in course, at anchor, in dock, or upon the careen, as there be days in the year ; here they can build a compleat Galley in half a day, and put her afloat in perfect equipage, having all the ingredients fitted beforehand ; as they did in three hours, when Henry III. pass'd this way to France from Poland, who wish'd, that besides Paris and his Parliament towns, he had this Arsenal in exchange for three of his chiefest cities."—" Familiar Letters," J. Howell.

The Russians and Swedes, in the Baltic, also used galleys of the same build as those of the south; otherwise they were rarely seen far outside the Straits of Gibraltar. No doubt the old galley was the origin of the frigate or frigata, and many years after the lateen-rigged galley was extinct, or rarely seen north of Finisterre, a class of low, straight, square-rigged ships, known as galleys, were built and used in England, both for war and commerce.

The term "galley," used for these vessels, probably originated from a custom among naval architects and seamen of that time of calling a ship "galley-built," when her upper-deck and rail was flush fore and aft, without a waist or break in the line of her deck amidship; while a frigate-built ship always had a quarter-deck and forecastle rising above this waist or middle-deck. But whether galley or frigate built, all this class of small vessels were provided with row-ports in addition to their gun-ports, through which long oars or sweeps were constantly worked in calms, to escape from, or come up with, any enemy.

And mention is often made by Captain Woodes Rogers, in his cruising-voyage round the world in 1708 and 1711, of the use of oars on board his little frigates, the *Duke* and *Duchess;* while he speaks of starting on his voyage in company with five or six of these galley-built ships, most of which hailed from Bristol, and were then known as "runners," or vessels which, owing to their speed, and the ease with which they would be rowed in a calm, were able to take care of themselves, without waiting for naval convoy, through the swarms of French privateers which at that time infested the "narrow seas."* Captain Shelvock also speaks of one of the two ships with which he started on a privateering voyage, a few years later than Rogers, as "a Thames-built galley."

But these Bristol and Thames galleys were no more like the lateen-rigged ones of the Mediterranean than was the "Luxemburg galley," which was accidentally burnt in the Atlantic in 1727, and which is shown by a painting of her at Greenwich, to have been a full-rigged ship, with even a second tier of guns upon a flush spar-deck above those on her main-deck.

I give on next page a figure of one of these galley-built sloops-of-war of the latter part of the eighteenth

* Pinkerton, in his account of Bristol, written in 1808, says that "in the late wars with France, they built here a sort of galley called 'runners,' which being well armed and furnished with letters of marque, overtook and mastered several prizes of that nation. Many of these *ships* were then also carriers for London merchants, who ordered their goods to be landed here, and sent to Gloucester by water, thence by land to Lechlade, and thence *down* the Thames to London; the carriage being so reasonable that it was more than paid for by the difference of the insurance and risk between this port and London."

century, showing the position of her row-ports between the gun-ports. The armed xebec of the Mediterranean, which carried from fourteen to twenty-two guns on one deck, with small ports for oars between each gun, appears to have been the connecting-link between the galley and the frigate. The English are said to be the first who used this class of vessel equipped for war as well as commerce on the ocean. But all the earlier frigates and sea-going galleys, or xebecs, were constructed with a view to an attack delivered from the fore part or forecastle of the ship. Their broadside-guns were few, while the after end and lofty poop was almost defenceless: a mode of construction due to the importance attached by early seamen, not only of obtaining, but of retaining, the weather-gauge of an enemy whenever it was possible to do so in a breeze.

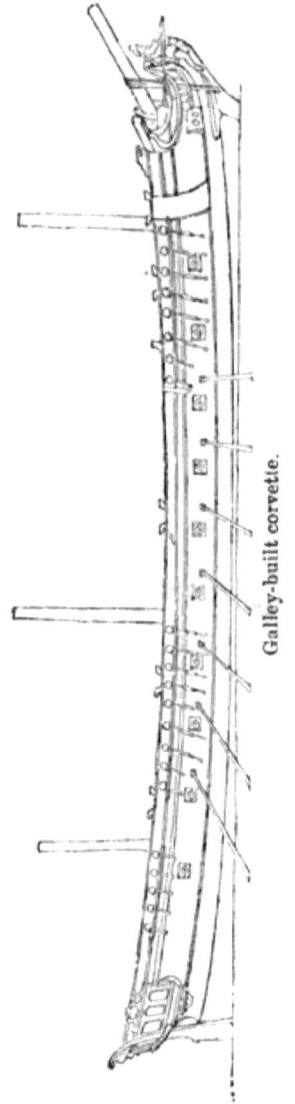

Galley-built corvette.

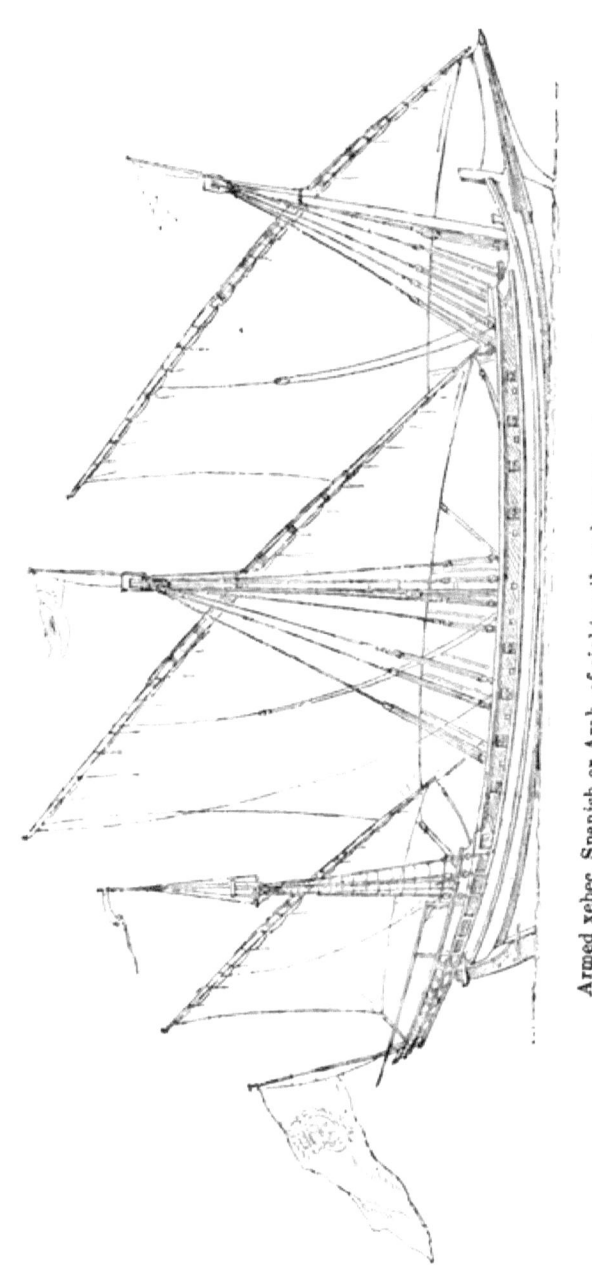

Armed xebec, Spanish or Arab, of eighteenth and seventeenth centuries.

From a circumstantial account of an action in 1545 between a French fleet of "a hundred and fifty large ships, sixty of inferior size, and twenty-five galleys," and an English fleet under Lord Howard, written by Sieur Martin Du Bellay, it is evident that both the English and French had at that date fast, handy ships capable of working and holding their own to windward. In this narrative we learn also that the English had then a "light sort of pinnace, longer than ordinary in proportion to beam, being narrower than the French galleys, but worked like them both under sail and oar. . . . Which vessels were so well handled by their sailors, among the tideways round the Isle of Wight, that in speed they proved as fast or faster than the French galleys, upon which they bore down, and so galled their sterns with their artillery that the destruction of the French galleys seemed inevitable. For, had the galleys ventured to turn, or haul their wind, these English vessels would have been over them instantly. Nevertheless, the *Prior of Capua*, no longer able to bear this disgraceful position, began to haul her wind in order to attack one of the enemy's foremost vessels, which was almost touching the stern-post of a galley. But the English vessel, being shorter, was round before her, and regained her consorts; after which the English discontinued the pursuit." In this action the English fleet was smaller than the French, and was acting defensively, having been attacked by the French galleys at Spithead in the morning, under oars, before the day-breeze sprang up.

But it is very significant that, after this, the mere fact of the English ships being to windward of them was enough to deter the French from attacking them; while a dread of following the French fleet too far, with the chance of the wind failing or changing, and so enabling the French to again use their galleys under oars, caused the English to give up chasing them.

It was this plan of attack that was adopted by the commanders of our handy little ships when they followed in the wake, and galled with the artillery of their forecastles the lofty sterns of the Armada galleons; our seamen, once they had the Spanish ships to leeward of them, taking good care, both by night and day, to keep them there. To ensure success in this mode of attack, speed, weatherly qualities, and handiness in the ships, with seamanship on the part of their captains and crews, were essential, and in each and all of these qualities, together with local knowledge, our men and ships were superior to those of the Armada. So that when Drake waited quietly to finish his game of bowls on Plymouth Hoe, he knew well enough that to put to sea before the

Spaniards had run past Plymouth would only be putting them in a position to give or refuse an attack; while, once he had them well under his lee in the narrower part of the Channel, they would only be able to do so in a calm with their galleys, in which case he had no doubt some of those narrow, light

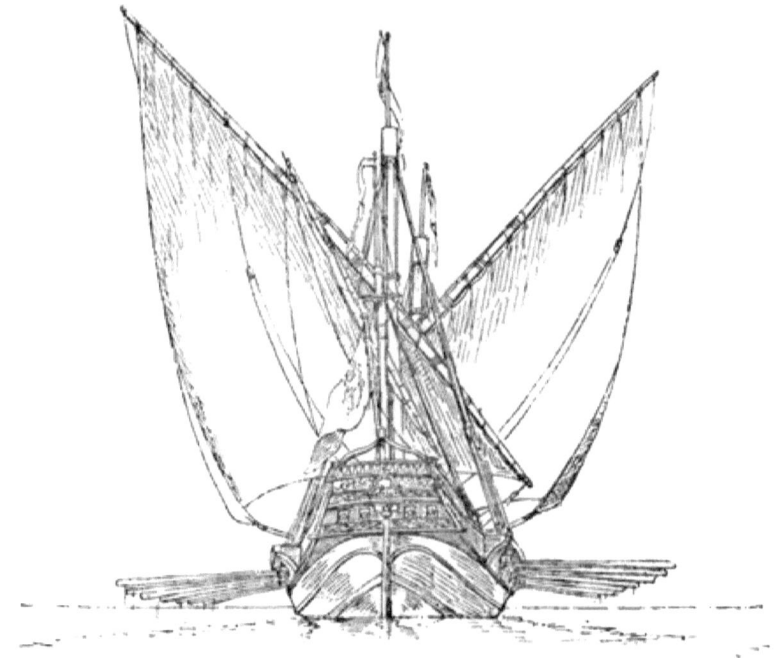

Xebec with sails "en oreilles de lievra" (hare's ears, or goose-winged).

pinnaces, worked with oars, ready for them, just as they were for the French, near the Isle of Wight, in 1545.

It is curious that the term "galley-way," or "give her good galley way," is still often used among Southampton watermen.

CHAPTER X.

FIGURE-HEADS.

"Old Friends"—Figure-heads ashore, on and off duty—Heads of "Fighting *Téméraire*" and *Victory*—The *Téméraire* at Trafalgar, and towed to her last berth—Turner's accuracy in certain details in this picture—The anatomy of a sea-going ship's beak-head, etc.—An early type of true stem—The upright American axe-bow—The old frigate bow, some advantages and drawbacks of it—Bowsprit gammoning—A naval figure-head out of place—From the eye of the Chinese junk to the highly developed human eighteenth-century figure-head, etc.

MR. H. STACY MARKS was certainly doing his duty as an historical painter when some years back he gave us, under the title of "Old Friends," his picture of three figure-heads of ships that may have fought at Trafalgar or the Nile. The scene is laid outside some large Thames ship-breaker's yard, and two Greenwich pensioners are fighting their battles again, as they stand below and recognize the ghost-like forms of all that remains of ships they may have fought in as boys. One of these relics is a portrait of Nelson, with a gas-lamp attached to, and projecting from it. A fact, no doubt, noted for us by the painter, and very significant of the value put upon such marine stores to-day.

In many outlying sea-coast hamlets, one often comes across an old figure-head, generally an armless

"Old Friends." From a drawing by H. Stacy Marks, R.A.

trunk, which stands grimly looking up to the sky in a small coastguard or fisherman's cottage-garden—a weather-stained cenotaph of a ship and her crew, carved for and carried by them proudly over the sea, years before it was washed up from the shattered hull of some eighteenth-century frigate or Indiaman;

while in such places the more enduring oaken ribs of the ship that bore the head, often form the principal beams of cottages, in which men still live with whom rests the only record of her wreck. Perhaps the largest collection of this class of figure-head is that in the Scilly Islands; where numbers stand about, and, as subjects of Mr. Augustus Smith, do their duty in his little kingdom as gate-posts, or supports of summerhouse, etc.

But owing to neglect, and still more perhaps to the material, mostly English elm, used by ship-carvers, very old figure-heads are not common; and many of us know more to-day of the look of a Roman emperor, or Greek warrior, than we do of the figure-head of such a ship as the "Fighting *Téméraire*," only broken up in the Thames fifty years ago.

But as shown in a fine old model of the ship, made for us by the French prisoners at Portsmouth, it is said out of their beef bones, this head—a full-length figure of the god of war—must have been a masterpiece of the ship-carver's art.

This vessel, the real "Fighting *Téméraire*" of Turner's great picture, must not be confused with the older French-built ship of the same name, of seventy-four guns, captured by Admiral Boscawen in 1759, and sold in 1794. The "Fighting *Téméraire*" was a ninety-eight-gun ship, built at Chatham, and launched in 1798, and was desperately engaged at Trafalgar, where she followed Nelson's ship, the *Victory*, into action. It is curious to find, from a model at Greenwich, that the figure-head of Nelson's favourite was a *facsimile* of the head of an older line-of-battle ship

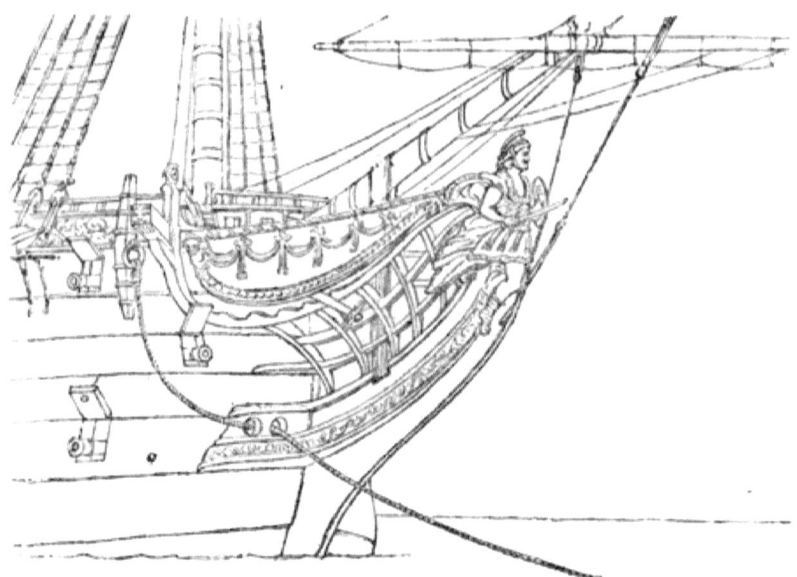

Head of "Fighting *Téméraire*" (Turner's), a 98-gun ship.

of the same name, lost with all hands in the Channel in 1744.

At Trafalgar "the *Téméraire* was commanded by Captain Elias Harvey, with Thomas Kennedy as first-lieutenant; her rigging and spars were almost entirely cut to pieces, the head of her rudder was shot off, and eight feet of the starboard side of her lower-deck, abreast the mainmast, was stove in. During the action the *Téméraire* was fouled by the French ship *Fougeux*, and was at once lashed to that ship; then

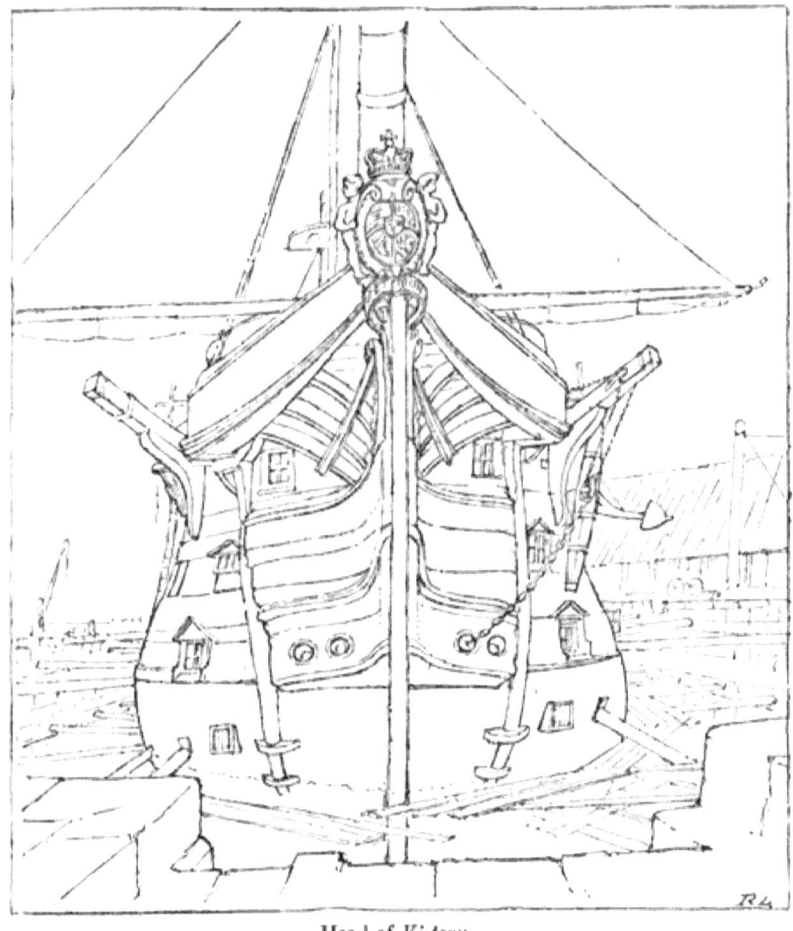

Head of *Victory*.

Kennedy, with James Arscot, mate, Robert Helgate, midshipman, twenty men and six marines, boarded the *Fougeux*, and in ten minutes she was taken."

I have repeated this noble story because Mr. Thornbury, in his "Life of Turner," states that, when a title was wanted for an engraving of the *Téméraire*, no history of the ship could be found. Turner insisted that the title ought to be the "Fighting *Téméraire*" (the title he gave in the Academy Catalogue); but, owing to the mistake of looking upon this ship as the older French seventy-four, which was broken up when Turner was a child, long before he saw the ninety-eight-gun ship "towed to her last berth" in 1838, this title was not considered historically correct, and with great reluctance Turner allowed the engraving to be called the "*Old Téméraire*," etc. How little was then known of the history of either ship is shown by Mr. Thornbury speaking of the *Téméraire* as having been taken from the French at the Battle of the Nile! The fact being that no ship of that name, French or English, was engaged in that action. Nautical critics of his time also fell foul of Turner for representing his ship as rigged, or jury-rigged, when being towed to her "last berth." But from Admiralty records it is now ascertained that, though an unusual thing, this vessel was actually sold to a ship-breaker with masts, yards, and rigging, all standing, in 1838, just as Turner saw and painted her. The truth is that Turner, who then spent much of his time upon the Thames in his own boat, and among watermen in riverside resorts, probably knew more of the history of the ship he painted than most of his nautical critics or Mr. Thornbury.

To naval architects the *Téméraire* is also interesting, as having been one of the last of our old line-of-battle ships built with a "beak-head," that is, with her upper

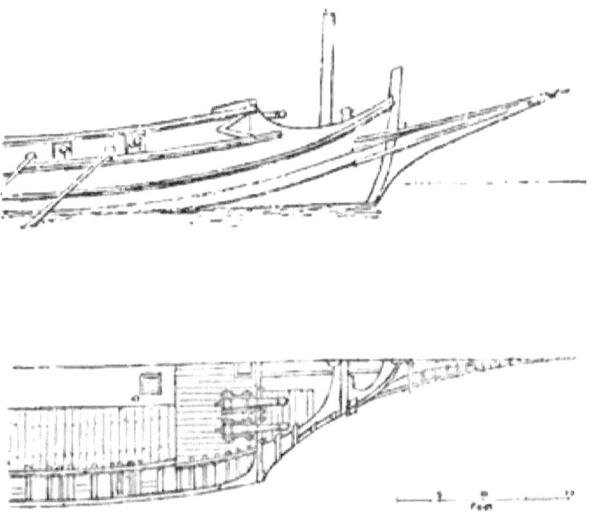

Head of eighteenth and seventeenth century war-galley, with half-deck plan of the same.

works cut square across forward in a line with the cat-heads, after the fashion of the old galley and galleon; a form of bow afterwards abandoned, as, from experience in the early part of the French War, it was found to expose the crew working the guns too much to an enemy's fire. This detail is also noted by Turner. Whether built in this way or not, in all the old wooden ships, that part of the vessel called the "head" was an independent structure built beyond the true stem, which, as it does now in most Norwegian, Italian, and Spanish small vessels, rose high above it.

In the ancient Roman and Greek war-galleys propelled by oars, and furnished with a ram projecting below the water-line, the head ornament was usually carved upon and carried by this inner or true stem; but upon the introduction of cannon, when war-vessels began to depend more upon sails than oars, the ram-bow disappeared, and figure-heads took the place they so long held on the beak itself, carried beyond the stem by the solid bracket-shaped timber or knee of the head, which supported all the complicated arrangements and decoration of this part of the old ships, like the overhanging gable of an ancient timbered house. So that the head of one of these seventeenth or eighteenth century ships might be entirely demolished without interfering in the least with the seaworthiness

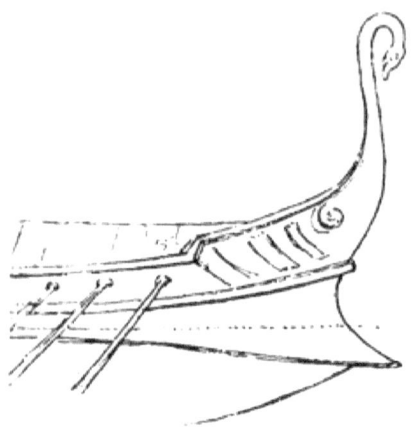

Head of Greek war-galley (old coin).

of her hull abaft it. But, driven by steam and pro-

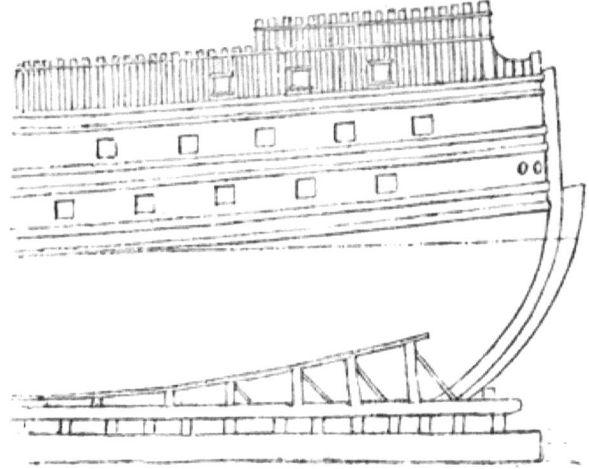

Bow of eighteenth-century line-of-battle ship on the stocks, before the addition of the beak-head.

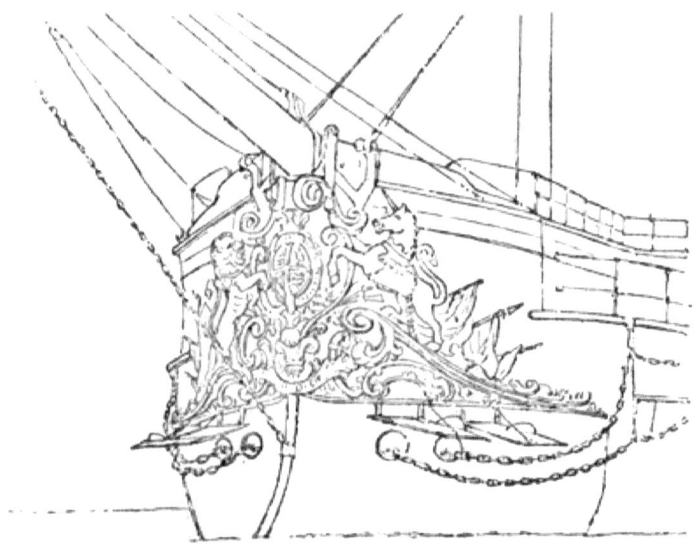

Decoration on stem of ram-bowed ironclad.

tected by armour, the modern war-ship has again reverted to the ram-form of bow; and figure-heads, or rather bow decorations, have once more found their place upon the actual stem of the ship's hull.

The word "stem," according to Johnson, is derived from the Icelandic verb *stæmma*, to oppose a current, or to go forward, notwithstanding a stream; and the Swedish word *stammen*, the prow of a ship, is of the same origin; while, in some early English books, "stem" is written the "stamine head." But one of the earliest recorded forms of boat, a model found, I believe, in some Egyptian queen's tomb, suggests another derivation for this word. Like all early types, this boat has both ends alike, and these take the actual shape of a thick stem, which, as it tapers upwards, bears a lotus or water-lily leaf; the disc of the leaf being the sole decoration of this entirely peaceful character of boat.

Early Egyptian boat, with lotus *stem* at either end.

Many changes and some improvements in modern ship-building are of American origin; and among these is the upright American axe-shaped head of our ocean steamers, which has almost superseded the old frigate-bow, as it was called, with its long flowing curve terminating in a gracefully carved figure. The American paddle-wheel steamships, *Fulton*, *Arago*, and *Adriatic*, were among the first vessels built in this way, and proved very fine sea-boats.

The *Great Eastern* had a bow of this kind; but in the Cunard liners, the frigate-bow was retained for many years afterwards.

The *Adriatic*, built by Steers, the builder of the yacht *America*, was not only one of the finest specimens of naval architecture of her date, but one of the most comfortable of Atlantic steamships. She, however, proved too large and expensive as a passenger-carrying vessel, and after being first sold to an English company, the Galway line, she was, when that company failed, converted into a sailing-ship for the Californian wheat-trade.

The long old-fashioned bowsprit, with its "gammoning," * or rope-lashing, upon which the safety, not

---

* Chain, or an iron strap, has long taken the place of hemp as the gammoning of a bowsprit, but in the days of rope-gammonings the whole affair was a most important one, and the boatswain always had a well-stretched nearly new rope ready for it, which had been used as a "heel," or "top rope," in hoisting up a main or foretopmast. A fine warm dry day was also chosen for the work, and eleven turns of the rope were taken over the bowsprit and through a mortise in the knee of the head, each turn being hove taut by capstan-power, and further tautened by cross or frapping turns taken round them. Is the word "gammoning" derived from the Italian *gambone*, to encourage, support? it also signifies the stout stem of a plant.

only of this spar, but of the foremast and maintopmast, formerly depended, led no doubt to the knee of the head being retained among sailing-ships for some years in its original weight and strength; but as bows increased in length and sharpness, the bowsprit in clipper ships became a shorter spar, and a lighter form of head, incorporated with the true stem of the ship, became the fashion. All extra weight forward is worse than useless in a seaway, while every inch of length adds to the difficulty of handling a ship in dock or in a crowded river.

But whether the old frigate-bow did not act at times, in cases of collision, as a form of buffer, is a question not altogether without value. In the case of one of the early Cunarders (the *Canada*) it certainly proved useful in this way, when in a dense fog, after crumpling up her bowsprit, figure-head, etc., forward, into matchwood against a steep wall of ice, her topgallant forecastle being lifted up like the leaf of a table, her hull still remained tight below water; so that she was able to reach Halifax, distant some five hundred miles, in safety.

In collisions between sailing-vessels of the old types, it was not uncommon for a ship to leave her figurehead on board the ship collided with, the captain of which, particularly if close-hauled on the *starboard* tack, was sure to take care of it, as a silent but reliable witness to the identity of the vessel that had fouled him. In a seaway, on the other hand, the overhanging stem, etc., once entangled in another ship's rigging,

Figure-head of H.M.S. *Warrior*.

was, after a collision, not easy to get clear of, and often led to a succession of downward chopping blows even more fatal, in the days of wooden ships, to the ship run into, than the first shock. The first of our English ironclads, the (*Warrior*, had a frigate-bow with a magnificent figure-head, which she contrived one day, in manœuvring under sail, to deposit in the gun-room of the *Royal Oak*; probably the first and last figure-head likely to find itself in such a locality.)

Beyond being often the earliest head in the ship to practically discover the position of another vessel, figure-heads should have no more to do with collisions

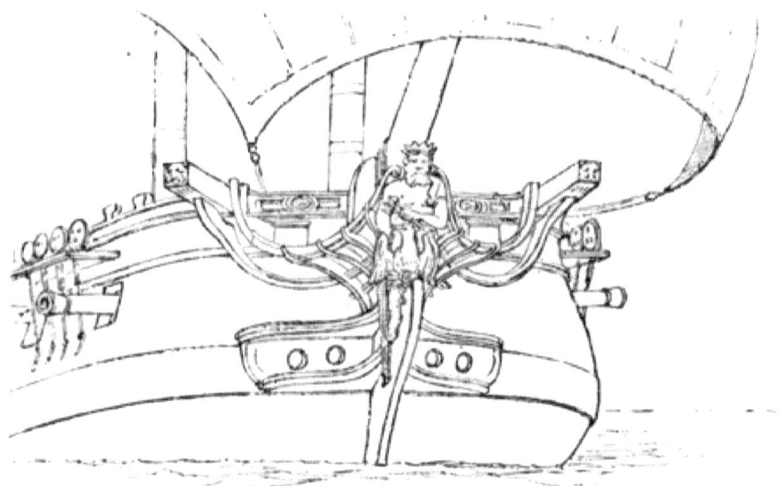

Figure-head, *Jupiter* (French 28-gun ship).

at sea than the big eye painted by the Chinaman on the head of his junk has in keeping her clear of them.

Scientific naturalists, however, tell us that all forms, human or animal, begin in some low type of eye. It is just possible, therefore, that this eye* of

---

* I believe I am wrong, or not up to date about this eye, and that we are told now to look to some simple form of sac, bag, or stomach, as the origin of all things, figure-heads, of course, included.

the junk, by a slow process of evolution, became in time the highly organized figure-head of our seventeenth and eighteenth century ships, which for so many years held its own above the waves, plunging into, and rising from the foam, below the great arch of the spritsail.

CHAPTER XI.

FIGURE-HEADS (*continued*).

> Strange head of New Zealand war-canoe—How did it get there?—
> The old rampant lion-head—"The lion's whelps"—"The sweep
> of the lion"—A Frenchman's description of and objection to—
> A Yankee skipper's objection—An equestrian figure-head, and
> its connection with the fate of Charles I.—The *Sovereign of
> the Seas*—Her knight-heads, apostles, and cat-heads—Career and
> fate of this ship—A later equestrian head, the *Royal George*—
> Why she was lost—Coloured figure-heads of old war-ships—A
> figure-head laid up in ordinary—Figure-heads and their re-
> movable limbs in action—The modern steamer's geographical
> head—The respectable nineteenth-century merchantman's head
> —A very humble little lady-head—A revival of her in other
> forms among yachts, etc.—Figure-head in repose.

It is curious to note that while the ships of the Chinese and Japanese remained almost figure-headless, how a more warlike, but almost isolated, race of men in New Zealand decorated their canoes with a figure as highly developed as any of those upon our own sixteenth-century ships; to which, indeed, with its wonderfully executed carved open-work supports, etc., this grotesque head of a New Zealand war-canoe bears a striking resemblance. If a nation is to be judged as to its civilization by the amount of carving and decoration upon its weapons and war-ships, the New Zealanders ought to take a high rank.

When these canoes were first found and described by Captain Cook, the people who carved them could have had no idea of any animal of the lion character, and it is not easy to account for this strange form upon their canoes, unless it may have been suggested

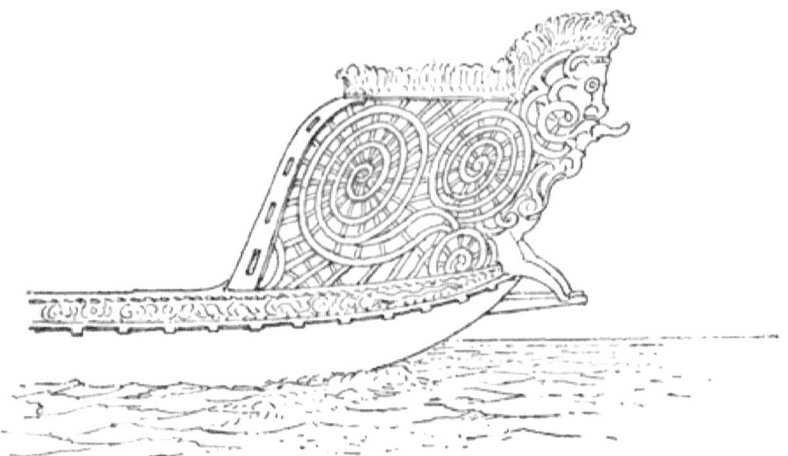

Head of New Zealand war-canoe.

to them by the derelict head of some early sixteenth-century navigator's ship cast up on the shores of their islands. It is certain that a lion rampant, sometimes crowned, and bearing on a shield the arms of his country, was the most usual decoration of the prow of sixteenth and seventeenth century vessels, especially those of the smaller class. But ships were then so loaded from stem to stern with carvings as to greatly diminish the importance of the leading figure of the head, which was also at that time more built into, or incorporated with, the beak of the head itself than the figures upon the heads of ships of a later date were. This was no doubt a necessity in the long projecting heads of ships of the period of the lion's first, second, third, fourth, and fifth whelps, etc., to enable them to

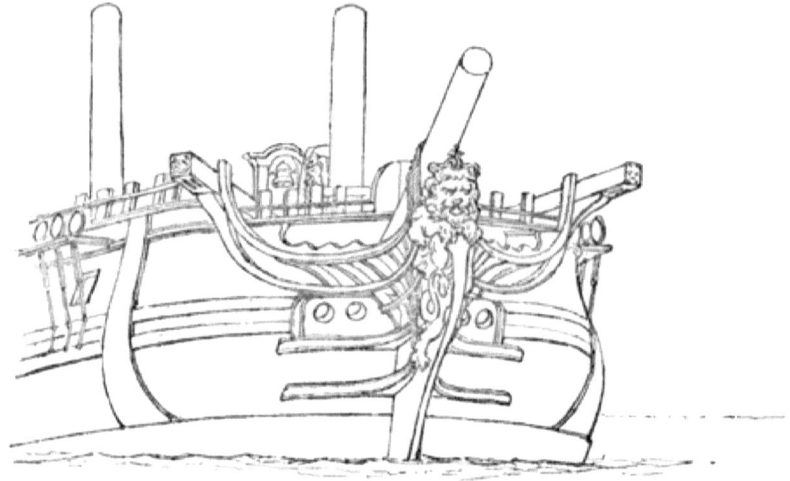

One of the lion's whelps.

better withstand a playful dive now and then into a wave. In an old French work on ship-building, great stress is laid upon, and a whole page of illustration is devoted to, the exact curve of the head, or, as it was then called, "the sweep of the lion;" and this particular curve was retained as the only right one for figure-heads for years; so that, no matter what the celestial or terrestrial rank of one might be, it was always so arranged as to flow of drapery, or disposition of limb, as to conform to all the cat-like curves of this old ship-carver's inexorable "sweep of the lion." From some remarks also of the French writer, Lescallier, who wrote upon this subject in 1780, it appears that about that

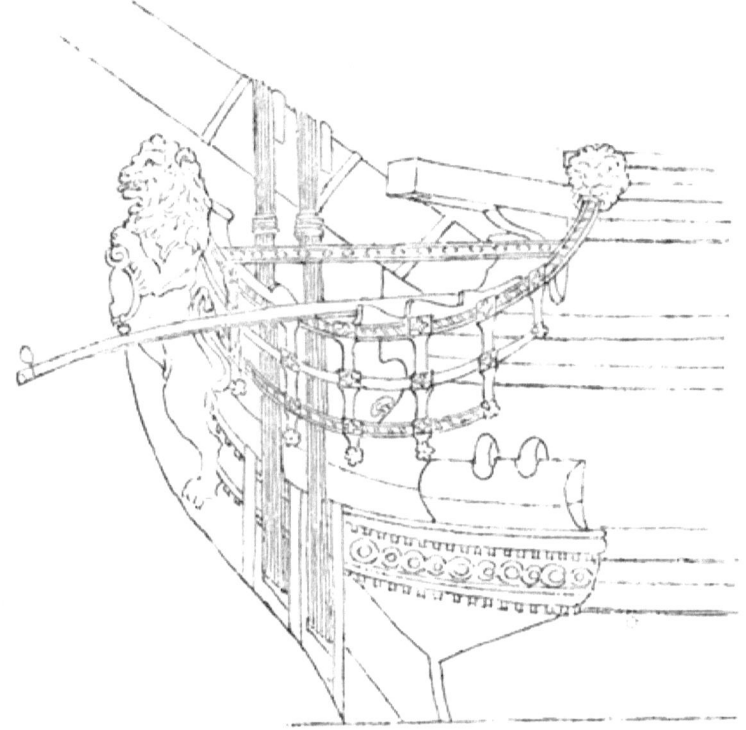

Lion-head, eighteenth century, French.

time it was customary to give many French men-of-war a lion-head, with a view of hiding their nationality; for, after remarking "that a ship's figure-head should represent some deity or hero having a connection with the vessel's name," he says, "but this rule cannot be followed so long as we persist in trying to make our vessels look like those of the English, by giving them a lion-head, which," he adds, "is always placed astraddle, and in a very forced attitude, painful enough to look at even in an animal; but little less than ridiculous when a figure of Flora, Pomona, or Atalanta is seen in such a position."

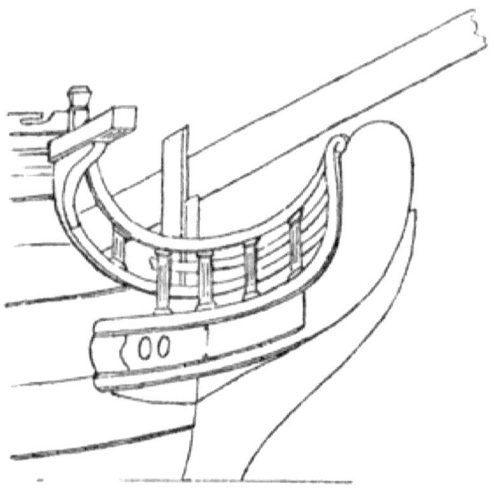

English frigate-head, eighteenth century.

I give, from Lescallier, one of these old French lion-heads, in which drawing also the arrangement of the gammonings of an old bowsprit, described in the last chapter, are well seen.

In the above cut of an English frigate's head is shown the timber conforming to the "sweep of the lion;" to either side of which the carving, in alto-relievo, of the figure-head was attached. The position is also seen here of the timber or scroll-shaped bracket of the head, always called "the hair-bracket," from its rising just abaft this timber, and meeting or supporting the lion's mane, or the hair of a figure-head.

It was of course a Yankee skipper who, some fifty years ago, first attempted to resist this old "sweep of the lion," and being a large owner in, as well as commander of his packet, actually had carved for her a full-length figure of our Queen, with drapery and robes about her just as they would hang in a calm; giving as his reason for this tremendous innovation that "he guessed she looked nicer so, and that he didn't want to see his ship look as though she always had the wind dead ahead." But a head-wind was of more consequence to a seaman then than it is to-day, when a steamer always makes a head-wind for herself out of a calm, or even a moderately fair one.

How and why, during the troubled reign of Charles I., figure-heads, with their numerous accessories or retainers, came at last to have an influence upon politics, will be best understood by a glance at the head of the *Sovereign of the Seas*, built for Charles by the celebrated Phineas Pet, and launched in 1637.

This was the year after John Hampden's resistance to the king's arbitrary levy of ship-money; and

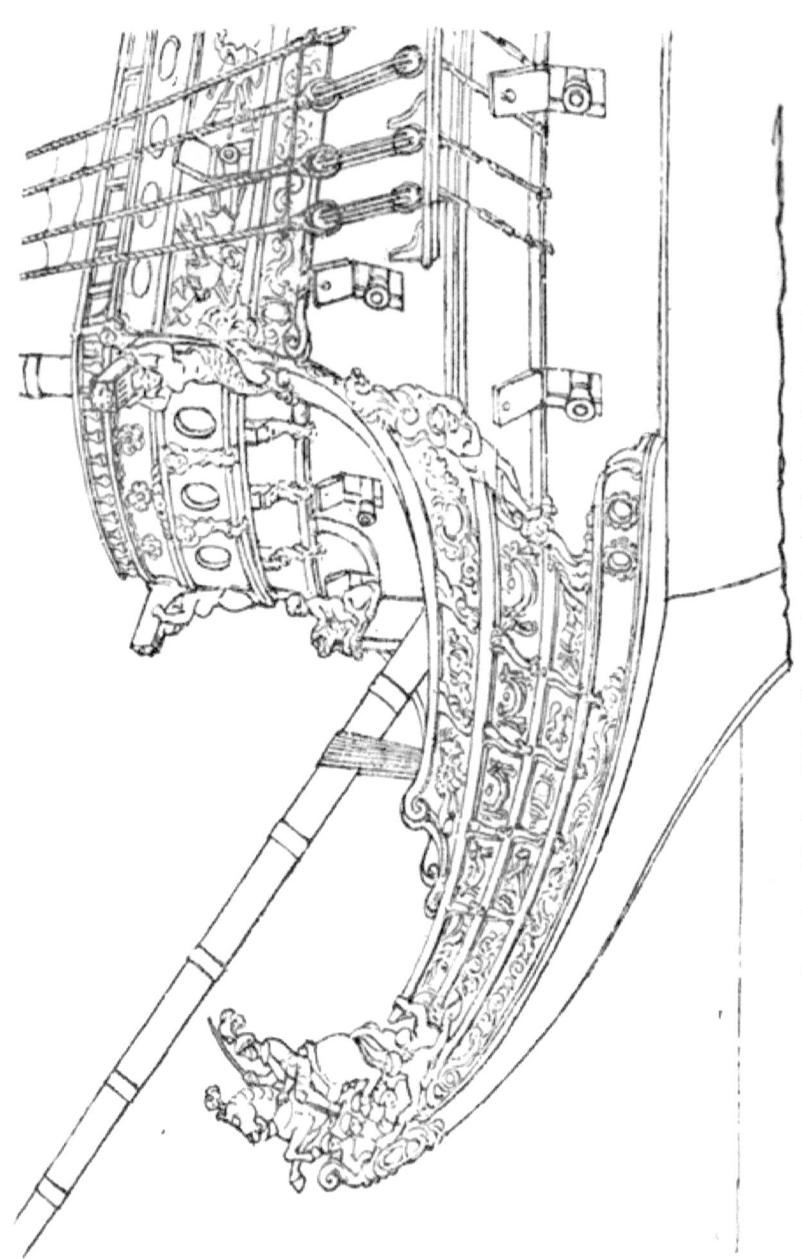

Sovereign of the Seas, 1637. From a drawing by the elder Vandervelde.

though since then larger sums than this really useful old ship cost have been squandered by Governments upon war-ships and big guns, very little of it has been devoted to outside show. We are told by Thomas Haywood, the designer of her decorations, that the leading figure-head, or, rather, equestrian statue, "which sitteth upon her beak-head, is the Royal King Edgar on horseback, trampling upon seven kings—alluding to the story in the Saxon chronicle of his having been acknowledged supreme lord by the other kings of Britain." So that this monarch (who appears to have been fond of yachting, but of doubtful morals), when he made his annual cruise round England, was rowed in his barge on the Dee by eight of his subject kings: viz. of Scotland, Cumberland, Westmorland, Anglesey with the Isle of Man and the Hebrides, Galloway, and North, South, and Middle Wales.

It is curious to note in this ship, that while her outer beak or prow bears an emblem of sheer might as right, her stem, or, as it is written, the "stemine head" (the true stem of the ship), bears upon it a figure of Cupid astride of a lion; "emblematical," says Haywood, "of the higher Power whose majesty is over all, and rules all His works." After being cut down one deck, this *Sovereign of the Seas* proved herself, for nearly sixty years, one of England's best men-of-war.

But after a long and most successful fighting career against France and Holland, she was accidentally burnt in Chatham Dockyard, when laid up there in order to be almost rebuilt. Naval architects in those days had evidently little doubt as to the best type of war-ships. In addition to the central or leading figure in all these old ships, the upper ends of the principal bow-timbers which, rising above the forecastle rail, are still known as "knight-heads," were carved into the actual form of helmed knights. The old French sea-term, "apôtres" (or apostles), for these timber heads, seems to show that originally the number of these carved bollards must have been twelve.

The term "cat-heads," used for the two stout projecting timbers on either bow, from which the anchor hung clear of the ship before it was let go, was no doubt connected with the face of a lion, or large cat, usually carved upon the square ends of them.

This head of the *Royal George* gives the position of some of these knight-heads, or apostles, as well as the lion's face upon the cat-head. Like the *Sovereign of the Seas*, this ship was one of the finest line-of-

IN THE DAYS OF OAK AND HEMP. 155

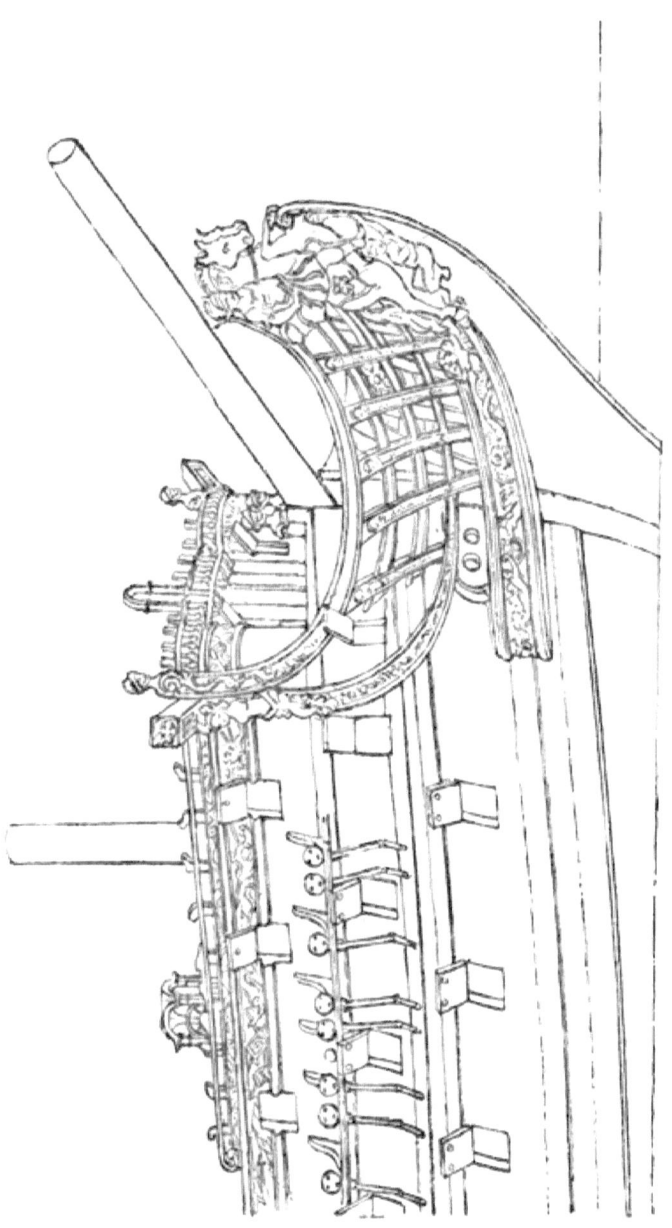

Head of *Royal George*, 1756.

battle ships of her time, and a comparison of her beak-head with that of the older ship, gives a good idea of the changes that had taken place in this part of a ship after the lapse of a hundred and twenty years. The *Royal George* was launched at Woolwich in 1756, and, as we all know, was capsized and sunk at her anchorage, Spithead, while heeled over to repair an old worn-out sea-water tap in her bottom. Enough of her recovered timber and copper has, I believe, since then been sold at Portsmouth, in the shape of relicts, to have built two such ships. In speaking of the fate of this fine old ship, it is always said that it was due to a sudden squall. But from a circumstantial narrative of the disaster by a survivor, published in 1834, in that mine of information, the good old *Penny Magazine*, it seems that her loss was really owing to the obstinacy, or worse, of a lieutenant of the watch. In this account we are told how, with the ship inclined at an angle of between twenty and thirty degrees, her topgallant masts on end, and the ship in charge of a second or third lieutenant, Admiral Kempenfeldt, of the blue, then over seventy, was being shaved in his cabin by the ship's barber, while most of the hands below were busy stowing rum-casks—hoisting them in from a lighter lashed to that side of the ship into which the short Spithead sea was already washing through the lower-deck ports; these ports having to be all open to allow the great guns to be run out on that side to help give the ship the required heel. Yet, so far, no anxiety about the stability of the ship seems to have been felt by any one; and, sailor like, the men on this lower deck " were enjoying," says the writer, "a rare game hunting mice that had been driven up from below by the water in the ship's bilge!"

The carpenter, who was superintending the work outside the ship's bottom, appears to have been the first person to think it time to make some change in the ship's position, and mounted to the quarter-deck to ask the lieutenant in charge to give the order " to right ship." The lieutenant, however, gave him a very short answer, and the carpenter left the quarter-deck, but soon afterwards returned and repeated his request and warning. This time the reply was, " D—e, sir, if you can manage the ship better than I can, you'd better take command." However, shortly afterwards the lieutenant ordered the drummer to be called to beat " to right ship." It was too late, for the writer says "there was no time for him to beat his drum, and I don't know that he even had time to get it."

In the peaceful years that followed the times of Howe, Vincent, and Nelson, the ship-carver's art gradually became less florid in character, and the bright colouring which was a strong feature in all eighteenth-century figure-heads, slowly went out of fashion, particularly among the more aristocratic classes of them in the navy and larger merchant-ships. But in Lutherburg's picture, at Greenwich Hospital, of the action of

Trafalgar, 190 guns.   Lord Nelson housed.

the 1st of June, 1794, the figure-heads of the two leading vessels, the *Queen Charlotte* and *Le Montagne*, are as brightly coloured as the figures of saints, etc., are in Roman Catholic churches.

Many of these old coloured figures are still preserved in a room at Devonport, removed, no doubt, from some of the venerable hulks which lie near them, moored in Hamoaze. Perhaps it was found more economical, as well as better for these figure-heads, to house them thus together under one roof, than to give them that individual outdoor protection which, for some years after the war-time, it was customary to build over them, like this figure of Lord Nelson upon the *Trafalgar*, 190-gun ship, laid up at Chatham in 1824.

In order to economize timber in construction, and that they might be less in the way of the fire of the bow-guns, all the arms, wings, or other lateral projections of figure-heads of gods, saints, heroes, etc., when engaged in active service, were ingeniously contrived to unship.

A glance at the confusion that raged about the heads of these old ships at such times—shown in the central portion of a sea-fight by Lutherburg—explains how convenient this crab-like facility of parting with and replacing limbs must have been.

As commerce extended, and our ocean lines of steamers began to run east, west, and south, the figure-head of the nineteenth century rapidly grew less warlike, and became distinctly geographical in character: the heads of the large steam-companies' ships often taking the embodied shape of a river, nation, or even of one of the quarters of the globe. But on private merchantmen, especially among sailing-ships, so long as a frigate-bow was retained to carry him, it was usual to meet, in walking round the London Docks a few years back, the highly respectable and well-dressed

Figure-heads in action.

portrait and complacent smile of some hard-featured, well-to-do merchant or ship-owner, or perhaps even of his wife, as the figure-head and true ruler of the nineteenth-century waves.

But even these prosperous ladies and gentlemen have, most of them, now become marine stores; and the only figure of their class which survives is the less aristocratic, stout little North-country lady, which, in a short-waisted, bright red-and-blue bodice, still now and then peers out before the gammoning of a bluff-bowed old collier's bowsprit.

It may be noticed that the arms of the little

A nineteenth-century ruler of the waves.

guardian angel of this old brig (see p. 162) are absent, or, as sailors say, are unshipped; in fact, owing to the shortness of the brig's voyages, and length of time spent in crowded ports, loading or unloading coals, these precious limbs are mostly kept carefully stowed away in the skipper's cabin, along with his best hat and shore-going togs.

Before closing this chapter I must not omit to say that of late years there has been quite a revival of the ship-carver's art—which may be seen and studied by all who go down to the sea at Cowes or Ryde—in the shape of figure-heads of delicately and artistically

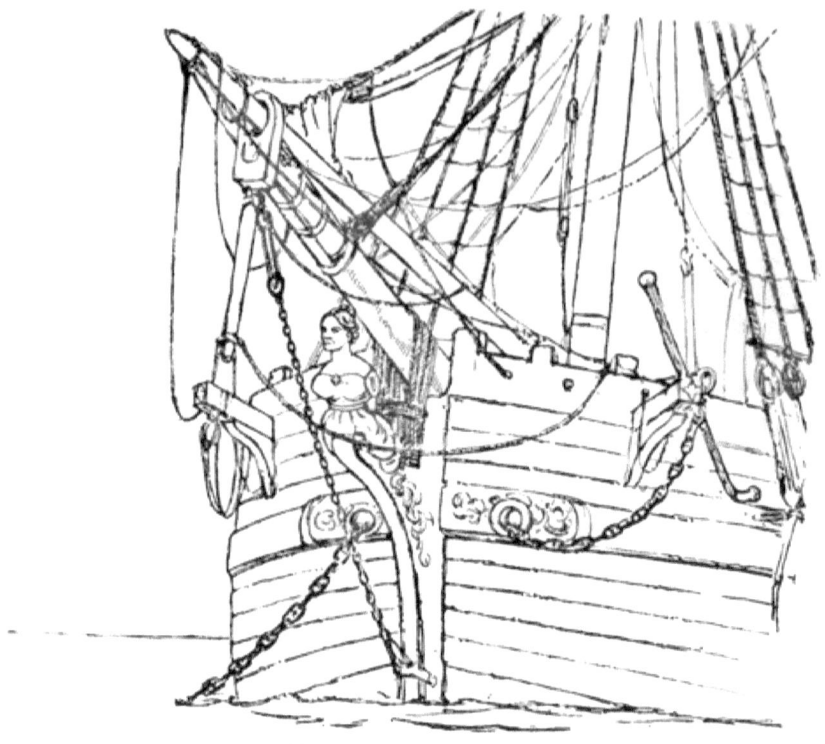

Figure-head of collier brig.

carved water-sprites and sea-nymphs; which, securely perched upon the stems of our modern big steam and schooner yachts, there idle away most of their time; too often, I regret to add, with that most unseamanlike sight below them, of two round turns in the hawse of the ship they decorate; which may partly account for the fact that none of these modern sea-nymphs look as much at home, or at their ease as figure heads, as this jolly young waterman of old did, when, seated on the bow of his skiff, he watched upon a common hard for a fare to or from an outward-bound man-of-war.

Figure-head in repose (Tom Tug).

CHAPTER XII.

OLD SEA-LIGHTS.

The sea-chandelier—Great size of early poop-lanterns, and reason for it—Importance of the ship-chandler and art of candle-making to old seamen—Night-signal at Battle of the Nile—Rodney's night-action off St. Vincent, and naval manœuvres in 1781—Code of old naval night-signals—How St. George's Channel was lighted a hundred and forty years back—Between-decks and below in the cock-pit during a night-action, etc.

In a "true description of His Majestie's Royal ship, *Sovereigne of the Seas*" (date 1637), we are told "that she bore five lanthorns, the biggest of which would hold ten persons to stand upright without shouldering or pressing one the other." From the great height and narrow form of the poop of sixteenth and seventeenth century ships, and the arrangement of the three lanterns there upon iron crutches, or, as they were always called by the French, "chandeliers," seen in the sketch, it is evident that when the large central light was hidden by the ship's masts, etc., the other two would be visible upon a ship bearing down, or exactly end on to another vessel, and would therefore be a danger-signal to that vessel; while the shutting in of one of them would indicate to her, either that she had passed the line of the approaching ship's

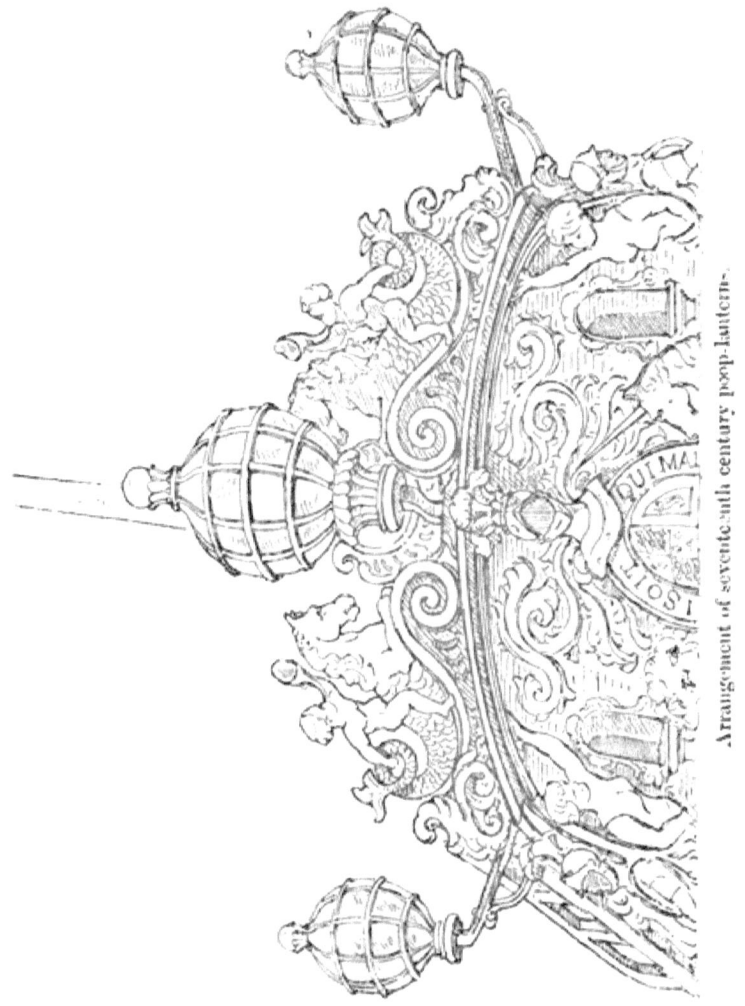

Arrangement of seventeenth century poop-lantern.

course, or that the ship had turned to starboard or port, according to which of the lights had first become invisible.

Again, with the three lights in one, or nearly so—the larger one being always above the other two—a ship would be known to be nearly broadside to the spectator. We still use the light of a candle as the standard measure of illuminating power (even of the electric light), and that these three chief lights of the old ships were of considerable power is shown, I think, by the enormous dimensions of all the earlier poop-lanterns, which allowed candles, not only of a large size, but in considerable numbers, to be used in them. With smaller lanterns this would have been impossible, as, owing to the heat generated, the candles would have rapidly melted down instead of burning. No doubt, soon after the discovery of the Spitzbergen whale-fishery, early in the seventeenth century, sperm oil may have slowly superseded the candle in these fixed or "constant lights," as the poop and top lanterns were called; for the later poop-lanterns of the eighteenth century were much smaller. Still, owing to the lively motions at sea of our small old-fashioned ships, and the difficulty of keeping oil in its place in a sea-lamp, sailors, and especially fishermen, have always had a strong bias toward the use of a candle-lantern.

Though thought little of to-day (in Protestant England), candle-making was once a most important art—older, of course, than Candlemas Day itself; and no doubt, in the bigger ship's lanterns, the candles

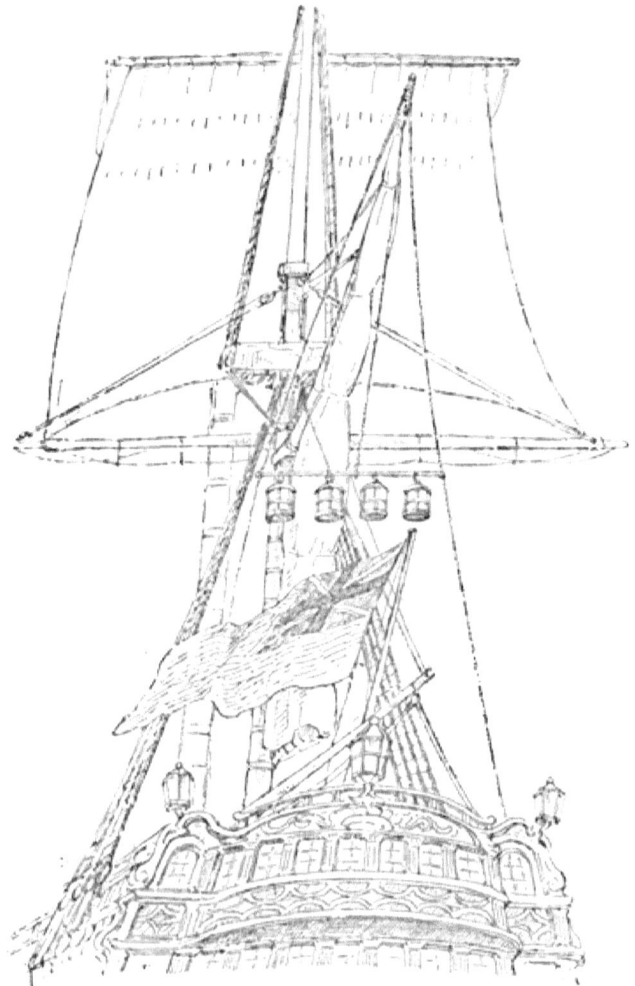

Night-signal lanterns, Battle of the Nile.

burnt were of a very superior make compared to the purser's dip, by light of which petty officers and men of eighteenth-century ships had to grope about their work below. The term "ship-chandler," still in use, also points to the importance formerly attached to this industry and class of marine stores.

In order to give an idea of the way in which the ordinary signal-lanterns were used, I illustrate on p. 167 a night-signal as shown at the Battle of the Nile, from Lutherburg, in whose picture the same signal is seen repeated in a more distant vessel lying in the glare of light caused by the blowing up of the French ship *L'Orient*.

The Nile was a night-action, but it was fought in comparatively smooth water and moderate weather. This was not the case in another very memorable night-action fought eighteen years earlier by Sir George Rodney, when, on his way to relieve Gibraltar, he fell in with a Spanish squadron, under Don J. de Langara, on the night of the 16th of January, 1780, when, "out of eleven ships of the line, five were taken and two destroyed; but the action being at night, and the weather tempestuous, the rest escaped." This short but suggestive paragraph occurs in the *Naval Chronicle* of November, 1801, in an account of the services of "the late Captain Edward Thompson, of the *Hyæna*, repeating frigate in that action, which," adds the old *Chronicle*, "was fought, it may be remembered, under circumstances of peculiar difficulty: a gale of wind, a dark night, upon a lee shore, and on the enemy's coast."

The distinction between what seamen then termed "landmen" and sailors, was far more sharply defined in those days than it is now, and few people ashore, unless they had actually served on board a man-of-war, knew what kind of work handling ships and fighting an enemy off Cape St. Vincent meant on such a night. To-day, however, there are plenty of "landmen" who, having spent a few hours in "the Bay," on board some modern 5000-ton steamship in heavy weather, may be able to realize to some extent the conditions under which such work had to be carried out on a January night by a fleet of line-of-battle ships, though in doing so it must not be overlooked that with the fleet of old liners it was not the case of a single vessel making the best of the gale, and taking care of herself under steam, but of twenty great ships bound to keep in station for fighting purposes, etc., under sail-power only, and all regulated by night-signals, carried from one division of the fleet to another by the "repeating frigate" or frigates of the squadron.

The dazzling electric search-light and flashing signals were then (perhaps fortunately) unknown, and beyond an occasional blue light or "false fire," or a gun or two fired when not in action, all night-signals were given by candle-light in horn lanterns, shown in various parts of the ship's rigging, at times combined with a flag or two—a form of light which, at any rate, left the old seamen's eyes clear and steady to make out the all-important movements of hull and sail by which they were surrounded, often in very close order. The following code of night-signals, forming an article in the "New Royal Cyclopædia, or Modern Dictionary of Arts and Sciences," 1788, will give a fair notion of how our fleets were handled at night by men like Rodney.

When an admiral would have the fleet unmoor, and ride short, he hangs out three lights, one over another, in the maintopmast-shrouds, above the *constant* light in the maintop, and fires two guns, which are answered by flagships, each private ship hanging out a light in her mizzen-shrouds. All guns for night-signals to be fired on the same side, to avoid confusion of sound. When he would have them weigh anchor, he hangs one light in the maintopmast-shrouds, and fires a gun, which is answered by flagships and private ships as before. The signal to tack is two flags on the ensign-staff of the admiral, over the constant light on his poop, and a gun, which is answered by all flagships; each private ship hanging out an extra light not to be taken in till the admiral takes his in. After this signal is made, the leewardmost and sternmost ships must tack as fast as they can; and when about, the sternmost flagship leads the fleet, the rest to follow her to avoid fouling of one another in the dark. When sailing close hauled, if the fleet is required to veer, and bring to on the other tack, the admiral hoists one light on his mizzen-peak, and fires three guns, which is answered by flagships, each private ship answering with a light at her mizzen-peak. In blowing weather, when the admiral wishes the fleet to lie a-try, short, or a-hull, or with head-sails braced to the masts, he forms lights of equal height, and fires five guns, which are answered by flagships, each private ship showing four lights; and when he wishes them to make sail again, he fires ten guns, which are answered by all flags, the weathermost ships making sail first. When a fleet is sailing large, or before the wind, and the admiral desires them to bring to with starboard tacks aboard, he shows four lights in his fore-shrouds, and fires six guns, which are answered by flagships, private ships showing four lights; the windermost ships bringing to first. Whenever the admiral alters his course, he fires one gun, without altering his lights, which is answered by all flagships. Should any ship require to lie by, after the fleet has made sail, she must fire one gun, and show three lights in the mizzen-shrouds. When a ship discovers land or danger, she is to show as many lights as possible, fire one gun and tack, or bear away from it. If a ship spring a leak, or is disabled from keeping company, she hangs out two lights of equal height, and fires guns till relieved by one of the fleet. A ship sighting a fleet is to fire guns, make false fires (blue lights), put one light on his maintop, three on the poop, and steer after them, unless called off by the admiral steering another course and firing two or three guns, when he must follow the admiral. When the fleet is to moor, the admiral puts a light on each topmast-head, and fires a gun, which is answered by flagships, all private ships hoisting one light. If the admiral wishes the fleet to lower yards and topmasts he hoists one light on his ensign-staff, and fires a gun. The signal to hoist them again is two lights, one over the other, in the admiral's mizzen topmast-shrouds, with one gun, which is answered by flagships, private ships showing one light in their mizzen-shrouds. Should a strange ship be seen coming into the fleet, the nearest ship must try and speak her, and not suffer her to pass through the fleet; but if it blows so hard that he is unable to give the admiral timely warning, he must hang out a number of lights, and continue firing gun after gun till he is answered by the admiral. When an admiral would have the fleet to cut (cables) or slip, he hangs out four lights, one at each main and fore yardarm, and fires two guns.

That these eighteenth-century night-signals among ships at sea were in advance of the means then in use to guide seamen after dark as they drew near home ports, is clear from a glance at an old pharos, or light-

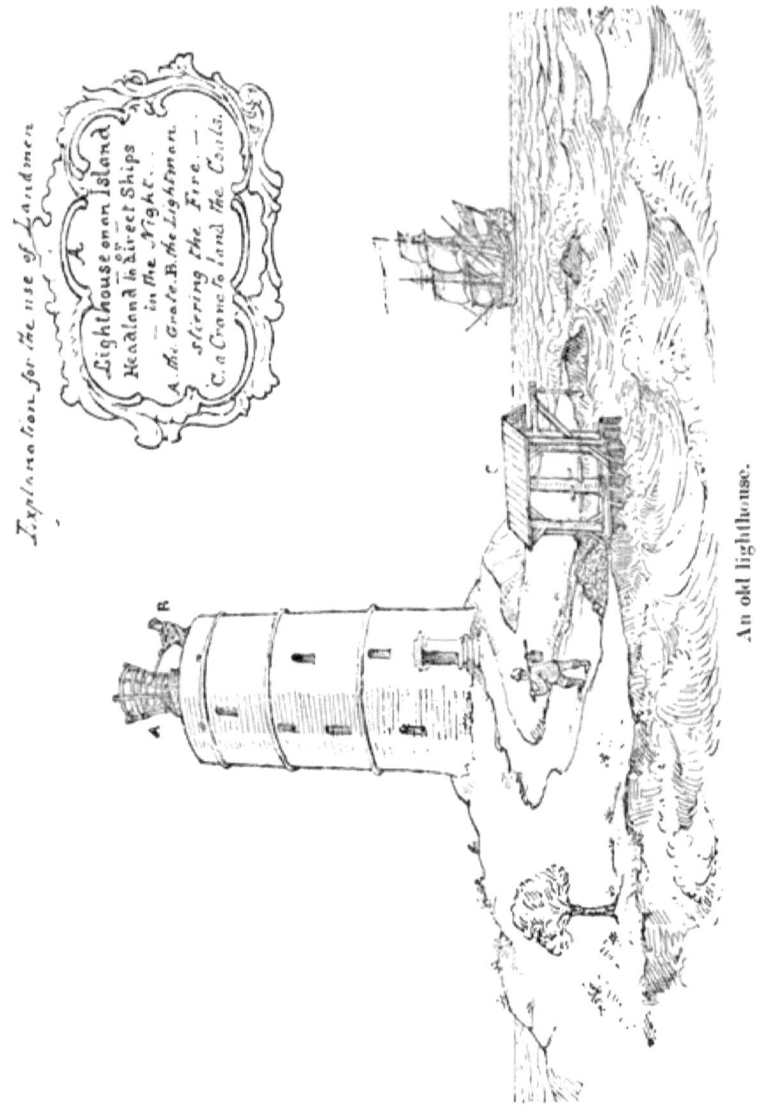

An old lighthouse.

house, "with an explanation for the use of landmen," from a book of "Plans of the harbours, bays, and roadsteads of St. George's Channel, lately surveyed under the direction of the Lords of the Admiralty, and published with their permission by Lewis Morris in 1748."

The huge grate for a beacon-fire at once also suggests how easily master-mariners might then be misled by forged or false beacon-fires of the same kind, kept well stirred for them by the natives of some parts of those wild shores without either permission of the Lords of the Admiralty or Elder Brethren of the Trinity House. Truly, Jack then had to keep a bright look-out for himself, and feel or grope his way by night with the soundings of the narrow seas at his finger-ends, so to say.

But if our ancient mariners had little in the shape of artificial light to dazzle or help them on deck, they were certainly not better off below upon the orlop, in the powder-rooms, cable-tier, or cock-pit, where, even by day, the glimmer of the purser's dip was the only working light.

Imagine, then, the beat of drum to quarters, and what a scene it must have produced on the night in which Rodney engaged that Spanish fleet. The men from below all hurriedly tumbling up one after another, with hammocks hastily rolled together for stowing; the magazines dimly lighted through iron-barred sliding scuttles from certain adjoining dens, known as "light-rooms," by light borrowed from which, cartridges are being filled and handed up by powder-monkeys to the fighting-decks above; along which are ranged at intervals " match-tubs," with scores in their brims to receive the slow matches used in firing the guns, the lighted ends as they hang in these scores all reflected in the water washing to and fro in the bottom of the match-tubs. Then by lantern-light, hung from beams

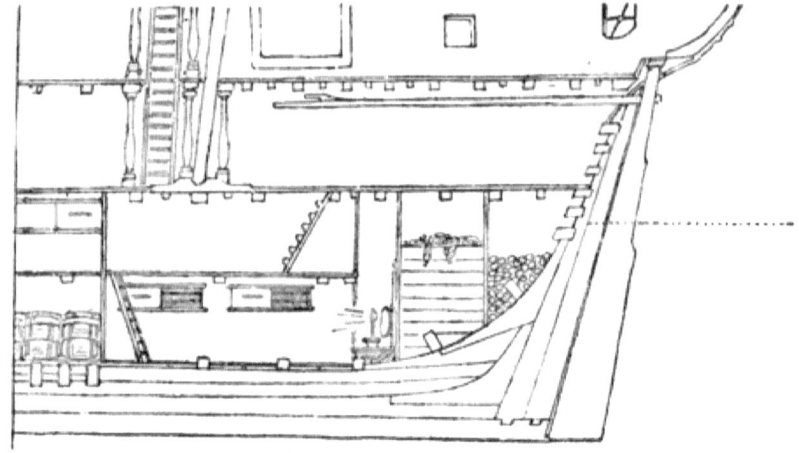

Light-rooms and magazine.

barely five feet six inches from the deck, the men are loading the great guns; and as the order from those on deck, watching the ship's roll, comes to fire, broadside after broadside is poured in upon the Spaniards' passing ships. All this, too, on a lee shore, an enemy's coast, in a gale of wind, and dark night; and the whole pack of twenty ships of the line kept in hand by the will of one man—Rodney (he went to sea from Harrow

School at twelve). It was a hard life; but what a splendid scene of fire-lighted wave, and smoke driven by the gale, must he have overlooked from his lofty poop, as each of his great ships opened her fire upon the enemy that stormy night.

Then, while all this is passing above, or on the fighting-decks, the surgeons, their mates, and loblolly boys, away below almost the roar of the battle, are at work in the cock-pit manufacturing, by unsteady lantern-light, as best they can, in an air heavy with fumes of sulphur and rolling bilge water, those one-legged and one-armed pensioners, many of whom were still with us at Greenwich less than forty years ago.

CHAPTER XIII.

THE OLD SHIP-FARM.

A luxurious voyage about the Cape in 1682—A New York packet-ship's long-boat forty years ago—The old sea-cow—Stock not always home-fed at sea—Great value of the pig as sea-farm stock, and superiority of ship-fed pork—The goat and his appetite on board ship—Naval model sea-farm—Poultry bred at sea—A crowing hen—Root crops in the lower hold, and other crops in the jolly-boat.

In a letter written on shipboard by John Fryer (M.D., Cambridge), on his arrival from India, he says, " That though a tedious voyage of seven months, it passed away merrily, with good wine, and no bad musick: but the life of all good company, and an honest commander, who fed us with fresh provisions of turkies, geese, ducks, hens, *sucking* pigs, sheep, goats, etc. . . . and, to crown all, the day we made England, kill'd us a fatted calf: so that you may spare that welcome when you receive yours, etc."

This was written more than two hundred years ago—a time we are accustomed to regard life at sea as something too tedious and terrible to be endured by ordinary mortals.

But this John Fryer was a cultivated gentleman and scholar, and his honest testimony to the comforts and pleasures of a voyage round the Cape in the year 1682 is invaluable. Of late, steam, the ice-house, canned-meats, and the refrigerating-chamber have changed the character and limited the extent of stock-farming on shipboard, which even fifty years back, in the hands of the ship's butcher and his mate, "Jemmy Ducks," formed an important part of the economy of our old East Indiamen, or men-of-war engaged in a long blockading cruise. In those happy Board-of-Tradeless days, the heavy long-boat of even a fast "line-of-packet ship," bound only for a short trip of five or six weeks between London and New York, looked more like a working model of Noah's Ark than anything likely to save life at sea, or even to live upon it. Always securely stowed amidships, well lashed down and housed over, the boat, as she lay upon the ship's deck, was full of live provender; being divided as to her lower hold into pens for sheep and pigs; while upon the first floor, or main-deck, quacked ducks and geese, and above them (literally in the cock-loft) were coops for another kind of poultry.

This great central depôt was closely surrounded by

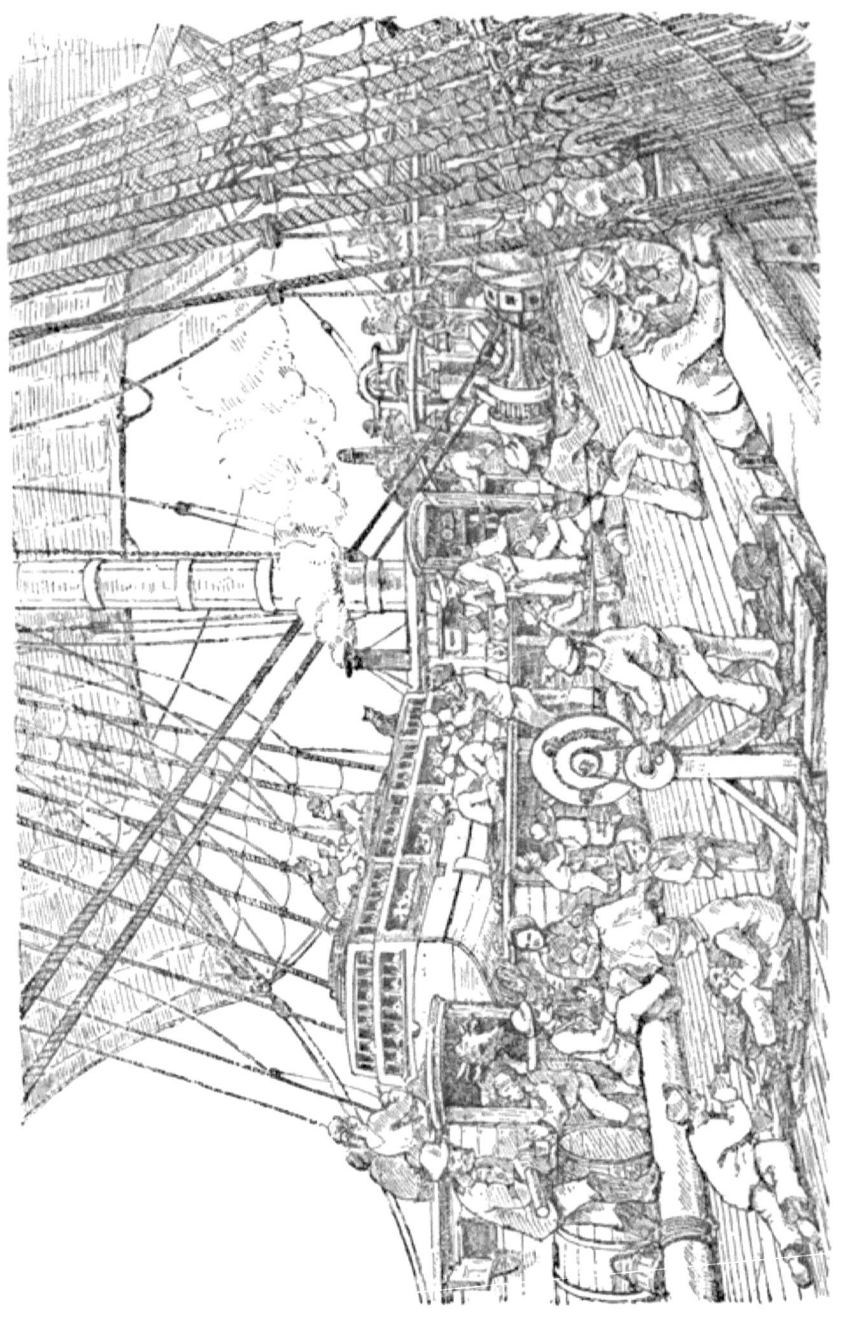

other small farm-buildings, the most important being the cow-house, where, after a short run ashore on the marshes at the end of each voyage, a well-seasoned animal of the snug-made Alderney breed, chewed the cud in sweet content.

In fact, when in old days a passenger-ship began her voyage, the hull of her clumsy long-boat was nearly hidden by the number of temporary sheds and pens required to house the live stock for the supply of her cabin-table; and with its many farmyard and home-like sounds, a ship was even then more like a small bit of the world afloat than it is now. Various forms of life appeared and passed away during the voyage—expended, so to say, like the marline spun on board—in the narrow world it began in.

In smaller vessels, carrying no passengers, the skipper's live stock was not always home-fed—pigs and goats being often turned loose to cater for themselves among the odds and ends in the waist, or deck, between the poop and forecastle. Some of the poultry, too, soon became tame enough to be allowed the run of this part of a ship; the ducks and geese finding a particular delight in paddling in the wash about the lee-scuppers.

It does not, however, always answer to turn down sheep to feed with pigs at sea, for the last-named animals are apt to develop a taste for live leg of mutton after a few weeks afloat.

Pigs—or as the old seamen usually called them, "hogs"—have always proved a thriving stock on a ship-farm, and the one that pays best. Some old sea-captains assert, indeed, that, like Madeira, pig is improved greatly by a voyage to India and back, round the Cape; and that none but those who have tasted boiled leg of pork on board a homeward-bound India-man know much about the matter.* But here also, as in so many other things, there was a drawback. For pigs are such cheerful creatures at sea that, as a soft-hearted old skipper once remarked, "You get too partial towards them, and feel after dinner sometimes as though you had eaten an old messmate."

Next to the pig, the goat was the most useful stock on a sea-farm. This animal soon makes itself at home on shipboard; it has good sea-legs, and is blessed with an appetite that nothing in the shape of vegetable fibre comes amiss to, from an armful of

* As tending to prove what a favourite dish this was among old sea-captains, it used to be related by an ancient waiter of the old Quebec Hotel, Portsmouth, that upon a certain memorable day, years ago, when three brothers—all skippers of ships then wind-bound at Spithead—met, and agreed to dine together, the dinner to consist only of three dishes ordered independently by each captain, that on removing the covers three smoking legs of boiled pork graced the table.

shavings from the carpenter's berth to an old newspaper or log-book.

Preserved milk was, of course, unknown in those times; and the officers of a large passenger-ship would rather have gone to sea without a doctor (to say nothing of a parson) than without a cow or some nanny-goats. The ship's cow and her health was always a most important matter in large passenger-ships, and the author remembers a case when, after a long spell of very bad weather, one of these creatures fell off in her supply of milk for the cabin-table, how she was brought round again by a liberal supply of nourishing stout, wisely prescribed for her by the ship's doctor. Even on board a man-of-war, the admiral or captain generally had at least one goat for his own use, while space was found for live stock for other wardroom officers. But model-farming and home-feeding was the rule then as now in the navy; and it is related that on board one of these vessels, the first lieutenant ordered the ship's painter to give the feet and bills of the admiral's geese, that were stowed in coops upon the quarter-deck, a coat of black once a week, so that the nautical eye might not be offended by any intrusion of colour not allowed in the service.

The general absence of colour among the true sea-fowl is very marked; and when, as it sometimes happened, a gay rooster, after an exciting chase round the decks by Jemmy Ducks, escaped overboard, and fluttered helplessly down upon the bosom of the sea, his glowing plumage looked strangely out of harmony with things as he sat drifting away astern upon the waste of waters.

The administration of a farm, even on shore, is not always unruffled; so that it was not to be hoped that the management of live stock afloat should be carried on without some grumbling and discontent.

Passengers' stock, shipped either for use at sea, or with a view to speculation upon its arrival at a distant colony, was often tended by a sort of private farm-servant, whose notions of feeding, water supply, etc., often clashed violently with those of Jemmy Ducks and the ship's officers generally. On board a man-of-war, when an enemy hove in sight, and the order to clear for action came, short work was made of the farm-buildings and their population. But, even in this extreme case, some of the admiral's geese and pigs often survived—stowed away on neutral ground among the water-casks in the lower hold, whence their squealing and cackling could at times be heard amidst the roar of artillery above them. Short keep and bad weather made sad havoc among the live stock of a ship-farm. And this little quotation from the narrative of a South Sea whaling captain, in the year 1794, will give some idea of the trouble attending the rearing of poultry in low latitudes after two years spent at sea. "In every awkward circumstance in which we found ourselves, all on board, from the whaling-master to the lowest seaman, had perfect confidence in my opinion. But the superstition of a seaman's mind is not easily subdued; and it was with some difficulty that I could preserve an hen who had been hatched and bred on board, and who at this time was accompanied by a small brood of chickens,* from being destroyed in order to quit the ill omen that had been occasioned by the unexpected crowing of the animal during the preceding night."

In ships bound upon long voyages in ballast, such as those engaged in the North American timber trade, it was not unusual for the captain to do a little practical farming in the hold of his ship by planting out upon the freshly trimmed ballast, cabbage, lettuce, spring onions, or any edible root that was likely to thrive in the soil he chanced to carry across the Atlantic with him. Most ships, some years back, had a small kitchen-garden planted in boxes of earth in the jolly-boat, which boat was further crammed to her gunwales with greengroceries of every sort; and, weather permitting, this little garden was a source of great pleasure to a solitary skipper on a long voyage.

* We have here two generations of ship-bred poultry.

CHAPTER XIV.

OLD GROUND-TACKLE.

From hemp and sails to chain and steam—A lost art—Keeping a clear hawse—Size and weight of old hemp cables—The old wooden-stocked anchor—Some advantages of it—A ship's "manger," and what she disposed of in it—A foul anchor—Two round turns in the hawse—Consequent troubles—"The bitter end"—Anchoring under sail and steam—Big and little ships as roadsters—Dragging, etc.—Proceedings on board Lord Anson's ship, *Centurion*, anchored off the island of Tinian—Wind against tide—Pooped by her long-boat—Drives to sea with three cables hanging in her hawse, etc.

IF there be one thing on which the modern steam seaman should congratulate himself, in comparing his lot with those who manned our navy when, "All in the Downs the fleet lay moored," it ought to be his freedom from the many small cares and worries attending the use of hemp, or even chain cables, before the introduction of steam.

Almost the last words of Nelson to his sailing-master were, "Anchor, Hardy; anchor!" Owing to the gale then threatening, this advice of the dying hero could not be followed out. But it is not easy for even a sailor to-day to realize all the troublesome details which had to be looked to on board an old line-of-battle-ship like the *Victory*, before this simple command could be rightly carried out, or the various acts of seamanship required in those days in mooring or unmooring ships on entering or leaving crowded roadsteads like the Downs or Spithead. Something of this old nautical lore, no doubt, still lingers among us here and there, bottled up in the brain of a collier-brig's skipper.

But as these old mariners pass away with their ships, so these small but important details—such as keeping a clear hawse by tending a ship with forestay-sail or spanker each time she swings to her anchor with a change of tide—will, for sheer want of practice, come to be reckoned among some of the lost arts of seamanship.

The change from hemp to chain cables was an enormous boon to seamen and shipowners; relieving them at once of the great trouble, anxiety, and expense entailed by the perishable nature of the cumbersome hempen cables, which, when coiled down in a frigate's cable-tier, filled nearly a fourth of her hold.

Less than forty years back, one often saw, standing

as a sign outside the marine-store dealer's warehouse, facing the figure of a little post-captain and his sex-

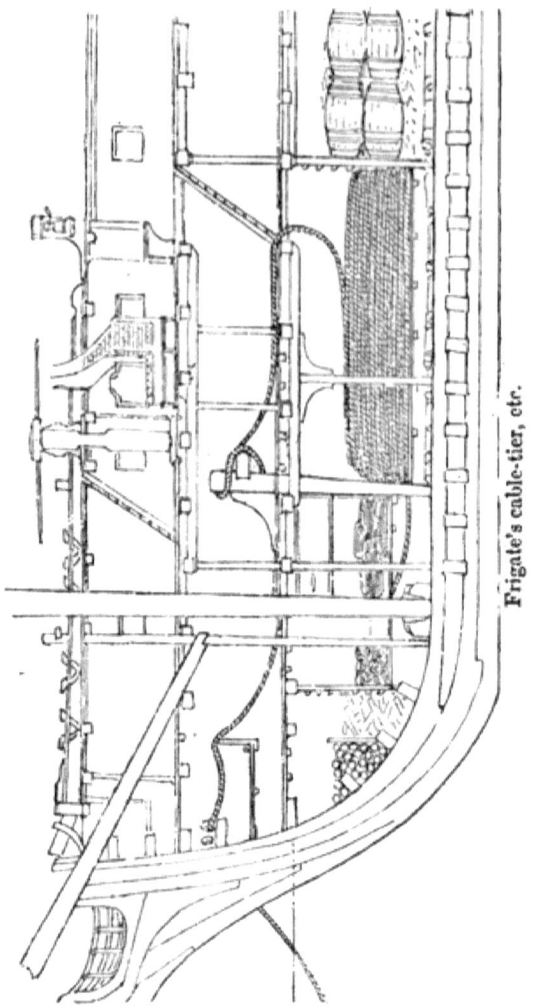

Frigate's cable-tier, etc.

tant, a short junk of one of these cables, and from the size and texture of such a specimen, might form some idea of the difficulty of handling these great hemp cables,* now long since all picked to shreds as oakum. But at places like Deal or Yarmouth, one may still often see some of the big wooden-stocked broad-palmed anchors, with rings over two feet in diameter, through which these stout cables once passed and were bent, or clenched, after the ring had been scientifically "puddened" by "serving" round it much small rope and canvas, to save the cable

Old wooden-stocked anchors lying in state.

from chafe; while the cable, when an anchor was let go upon foul or rocky ground, was also defended by "keckling," or winding rope, or even small chain, about it. In such cases the cable, too, was at times buoyed by casks, lashed to it at intervals, so that it

* The hemp cable of a ship of a thousand tons was over eight inches in diameter; a hundred fathoms of it weighed about six and a half tons, and was tested to a strain of sixty-five tons; equal to the strength of a $2\frac{1}{8}$-inch chain cable, a hundred fathoms of which weighed twelve and a half tons. The largest anchor used with such a cable weighed about five tons.

floated safely above the rough sea-bottom at some distance from the anchor.

The big wooden stocks of these ancient anchors possessed one advantage over the more slender iron stock of the ordinary modern one, especially when one was let go upon a soft muddy bottom, or upon what seamen sometimes call "rotten ground," into which the slender iron stock is at times apt to sink, in place of canting the anchor. In which case the ship rides to, or is held only by the stock of her anchor, and should a gale spring up, will steadily drag it through the soft ground until it is brought up by something harder, when the chances are it either bends, or breaks, at the point where it passes through the shank of the anchor. With the stouter, old-fashioned timber stock, this was less likely to occur; while, if the timber stock did enter the ground, the great size and strength of it was more likely to hold on than the slighter iron one. Most fishermen, hailing from the muddy-bottomed south hams of England, still use strong oaken stocks, fitted to their anchors, which have also rather broad palms; while old seamen had a method of increasing the holding power of an anchor in oozy ground, by enlarging the palms of it by means of flat pieces of wood secured to them.

The great size of hemp cables, compared with

chain, required very large openings, or hawse-pipes, in the ship's bows; which, when riding bows under, with a heavy sea, caused her to take in much water for'ard. It was to receive and check the flow of this water, and that which ran off the cable itself when hove in, that ships had a large compartment just abaft the hawse-pipes, called the "manger," furnished with a breakwater and scuppers, through which the sea passed out of the ship, instead of flooding her between decks. This manger is shown in the section of a frigate's bow, page 186.

A foul anchor—that is, one entangled in its cable—which, curiously enough, is the strange device upon our naval button, always was, and perhaps is now, when seen, regarded by seamen as a thing that marked a careless lubber or lazy shipmaster.

Except when riding to a permanent swivel-mooring, the greatest attention was always given to a ship with more than one anchor down to keep a clear hawse; a foul one meaning that, for want of this care, the ship in swinging for several days or tides had taken first "a cross," then "an elbow," followed by "a round turn;" while more turns than these were spoken of as "a round turn and an elbow," or "two round turns."

Captain Marryatt, in "Peter Simple," draws a

touching picture of the feelings of an old salt upon this subject, when he makes the master of the *Sanglier* frigate say, on declining to join his brother officers at the Governor's ball at Barbadoes, that "he'd as soon have *two round turns in his hawse*, as go to see people kick their legs about like fools," and that "he'd stay and take care of the ship."

I regret to have to record it, but during the late naval evolutions, spite of the facilities one would expect steam to have given modern seamen in keeping a clear hawse, several ships were much delayed when getting under way, by having first to clear their hawse. It is easy to understand that in real warfare, or with bad weather coming upon them suddenly, such a state of things might mean something more than the slipping a cable, or the loss of an anchor and some chain. In the old days of hemp cables, a few blows of an axe quickly solved this problem of clearing hawse in a hurry; hence, no doubt, the term, "He cut and ran."

The chain cable has to some extent made this work of untwisting a foul hawse easier than it was when a hemp cable, say of eighty-five fathoms in length, had to be unspliced from the next length before doing so, or if, riding to forty fathoms of a cable, the whole remaining forty-five fathoms had to be passed out through one hawse-hole to its "bitter end"* before a single turn could be cleared. With the chain cable one length is easily and quickly unshackled, at the nearest shackle or connecting-link, usually not more than ten fathoms apart, within the ship. But, with her engines always at hand to assist her anchor, a modern steamer or man-of-war seldom has need to perform this operation, as she rarely rides to more than single anchor.

The mere act of bringing up and selecting a good berth with a large ship under canvas, especially in a crowded roadstead, is an actual fine art, compared with doing the same thing under steam, however large the ship may be. And to do it rightly under all conditions of weather requires accurate judgment of distance, and the effect of wind and tide upon a ship's sails and hull. The captain of a steamer, when choosing his berth, has only to move a handle in order to give his vessel the requisite head or stern way; while, after his first anchor is down, he has his steam to help it, or to move his ship a few yards to right or left before mooring her with a second anchor; all which, in a

---

* "The bitter end" of a cable (an old sea-term now obsolete) was that part which remained abaft the bitts within board. "To veer away to the bitter end" meant, therefore, to the extreme length of one cable, and hence, I believe, the origin of the phrase, so often used by landsmen, "to the bitter end."

sailing-ship, has to be done by much bracing about of yards, in order to obtain the necessary head or stern way.

The same remarks apply to heaving in and getting under way; which, with steam to help both crew and master, is a very simple business compared with the old way of heaving short by capstan, or windlass, and "casting," or turning the ship's head at exactly the right moment, in the right direction, by sail-power only. Again, upon letting go an anchor, the friction set up as the hemp cable passed over the bitts, and through the hawse-pipes, made it so hot that the tarry surface often took fire, and men were always stationed at these points, with buckets of water, to prevent this "firing of the cable," or even of the bitts and timbers round the heated hawse-pipes. It may be said by modern seamen that ships are much larger now, and altogether less handy than the old ones, and that they require far more care in bringing up than those of our ancestors. This is true enough, if one of these masses of iron is once allowed, as sailors say, "to take charge," or an attempt is made to check her weight and way too quickly; but once at rest, it is well known to seamen that a long heavy ship actually rides far easier in a seaway, and with less strain upon her anchors and chains, in proportion to her size, than a short beamy one, which, as she tosses her bluff bows to the sea, continually throws an uncertain surging strain upon her cables; and such a vessel often requires better ground-tackle to hold her than a larger one.

Brig riding in the Downs.

This is a fortunate fact for our ponderous iron-clads; for, if they were not better "roadsters" than our line-of-battle ships were, no anchors or chains yet forged would bear the strain of their weight in a jump. As dragging an anchor in a crowded tideway generally meant falling foul of other vessels, and the consequent dragging or slipping from their anchors until an entire fleet was often started in hopeless drift and confusion by the neglect or incompetence of one careless ship-master, seamen had, before the days of handy tugs, and steam, to be more wide-awake to the proper use of the ground-tackle than seems to have been the case with certain officers in charge of some of her Majesty's ships in the late Naval Manœuvres.* After reading the following account, by Mr. Richard Walters, of some "proceedings" on board Lord Anson's ship, the *Centurion*, when driven to sea from her anchorage off the island of Tinian, in the Pacific, one really wonders that, after a long voyage, our old sailors ever had an anchor or single serviceable cable left on board their ships. It is also an excellent

---

* "An error of judgment in not making sufficient allowance for the strength of the tide" was the only reason given by the First Lord of the Admiralty in answer to a question in Parliament for the fouling of the North Goodwin lightship by H.M.S. *Rodney*, and of the Newark lightship by H.M.S. *Elk* during the mobilization of our fleet in August, 1889. Neither vessel had a pilot on board, but were *navigated* (?) by their own officers. About the same time the *training*-brig *Nautilus*, in moving out of Portsmouth Harbour to Spithead, collided with the *Martin*, tender to the *training*-ship *St. Vincent*, which was moored in the waterway. The *Nautilus* carried away her fore-royal, and the *Martin* lost her flying-jibboom. After the vessels got clear, the *Nautilus* was towed out to Spithead by the Government tug *Malta*. Another *training*-brig, the *Liberty*, also of Portsmouth, ran ashore soon afterwards upon the Admiralty bank, but was subsequently got off. We read also, among the more fashionable shipping disasters of this period, how Lord Brassey's steam-yacht *Sunbeam* took the ground at Ryde, and lay on her beam ends for many hours, until towed off on the following day by the tug *Victoria*. Among those on board the *Sunbeam* at the time were Sir M. Hicks Beach, Mr. Ritchie, Mr. and Mrs. Chamberlain, Lord Charles Beresford, Mr. Forwood, Sir F. Leighton, and Lord Claud Hamilton.

picture of the perils and labour attending the use of hemp cables in exposed roadsteads without steam to fall back upon. The *Centurion* had been at anchor for some time off the island of Tinian to refresh her scurvy-stricken officers and men, and her water-casks had just been sent ashore, after which, Mr. Walters says, " we weighed our anchors, to examine our cables, which, owing to the bottom of this road being full of sharp-pointed coral rocks, we suspected had by this time received considerable damage. And as the new moon was now approaching, when we apprehended violent gales, the commodore, for greater security, ordered that part of the cables next the anchors to be armed with the chains of the *fire-grapnels;* * besides which they were cackled twenty fathoms from the anchors and seven from the service " (*i.e.* where they passed through the hawse-pipes) " with a good rounding of $4\frac{1}{2}$-inch hawser; while to these precautions we added that of lowering the main and foreyard close down, that in case of blowing weather the wind might have less power upon the ship to make her ride a strain.

* This was a special form of grapnel fitted with chain, and so called because they were not only used to secure one ship to another in boarding, but were hung about the bowsprit and rigging of fireships when started to run before the wind upon an enemy's fleet. The yardarms of a fire-ship were also furnished with iron hooks.

"Thus effectually prepared, as we conceived, we waited till the new moon on the 18th of September, when riding safe that and the three following days (though the weather proved very squally and uncertain), we flattered ourselves that the prudence of our measures had secured us from all accidents. But on the 22nd the wind blew from east with such fury that we soon despaired of riding out the storm. In this conjuncture we should have been glad if the commodore and rest of our people on shore had been on board; our only hope of safety seeming to depend upon our putting to sea at once. But all communication with the shore was now absolutely cut off, for there was no possibility that a boat could live, so that we were necessitated to ride it out till our cables parted. Indeed, we were not long expecting this dreadful event, for the small bower parted at five in the afternoon; while, toward evening the violence of the wind still increased, though, notwithstanding its inexpressible fury, the tide ran so strong as to prevail over it, forcing the ship before it in spite of the storm.

"The sea now broke most surprisingly all round us; and a large tumbling swell threatened to poop us, by which the long-boat, at this time moored astern, was on a sudden canted so high that it broke the transom of the commodore's gallery, whose cabin was

Centurion riding in gale off the Island of Tinian.

on the quarter-deck, and doubtless would have risen as high as the taffrail had it not been for the stroke; and yet the poor boat-keeper, though much bruised, was saved almost by miracle.

"At eight p.m. the tide slackened; but the wind not abating, the best bower, by which alone we rode, parted at eleven. Our sheet-anchor, the only one left, was instantly cut from the bow, but before it reached bottom we drove from twenty-two into thirty-five fathoms, and after veering away one whole cable and two-thirds of another, we found no ground at sixty fathoms, a plain indication that our anchor lay near the edge of a bank, and would not hold us long. In this pressing danger, Mr. Saumarez, our first lieutenant, ordered guns to be fired, and lights shown as a signal of our distress to the commodore ashore. About one o'clock, the night being excessively dark, a strong gust, with lightning and rain, drove us off the bank, and forced us to sea, leaving Mr. Anson, with more of our officers and crew, to the number of a hundred and thirteen, behind us.

"Our condition was truly deplorable; in a leaky ship, with three cables in our hawses, to one of which hung our only remaining anchor. We had not a gun on board lashed, or a port barred in" (the *Centurion* was a sixty-gun ship), "our shrouds were loose, our topmasts unrigged, and our fore and main yards close down; so that we had no sail to set except the mizzen. We had scarcely a fourth of our complement on board, and of these most were either boys, or those lately recovered of scurvy. The ship made so much water by working, and through our open hawse-holes, ports, and scuppers, that we found our pumps alone sufficient employment for all."

An attempt "to sway up the mainyard" ended in the breaking of the jeers.

"This turbulent weather continued for three days, and it was not till the fourth day after our being driven from our anchorage that, after twelve hours' severe work, we were able to heave in upon our cable sufficiently to bring our sheet-anchor in sight; when, darkness coming on, and being excessively fatigued, we had to leave our work unfinished till next morning. Thus, it was the 27th of September, five days after leaving Tinian, before we had secured our only remaining anchor."

CHAPTER XV.

EARLY NAVIGATORS AND THEIR NAUTICAL INSTRUMENTS.

An early training college for young gentlemen at Wapping New Stairs—The whole art of navigation as taught there by Joshua Kelly, mariner—Domestic navigation—A Dutch picture of sea-bottom—Five ways of finding the longitude—A sand clock—Its chimes—Making eight bells—" Flogging the clock " or glass—One that was never flogged, painted for us by Mr. Hogarth—A good rule for all master-mariners—The old binnacle—Captain Cook's compass—Davis's quadrant—The cross-staff—A star clock—A frigate's day's work at sea in 1742—The traverse-board.

An advertisement of about the year 1720 tells us that "In Broad Street, Wapping, near Wapping New Stairs, are taught the mathematical sciences, navigation, astronomy, dialling, gauging, gunnery, fortifycation, the use of the globes, and the projection of the sphere upon any circle, by Joshua Kelly, mariner. With whom young gentlemen and others are well boarded, and compleatly and expeditiously qualify'd (on reasonable terms) for any business relating to accompts and the mathematicks."

This Joshua Kelly was the author of " The

Compleat Modern Navigator's Tutor; or, the Whole Art of Navigation;" which art, Kelly says in his preface (dedicated "to the Master, Wardens, and

Master-mariner costume of 1710.

Elder Brethren of the Trinity House, Stroud, Depfort"), "is allowed by all, and well known by those of the noble tribe of Zabulon, to be one by which islands are enrich'd and preserv'd from invasion, the wonderful works of an omniscient Creator in the wide ocean, and remote nations delightfully beheld, etc.; while 'tis no mean accomplishment to be capable of conducting a ship richly laden round the world." The preface concludes with the words of the poet—

> "He that hath art,
> And can impart
> That art with art,
> Is master of his art."

The first part of Kelly's book treats of what our master-mariner quaintly calls "domestic or coasting navigation." From which essay it appears that the deep-sea lead of that time was almost a third eye to these old seamen, and so frequently and carefully used that, through its tallowed retina, the actual bottom of the channel from Scilly to Dunnose was almost a visible reality. And every little detail of this leaden eye's view is carefully recorded by Kelly in a table, from which we learn that "twenty-five miles east by north of Scilly Islands, in seventy-two fathoms," the sea bottom was then "pepper sand, black and yellow, passing into branny sand like ground wheat." Then comes "ouse sand, with Queen shells; white sand, with ouse and nits," followed by "branny sand, herring-bones, and small stones." Further up Channel, near the Lizard, the lead showed "marshy shells, like oatmeal husks;" while off the (at that time old wooden) lighthouse upon the Eddystone, the bottom resembled "the dust off a grindstone with hake's teeth." What a contrast is this minute investigation, and almost Dutch picture of the sea bottom, to the hasty glance of a modern seaman, taking an occasional flying shot at it, with Sir William Thomson's sounding-tubes, as he rushes up Channel at sixteen or eighteen knots!

For want of correct time-keepers, a ship's longitude at sea was then an unsolved problem; but Kelly describes what he calls "five of the most rational ways of finding it;" wisely, however, advising "no one to confide too much in them, or to omit any of the methods of a journal, or other precautions, to preserve a ship when she nears land."

Among these five methods, eclipses of the moon, and of Jupiter's satellites, of course come first. But of one of these he says, "this method would be accurate and useful if we could have an eclipse of the moon every night;" while of the other, he remarks "that the impracticability of managing a telescope twelve or fourteen feet long in the tossing rolling motion of a ship at sea, surrounds it with difficulties scarce to be remedy'd."

The craving of these early navigators for some

form of good sea time-keeper, is shown by Kelly's fourth "method of finding the longitude by automatas, or unerring clocks, watches, or hour-glasses;" where directions are given for preparing and using a "very perfect and true-running sand-glass, which may precisely run twenty-four hours without error, to be set exactly at noon on leaving the land; which upon being run out is to be turned instantly, not losing any time in the turning of it." "And so," says Kelly, "having very warily kept the said glasse 'til you think good to make an observation at noon, and having in readiness an half-hour, minute, and half-minute glasse, you may thereby know exactly how much the twenty-four-hour glasse is before or after the ship's time; the difference being your longitude east or west, according as the time by the sun is afore or after the time by the glass."

Time on shipboard was then always estimated by the glass, and in old accounts of sea-fights such expressions as, "We engaged the enemy over three glasses before he hauled down his ensigne" often occur. Strong time-keepers, or cabin-clocks, with balance-wheel escapements, like those used in carriages ashore, are plentiful enough on board ship to-day; but less than fifty years ago, a sand-glass, running half an hour, or one that ran an hour, but which indicated the half-hour by a mark or band round it, was the only clock by which sea time was kept.

The chimes of this clock were of course the ship's bell, struck by the man at the wheel or quartermaster, who eight times in each watch turned his half-hour glass, marking at the same time, by strokes upon a small bell near him, the number of half-hours that had passed since he took charge of the helm; these strokes being repeated by the larger bell in the belfry forward.

Time and longitude are synonymous terms at sea, and, unless the weather is very thick, the officers of a large ocean-steamer are almost constantly busy with their sextants, and are able by night or day to tell to a minute the exact change in a ship's longitude or time. But in those days the taking of even the sun's meridian altitude was a solemn business; and the captain and mate's old weather-stained quadrants rarely appeared on deck except toward the close of the sea day—that is, about half an hour before noon. Nowadays everybody on board ship knows all about such matters; but in those times few but the captain or

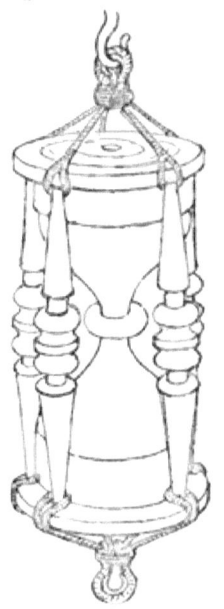

Old sea-clock.

mate had the remotest idea of how, after screwing up his eye at the sea-line, and swaying the lower part of his ebony quadrant to and fro for five minutes or so, the skipper knew when to say in an impressive tone to his mate, "Make eight bells, Mr. So-and-so." All that even the ship's company knew was that their captain "'ad took the sun," and that he never failed to do so whenever he hove in sight at noon. Though the "old sea-clock" is now superseded by a clock or big watch in the binnacle, the term "flog the clock" remains among sailors when putting it forward or back, and is evidently derived from the much older one of "flog the glass," or turn it before all the sand had run through, in order to shorten a watch on deck.

I have one of the older forms of these glasses before me, which is of the pattern of those used as emblems upon headstones in old churchyards, placed over a skull and cross-bones.

A good picture of it is to be seen on the left side of the parson's pulpit (with the sand all run down) in Hogarth's plate of "The Sleeping Congregation," showing that in small churches of that date the clergyman regulated the length of his discourse by a sand-clock; which in Hogarth's print is supported upon an iron-hinged bracket, like those for a candle, and arranged to move aside or forward at pleasure.

These oldest forms of land and sea glasses differed from some of more recent date, in the way the sand was introduced; for while in the latest forms of them this was done through a hole in the top or one end (both parts being in one piece), the older glasses were made in two pieces connected by a putty joint at the waist, with a small thin bit of card or metal placed between them, having a hole in it just large enough for the sand to run through.

As shown in the cut, these old sea-glasses were often harnessed with small line, ending in an eye at top and bottom, which enabled them to be hung to any convenient beam, and as the sand in them was heavy, there was, when so slung, less chance of the ship's roll interfering with the steady flow of it.

Navigation by account, or dead-reckoning, has changed little since Kelly's time. Indeed, the introduction of chronometers, and the almost perfect accuracy of observations taken with the modern sextant, have very much superseded it, except in the case of small coasters, etc. But in Kelly's day, and for years afterwards, the log-line, log-chip, reel, and half-minute glass, were almost a mariner's only means of estimating his longitude, or distance sailed east or west. Steam and patent logs have much simplified calculations which in his time required numberless corrections, not only for leeway, etc., but for errors in the log-line and glasses; and Kelly tells us that "shortness of the knots in a line are on the safer side, that a ship be not ahead of her reckoning; it being better to look for land before we come at it, than to be ashoar before we expect it."

All these matters, as well as the compass, log-board, etc., were in the old ships stowed in the binnacle, or,

Old binnacle.

as it was then spelt, "bittacle," which was an affair about the size of a corn-bin, and quite unlike the brass pillar or stand now used for a ship's compass and lamps.

The ordinary form of compass, with its card and needle pivoted in a copper bole slung on gimbals, is an instrument of considerable antiquity, the inventor of it being unknown; but an ingenious method of keeping the card horizontal without gimbals was the use of a heavy, inverted, cone-shaped leaden bole attached to the lighter copper bole, and hung upon a pointed brass support; the compass-card pivoting upon a point rising from the centre of this leaden arrangement below.

This sketch is from an instrument now in the possession of Mr. Philip Hedger,

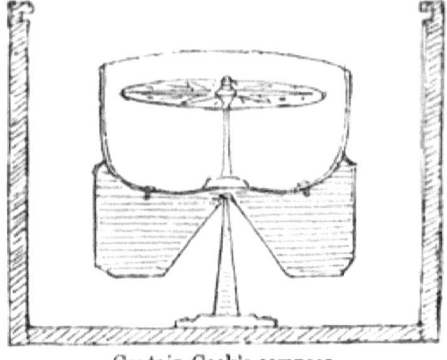

Captain Cook's compass.

of Southampton, and is interesting, as the compass from which it is taken formerly belonged to that famous navigator, Captain James Cook, and was probably used by him as a boat-compass when surveying and taking bearings in rough weather; for which, owing to its weight and consequent steadiness, this old instrument would be well suited.

Though our old shipmen had no means of finding the longitude at sea, they were fairly provided with instruments for latitude. And our master-mariner gives full directions for taking meridian altitudes with a cross-staff and the "sea-quadrant," known also as "Davis's quadrant," it having been invented by that early navigator in Elizabeth's reign. This was a much larger and more cumbersome machine than

P

Hadley's quadrant, being nearly three feet in length, with two distinct arcs of differing radius upon one frame; this instrument was also known as the "backstaff," from the position of the observer with his back to the sun when using it, and long after it ceased to be used at sea it remained in the hands of the little wooden midshipmen ashore, that stood outside the doors of London opticians.

Figure with Davis's quadrant.   Cross-staff, and manner of using.

The cross-staff or fore-staff was a still older and simpler contrivance for measuring angles between the fixed stars, or the sun and the sea horizon; being merely a four-sided straight staff of hard wood, with four cross-pieces of different lengths, made to slide upon it as the cross-piece does upon a shoemaker's rule. These cross-pieces were respectively called the ten, thirty, sixty, and ninety cross; and were used upon the staff according to the altitude of the sun or stars at time of observation. One cross only was used upon the staff at a time; the angle measured being shown by a scale of degrees and minutes, intersected by the cross-piece on that side of the staff to which it (the cross-piece) belonged. It was with this simple but really effective instrument that Columbus, Drake, and other early navigators took their meridian sights for latitude, etc.

A fine specimen of one in boxwood and ebony is still preserved in the Naval Museum, Madrid, which is no doubt as old as the days of Columbus, if not indeed the very instrument that first crossed the Atlantic in the hands of that seaman. The astrolabe, or, as Kelly calls it, the "universal ring-dial," was also used by early navigators for taking altitudes of the sun, this instrument being more convenient than the cross-staff for meridian altitudes near the line, when the sun was almost vertical; while, when he was near the horizon, a little before sunset or after sunrise, a form of small quadrant, called an "almacantar-staff," was used to find his azimuth and the variation of the compass. Among the ancient mariners whose voyages did not extend south of the tropics, the "nocturnal" gave the time of night by observing with it the hands of the great star-clocks, Ursa Major and Minor, as they turned about the pole-star.

That great-circle sailing was not altogether unknown among comparatively early navigators is shown by the fact that some of them actually carried large globes to sea with them, upon which, as far back as the time of Sebastian Cabot and Davis, they marked their ocean courses and distances, or corrected them as laid down upon the old charts.

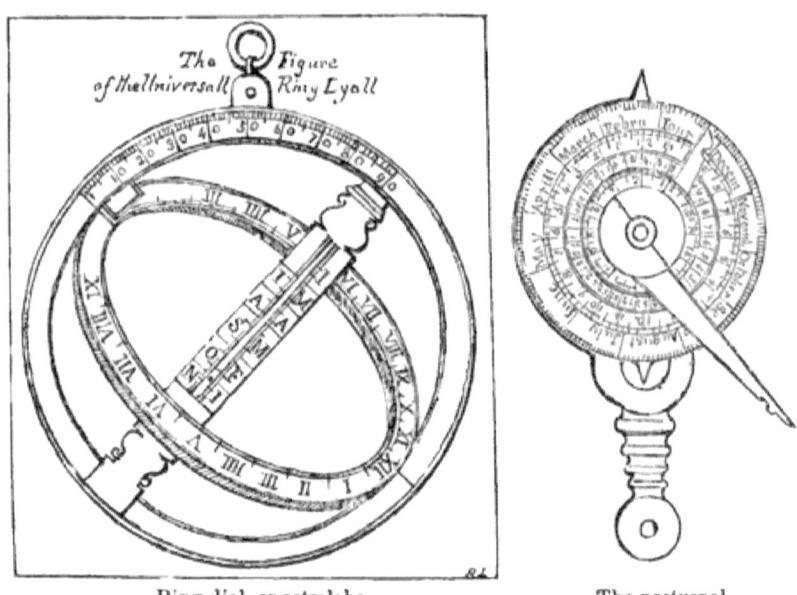

Ring-dial, or astrolabe.   The nocturnal.

The following copy of a page from the actual logbook of a frigate, acting as convoy to eight merchantmen from the West Indies to the Downs, in 1742, is of interest, as it shows exactly how a day's sailing and the results were recorded in a man-of-war nearly a hundred and fifty years back.

The old frigate and her convoy were then twenty-seven days out from "Watling's Key," from which she took her departure, and it was the 18th of May, or thirty-five days later, before she brought up in the Downs.

H.	K.	F.	C.	W.	Tuesday, April ye 13th, 1742.
1	2	–	N. ½ E.	E.N.E.	Moderate Gales & Cloudy.
2	2	4	N. B E.	E. B N.	The *Sophie* Transport Joyn'd
3	2	–			us.
4	2	3			
5	1	5	N. B E. ½ E.	E.N.E.	In 3rd R. B. T. S^ls.* The
6	1	4	N.W. B N.		*Britain* Transp^t Made y^e
7	2	2	N.E. B E.	S.E. B E.	Sign^l to speak us. Bore
8	2	–			Down to her, they In-
9	2	–			formed us of 3 Soldiers y^t
10	2	–	E.N.E.	S.E.	mutined. Brought too,
11	3	2			hoisted out ye yale and
12	3	3			Brought ye 3 Soldiers on
					B^rd. Made Sail.
1	4	–	N.E. B E.	S.E. B E.	Small Rain.
2	3	5			
3	2	4	N.E. B E. ½ E.		Shorten'd Saile for ye con-
4	3	–			voy.
5	3	2	N.E. B E.		Find ye Ship ahead of y^e
6	4	–	E.N.E.	S.E.	Log. By good Obs^vt
7	4	2			Lengthen'd ye Dist^ce 23
8	4	4			miles.
9	3	4	E. B N.	S.E. B S.	
10	4	3	E.N.E.		
11	5	–			
12	4	4			8 Sail in sight.

Course Cor^ted.	Dist^e.	Latt^d Obs^n.	Long^t.	Bear^ngs & Distance.
N.N.E. ¼ E.	102 m.	41° : 44 N.	31 : 53 E^n	Watlings Key.
Dep^t 44 E.	Merd^n Dist^ce 525 Lg^s E.		& 58 E.	S. 57° : 5 W. 640 Ligs.
			32 : 51	

* Abbreviation for "took third reef in both topsails."

In this log the first column marks the hour of the sea-day, counted from noon to noon; in the second and third, the number of knots and fathoms sailed are noted for each hour; the fourth gives the course or direction sailed; and the fifth that of the wind; the space beyond being filled in with remarks upon the weather, events on board, and evolutions of the frigate and ships under her convoy.

The spaces at the foot of this page of log are occupied, first, by the summing up of the day's courses into one; then comes the distance or easting made in the twenty-four hours, the latitude by observation, and the longitude by account or dead-reckoning; while, under the head of bearings and distance, we have the number of leagues which Watling's Key bore west and south of the old frigate at noon, on the 13th of April, 1742. It may be observed that, as Greenwich time had thus no existence on shipboard, longitude is only reckoned by this old seaman as his distance east of Watling's Key, which was the first land sighted by Columbus, being one of the most easterly points of the Bahamas.

In those days all the courses sailed during a watch of four hours were marked by the quartermaster, before they were entered upon the log-board or slate, upon a circular disc of hard wood, known as a traverse-board, which may still be found in the binnacles of some Norwegian or Swedish vessels. Upon this disc the points of the compass were clearly inscribed, and in the line of each point there were eight small holes, like those in a cribbage-board, while the board had attached to it eight pegs, one of which was placed in the hole corresponding to the course sailed every half-hour of the watch.

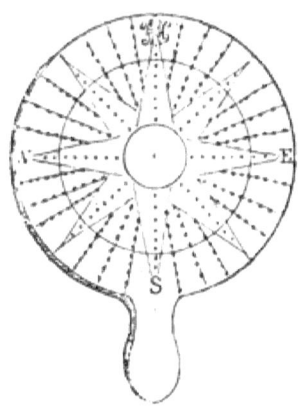

Traverse-board.

CHAPTER XVI.

THE BLACK X LINER.

Security of the Atlantic passage between Bristol and New York 150 years back—An extinct skipper and his ship—A popular and lucky captain—His precautions against fire—Useful passengers, mercenary seamen, and ungrateful owners—A steerage passage—Sleeping and cooking arrangements, etc.

IN the *Gentleman's Magazine*, of August, 1735, we read that "the vessels employed in the trade between New York and England make two voyages a year, and if instead of going to London they go to Bristol, the voyage (*i.e.* out and home) is performed in four months, and this indeed is generally the case, for Bristol is the port where the greatest part of merchandize for America is shipped. This voyage is, besides, attended with so little risk that insurance upon it is no more than two per cent." Trade with America, as it is to-day, was then almost entirely in our hands; but fifty years ago, and for some years before that, the following advertisement in the *Times* tells us that the "Only regular line of packets for New York," from London, were the American Black X liners, sailing monthly, and "the ship now loading, is the *Gladiator*, Captain Josia Joshua Champion, lying in St. Katharine's Docks; for freight or passage, apply to Messrs. P. S. & T., or to the captain on board."

Seamen fought their way then, across the North Atlantic, mile by mile, on the westward or uphill road, as it was called, against the prevailing westerly gales, making and holding on to some thirty or forty miles a day, when the wind was ahead, with little or nothing to help them but these foul winds and skilful use of them. Ships of five, or even three hundred tons, were at that time not thought too small for this work; and when, in 1840, to meet an increasing trade and number of passengers, vessels of eight hundred tons were built, they were spoken of as large unhandy ships. But in her four-hundred ton, or best day, with her fine wedge-shaped model, and practical fit-out of short lower masts, square (*i.e.* long) yards, big blocks, and grass-rope running rigging, the old Black X liner compared favourably in many ways with our heavier-sparred and larger Indiamen, as tide by tide, and tack and tack, they worked their way from Gravesend to the Downs or Spithead. Externally the New York built packet always had a cross of the Dutchman or Swede about her—having more beam than most English ships of the same length—while, in place of a row of painted ports, a broad band of well-scraped and varnished yellow pine ran fore and aft between her chain-plates and bends. The cut and fit of her canvas was also very Dutch.

New Jersey was at one time a Swedish colony, and it is noteworthy that the smart little vessels of Swedish and Norwegian build of to-day are more like the New York built ships of fifty years ago than anything now afloat. Old Channel pilots, after having been in charge of these little packets, used to tell marvellous tales about their handiness, and how they could turn them to windward through passages like the Gull stream on their way to the Downs, or through the Needles channel, as easily as one of their own pilot-boats.

People who had no idea of ever crossing the Atlantic, liked to have a look over "the New York packet;" and visitors were always welcome. Nothing so smart as to cabin fittings then sailed out of the port of London.

A clean-shaved, hard-fisted Yankee mate was ready with a helping hand for ladies at the gangway; and passing into the round-house on deck, some steep brass-bound stairs led you into the main cabin—saloons were seldom spoken of then on board ship. Here, at the end of the long cabin-table, was Captain

IN THE DAYS OF OAK AND HEMP. 219

Black X line of packet at sea.

Champion himself, a very young-looking man for one who had spent twenty years of his life, winter and summer, upon the North Atlantic. Near him were a basket of American crackers and a large bouquet of English flowers. He usually had an unlighted cigar in his mouth, which slowly became shorter and shorter as he rolled it about between his teeth when chatting to passengers. A black steward of very polished face and manner was also in attendance, and ready to show you the best state-room, with its dainty white dimity bed-curtains and cut-glass door-handles, or the pretty little white-and-gold lady's-cabin; everything looking bright and fresh, and so entirely innocent of salt-water or sea-sickness, as to give the idea that it had all been fitted up for this particular voyage only. Nearly every berth had a name pinned upon its white curtains, and to a lady's question as to "how many were going out this voyage?" the black steward answers, "De ship am full up, marm, in de fust cabum, and we hab to fix up two genelmen for de fust in de second. De *Gladiator*, Captain Champion, am nearly always full up for New York two or tree days arter she come into dock. Guess de *Mediator* take our berth to-morrow, with exactly same commodious accommodations in all respects."

Though young-looking, and with little outward

appearance of the sailor about him, Captain Champion was one of the oldest or best-known men in the line; and he liked telling how a timid lady-passenger, on being referred to him when she came to engage a berth, said that it was "old Captain Champion that she wished to see"! But, according to the captain himself, it was hard to lay out a hundred dollars more advantageously than in securing a passage to New York on board the *Gladiator*.

"The Atlantic at this season was a mill-pond, and the wind likely to hold on in the east for the next six weeks. No mistake about it, it was just yachting on a big scale, with board and lodging for three weeks or a month, and fed like fighting-cocks all the while. Yes, sir, I guess if I hadn't to go captain, I'd have taken a passage in my own ship for pastime. Why, sir, on a longish passage, a fellow might easy save enough to buy himself a nice little lot out West."

The easy way this Yankee skipper disposed of all little unpleasantnesses connected with the sea, when on board his own ship in dock, was wonderful; but when two young fellows, after going round the ship, said something about being able to sail to Australia for nearly the same money, the captain politely waved his hand toward the cabin-stairs with, "Well, gentlemen, I guess you can sail."

It was necessary to make a voyage to New York and back with Captain Champion before you learned that he had ever known rough weather; and even then he was shy of mentioning it. He did not believe in hurricanes or cyclones, and when he heard of ships being dismasted in them, always attributed such disasters to rotten rigging or spars. He had never been shipwrecked, of course, though he had once had his ship driven, with two anchors down, upon the Mother-bank from Spithead—getting off next tide. He had more than once spent a fortnight surrounded by icebergs, feeling his way among them in fog and light winds; but, though his mainyard at times nearly grazed them, he never considered his ship in any danger. Vessels were not compelled to carry lights then; but, for his own satisfaction, he always had a bright white light in a lantern fitted to the bowsprit-cap, "which, when fellows saw, they mostly 'bout-ship, taking it for lighthouse ashore."

Fire was the one thing the captain rather dreaded; and at sea, according to him, "it had one point only in its favour over fire ashore, viz. that water in a general way was plenty and handy. But," added the captain, "my carpenter is a smart man, and spends a'most all his spare time after leaving port between-decks among the steerage people. And no mistake about it, the yarns he spins down there about his escapes from ships afire, air not calculated to make them careless about lights, etc. No, sir, I never chanced on such times myself, thank the Lord; but as in a general way old Chips is the only survivor, feeding on his own boots for a week or so, it's hard to tell if they ain't all Gospel truth. Anyhow, them yarns act like a charm, setting all the wakefuller nervous people a-watching the other fellows like cat and mouse."

When a young man, the captain had once been pooped in running too long before a heavy gale, when something started about the stern-post; but "he was a young beginner then," and only remembers "how his owners grumbled" about some cargo that he jettisoned in order to lighten his ship aft, and get at the leak, or keep it above water. He was loaded with flour, apples, cheeses, and American clocks; the last-named goods unfortunately being the first they could get at. In consequence, over two hundred cases of these clocks went to the bottom before the cheese-boxes were arrived at. They followed the clocks, and altogether "he reckon'd he lightened his ship nearly a hundred tons aft in twelve hours;" some steerage passengers keeping the pumps going while the crew were busy handing up the clocks and cheeses aft.

"No, sir; I guess I didn't have to coax them passengers any. I just told 'em they'd got to pump or drownd. But you'd hardly believe me when I tell you that every one of those sailor-men that worked in my hold that night had at least one clock and a cheese stowed away in his bunk for'ard when we got into dock in London. Yes, sir, 'human natur strong in death,' as Shakespeare says. But when I got to home again in New York, and my owners asked, 'How was it, Mr. Champion, that it did not occur to you to select something of less value than them timepieces?' I felt pretty small; and only said, 'Well, gentlemen, I rayther wish you'd a-bin there yourselves, to pick and choose that night.' Yes, sir, that riled me; especially as my wife was with me that voyage, and her own private piannyforty was one of the fust articles that went overboard. Perhaps some of them owners would just as soon not seen anything more of me or my ship that winter."

These Yankee skippers nearly all hailed from the small State of Connecticut. Most of them left farm-work for the sea; and, long before they had attained the rank of captain, a good proportion of them were able to invest some small savings in the line of ships they navigated.

Steerage and even second-class passengers are apt

to growl to-day over the bad accommodation allotted to them on board a modern two-thousand-ton steamship, and even write grumbling letters to the *Times*, in which they describe discomforts, etc., which read like the height of comfort, cleanliness, and luxury, to any one old enough to have made a steerage passage

Steerage cooking-galley.

across the Atlantic fifty years ago; when a steerage passenger's fare to New York by sailing-packet was five pounds, and find yourself in everything except fire and water; of which last element something called "fresh" was served out in limited quantities by the ship, together with an unlimited allowance of salt water above and below in rough weather. Steerage passengers then had to cook their own victuals, weather permitting, at an open galley-fire on the waist-deck; which was lumbered up with the ship's long-boat, surrounded amidships by the cowhouse, caboose, for cabin-cook, sheep, pig, and poultry pens, with spare yards, topmasts, etc., on either side. So that of this deck there only remained two narrow alley-ways, which were nearly always reeking with the smell and drainage of this closely packed central farm-yard. With a dose of bilge-water now and then from the pumps, this was the state of things in fine weather; in foul, the waist-deck was kept sweeter, especially when a ship was deep laden, by the constant wash of the sea. The crew were housed in the top-gallant-forecastle, the doors of which opened upon the steerage promenade, just for'ard of the windlass.

But in anything like rough weather, all steerage passengers had either to run the chance of getting constantly wet with salt water or keep below. The space alloted to the steerage below in the larger class of the Black X liners was about 70 feet long, by 31 feet wide, and 6 feet high under the deck-beams; and here, according to the time of the year, were packed from a hundred to three hundred men, women, and children, most of them being hardy German peasants, with a sprinkling of English, Scotch, and Irish. Steeragestewards were not thought of then, and the whole arrangement and government of the place fell upon the ship's carpenter, whose chief business seemed to be to see that no one exceeded his or her proper allowance of water and fuel, and, as Captain Champion has told us also, that the ship was not set on fire by men smoking below, etc.

Sleeping accommodation was of the rudest kind, put up by the carpenter and his mate, according to the number of passengers, a few days before sailing. This was done by dividing the 'tween-decks through the entire length by a central partition, and then affixing to it on either side, and the ship's sides, *three* rows, one above the other, of shelves made of rough unplaned boards, each shelf being six feet wide, with ledges dividing it into three sleeping-places. The passages left between these rows of sleeping-shelves were very little over three feet wide; and here the chests and boxes of the steerage passengers, besides their provisions for the voyage, were stowed, so that it was rare to find standing-room; while, in order to pass from one end of the steerage to the other, it was necessary to crawl on all-fours above this lumber, between it and the deck-beams.

A few of the larger packets of the line had portholes here and there, about six inches in diameter;

but these only admitted light, for, being almost constantly washed by the sea, they were rarely opened after leaving port. Of other light there was little, and that only through a few narrow slips of glass let into the deck above, or from a dip-candle hanging here and there in a horn lantern from the deck-beams.

Fresh air on the Atlantic is plentiful, and said to be pure in quality; but the quantity of it allowed to find its way below among the steerage passengers was small, being confined entirely to that which was able to pass down the two rather small scuttles or hatches at either end of the steerage; the larger scuttle, or principal entrance, being in the main hatch, and the other in the fore. A wind-sail, or canvas ventilator, was, weather permitting, placed in one or both these openings, but in bad weather the forward one was always closed, if not battened down. An ordinary steep ship's step-ladder, with a man-rope to hold on by, was the only means of descent or ascent into or out of this gloomy place; but a tall man could, standing upon the main-deck hatch below, hand a child up to the deck-level with ease.

As the passengers found their own provisions, the only arrangement made for them on this head was to make sure that each on joining the ship had with him his proper quantity of sea-biscuit, flour, potatoes, tea, sugar, and treacle, together with two hams, a tin pot, frying-pan, tin mug, and teapot, with a knife, fork, and iron spoon; all which luxuries were supplied to the passengers, generally at the last moment, on the day of sailing, by a certain ship-chandler of Wapping, and were all duly checked and weighed by the carpenter or mate when brought on board.

The Black X line of packet carried no regular surgeon or doctor; and, unless one turned up by chance among the passengers, this duty in the steerage fell upon the carpenter, who dispensed all medicines required by this class of passengers. They were served out to him from the ship's medicine-chest aft by the black steward, according to the first mate's advice; an old, but very large "Dictionary of Domestic Medicine" being consulted in doubtful cases. Generally speaking, the carpenter was also the ship's dentist. But in spite of all these rule-of-thumb arrangements, and the laws of sanitary science, the steerage passengers in "the only regular line of packets" were generally healthy; and in the course of many voyages in ships of this class, I am inclined to think that the birth-rate usually exceeded the death-rate. What is more, I don't remember that there was more grumbling among the steerage passengers than there was in the cabin, though both classes had of course plenty of time allowed them for it on the voyage.

CHAPTER XVII.

FROM THE ST. KATHARINE DOCKS TO THE DOWNS FIFTY YEARS AGO.

Definition of a packet—The dock quay on sailing day—Those who live by seeing ships out of dock—Temperance ships—Christian knowledge and crime—Their diffusion and emigration—Latter-day Saint and ship-chandler—Sound and motion—"Any more for the shore?"—Too late—In tow—Brought up in the Lower Hope—A very quiet night—Under way again—Topsails *versus* steam—The pride of the morning—Feeling the way over the flats—A freshening breeze—Ready about—To windward through the Gull Stream into the Downs.

I HAVE gone much into detail about the Black X liner, her skipper, etc., because she was the last of ocean-packets as distinguished from more modern passenger-vessels built with a view to the combined carriage of cargo and passengers.

It is true that the earlier paddle-wheel Cunarder which ran these sailing-packets off the Atlantic, as the railway did mail-coaches, was a packet; for her cargo consisted almost entirely of the coal burnt in making each run. But as the screw superseded paddles, and ships rapidly grew larger, ocean-steamers soon ceased to be merely mail-packets; and at the present time I do not think there is a single line of ocean-going steamships built like these early liners were, with the model of a yacht or despatch-boat, and carrying cargo only as dead weight just sufficient to enable them to carry their canvas in good sailing trim. But this was so much the case with these sharp-bottomed little packets that they usually left London with nothing below two or three hundred steerage, and eighty cabin passengers, but a few hundred tons of chalk ballast and a full supply of fresh water for the passage, which, going West, at times extended to six or eight weeks.

The monthly sailing day of one of these ships was quite an event then in the St. Katharine Docks, where stood huddled together on the quay, first, a swarm of steerage passengers, or, as we should now call them, emigrants, with their worldly goods round them, besides bedding and provisions for the voyage. Then there were of course a number of those people who always have, or think they have, an interest in every outward-bound ship and her passengers, among them many tearful women, some, perhaps, wives of men going out alone to try and start a home for them in the West; other women, too, stood about quite as tearful, and more noisy, though only parting for a few mouths from some of the crew of the ship. Among these were men and women selling oranges, nuts, and other cheap fruit, and, as the Black X line of packets were temperance ships, a bottle or two of rum concealed under the fruit for the crew.

Then there were people bent upon diffusing the largest amount of Christian knowledge in the shortest possible time by distributing tracts to distracted men and women, who often asked in return for news of some missing bag or box. Besides these, there were always one or more detectives, quietly working like spaniels in cover among the crowd, with the object of nipping some Christian criminal or crime in the bud, before it succeeded in planting itself in other lands—a matter much easier done then, before the Atlantic cable was laid. Often too, just as the ship was on the point of being unmoored, a Latter-day Saint would rush frantically on board and insist on interviewing the captain, in order to persuade him to alter his sailing day; that so the end of all things, according to him now several days overdue, might not overtake the ship, passengers, and crew in the chops of the Channel. Not one of these, however, got a tenth part of the attention, or had a chance of a hearing against the stout ship-chandler of Wapping, mentioned in the last chapter, who was now busy mustering the emigrants, to see that none left the docks without his or her proper allowance of sea-stores. The Claimant, Sir Roger, hailed from Wapping, but the brain-power of even that remarkable man would, I think, have proved unequal to the rapid organization, command of temper, low Dutch and German, shown by this man as, helped by the ship's carpenter, he handled that mixed gang of steerage passengers as easily as an old Sunday-school teacher would a troop of unruly children; his rapid patter of Wapping-English, German, and Dutch, acting like magic in settling all disputes between them and those about them.

Ducks, geese, and poultry in general always sympathize with excitement near them, while pigs, and even sheep, thrown together for the first time, have a noisy way of their own. While at intervals, even the old sea-cow bemoans her lot in life. But all such home-like noises are now almost lost in the rapid click, click, click of a capstan, and regular tramp round and song of the red-shirted sailors as they reel in the warp by which slowly, but very surely, the ship is hauling out of dock. Yankee seamen (almost an extinct race now) were then noted for their capstan chants, and the chorus of "Good morning, ladies all," swells quaintly up at intervals above the other sounds.

A fussy little tug, with much steam roaring out of

her in one place, and rattling out in another, adds not a little to the difficulty the ship's mate has in making the pilot and dock-master's orders heard by his crew—commands which were never given directly to the men, but were, so to say, boiled down, concentrated, and strengthened before being poured out through the Yankee mate's speaking-trumpet on them.

The dock-master, for instance, would say, "That'll do, Mr. Storks, with our head-line; if you will be good enough to shift your starn-line to your port-quarter, and get a small pull upon it." Which, through the mate's trumpet, comes to the crew as "Vast 'eaving there for'ard; lay aft, som' of ye, an' tail on to that quarter-line. Lay aft! G—d d—n ye, lay aft there! Jump out quick, one of ye, and take it clear of the main-brace. In with it! smart now! run away with it, boys. Hurrah! hurrah! boys! there she slews." And as a great increase of noise almost invariably precedes the end of a fine piece of music, so the climax of uproar was always reached when the ship arrived at and stopped for a few minutes in the lock, or river entrance, of the dock. Here the ship's big bell rings impatiently as the Yankee mate roars out again and again, "Any-more-for-the-shore! Any one for shore!!"

There always is one more for the shore, and some time after the Latter-day Saint and stout ship-chandler have risked their lives in a tight embrace as they meet upon the tilting end of a gang-board, there comes from the crowded ship's deck a shrill cry from an Irishwoman of "Sure, an' it's myself am for the shore, yer honour. An' sure, I belaved it was the ship was the quay, an' the quay was the ship, win yer honour spake, an' now it's the quay's gone without me, an' it's myself that's lift behind in the ship altogither with my husband!"

But the tug ceases to blow off steam, and the flap, flap of her paddles, with a quiet "port!" "starboard!" or "steady!" from a Thames pilot, as the ship follows the tug through crowded pool, tells that the voyage has begun.

From the docks to Gravesend in tow of the tug was in those days a very stately procession, with an ever-increasing string of watermen's skiffs, etc., astern of the ship, which fully occupied the afternoon of sailing day, and gave time for most of the emigrants to tumble themselves, baggage, bedding, and sea-stores, down the main-hatch into the steerage below. And as Long Reach opens out, sailors, armed with short iron hooks, drag length after length of chain cable aft along the decks, and lay it fair in fakes ready for running out. The string of boats astern steadily grows shorter, until on passing old Tilbury Fort one only is left, into which, as it hauls up alongside, the Thames pilot and Irish-

Ship in tow of Thames tug.

woman scramble together down a rope-ladder, and leave the ship for Gravesend; just below which place, in the Lower Hope, the tug slackens speed, the tow-line is cast off and hauled in, and as the ship loses way some one shouts, "All clear there for'ard?" answered by "Ay, ay, sir, all clear;" and at the words, "Let go!" the anchor falls from the cat-head, and the ship, trembling from end to end as fathom after fathom of

Light colliers dropping down with last of ebb.

chain runs out, swings head to tide for the night. The tug also brings up close by on the Kentish shore, and at once fills the quiet evening sky with clouds of upstart noisy steam, as she blows off and banks up fires with a view to another job at daybreak.

After sundown, the lower reaches of the Thames were then wonderfully quiet. A light collier or two slowly driving down with the last of the ebb, telling very black across the twilight, take nothing from the stillness; and the bark of a dog on board one as she glides past the ship, answered by another far-off yard-dog ashore, is almost startling in effect. Quiet, also, so far as the upper deck is concerned, prevails on board the packet, broken only now and then by the cackle of a restless old gander, or a discontented squeal among the pigs, as they pack themselves away for night. Of cabin passengers there are as yet few on board; most of these choosing to travel by coach or post-chaise, and join the ship on her arrival at Portsmouth. And with the exception of one or two second-cabin passengers, and a German here and there smoking his pipe on deck, there is little more than the red glimmer of a deck-light in places to mark that whole families of emigrants of many countries are under that three inches of pine deck, like the pigs and sheep in the long-boat, making such arrangements as they can for a night's rest. In the main cabin, even the tick of the old Channel pilot's big watch can be heard, as well as his snore, from an adjoining state-room. Some time, however, before daylight, tramping overhead and a noise of heavy objects falling in all directions on deck tell that the pilot has turned out, and with a fair wind out of the river is getting the anchor, and making sail on the ship. London tugs of those days were feeble things compared to the fine powerful tug of to-day, which cruises in search of ships far down Channel below the Isle of Wight. And, though doing her best, the little tug barely held her own with the Black X liner, as under a fore course and two great topsails now sheeted home she moved fast before a fresh morning breeze through the greenish-grey water of sea reach. And the pilot's attention is divided between the tug's captain, the man at the wheel, and a hot cup of coffee on the quarter-deck capstan-head.

It was an ill wind indeed (unless it were an Irishman's hurricane) which blew a steam-tug any good below the Nore in those days. Nevertheless, as she paddles up alongside the ship, there comes a shout from the tug's captain standing on her paddle-box, with a hand on either side his mouth, of "Better make sure, sir! We'll give you a good hextra hour's tide while you gets the canvas on to her!" "Hour's tide! Why, you couldn't keep a taut hawser on us a minute with this breeze." And, turning to the mate, the pilot says, "Have the goodness, Mr. Storks, to look sharp with them topgallant-yards." "Ay, ay, sir! Fore-topgallan'-yard—ahoy! Gone to sleep there? Look alive, and lay down on deck! Now, then, hoist away! rouse 'em up, boys, smart!" And as each bellying sail is sheeted home, and yard after yard rises aloft, the ship rapidly forereaches on the tug, until her captain, with a last appeal of "It's only the pride of the morning," and a wave of his hand, turns her head up river, leaving, as she goes, a curving trail of brown smoke behind. And when the last curl of it blows clear of the packet's white canvas, the old pilot, sipping his coffee, says contentedly to the mate, "Done with him, Mr. Storks." "Ay, ay, sir—done with the steam, thank the Lord."

The low lines of shore on either side now quickly recede; and the orange-red Nore lightship is the only bit of positive colour upon a cold expanse of grey sky and water speckled with buoys and beacons of strange form and stranger names, all of which are a continued source of apparently artistic study to the pilot as he stands with upheld hand over the compass, taking the bearings of them. "I never omit, sir," he says to the mate, "taking as many bearings as I can on a fine morning like this, and they comes handy when I chance to pop on one of them buoys in thick weather or night-times."

A leadsman is now always in the chains with his long-drawn chant as the ship threads her way among the sandy banks, bars, and narrow channels at the mouth of the Thames. But soon after sighting the double tower of old Reculver Church the water deepens, and beyond Margate and the shelter of the Foreland, the little packet begins to roll in the short tidal sea; while,

Heaving the lead.

the wind drawing more abeam, the crew are busy bracing the yards to it until, as she feels its strength, she heels over to the breeze, and heads the sea with the long easy plunge of a great schooner yacht. A few hours of such sailing would soon have brought her nearer old Amsterdam than New York; and before noon, as the wind freshens, the fore-royal and flying-jib are taken in. Soon after which a quiet "Ready about" from the pilot causes quite a bustle among the watch on deck. Coils of rope are flung down in all directions ready for running; and nearly every passenger at once finds that the snug corner chosen by him has some rope, block, tack, or sheet near it, about which small groups of sailors gather, evidently waiting an important command. Very soon "All ready forward," from the pilot, answered by "Ay, ay, sir!" from a mate, is followed by "Put your helm down!" And at the words "Helm's a-lee! raise tacks an' sheets," the whole mass of canvas, ropes, and blocks, which a moment before stood as steady as though carved in wood, is banging, flapping, and rattling among the spars and rigging as the ship comes upright and head to wind; the men at the same time singing out, as they haul in and overhaul tacks and sheets, add to the noise; but now, clear and loud above their voices, rings out from the mate, "Mainsail-haul!" And as the long yards, almost with a jerk, swing round, gangs of sailors run along the deck, gathering in the slack of braces, etc. A few seconds of quiet follow as the ship turns from the wind and her after canvas slowly fills again, while her head-sails lie quietly, nearly aback against the foremast. Then comes another shout of "Let go, and haul!" And as the men run aft with the fore-braces the foreyards swing round, and the ship's head is toward the Kentish shore. "Steady your helm! Keep her full!" And after trimming the yards to the wind, and coiling down ropes ready for the next tack, the men obey the welcome order from the pilot of "Go below the watch, and let the people get their dinner, Mr. Storks."

Later in the day the wind steadily freshens, and more upper canvas is taken in until, tack after tack following one another in rapid succession, as a man in the chains feels the way, the little packet flutters her way against the strong wind through the Gull Stream into the Downs.

CHAPTER XVIII.

THE PILOT.

A Channel letter-box—A man found at sea—Pleasant flavour of the land about him—The pilot's hat—Sad Old-World prejudices of a through-and-out Trinity pilot—A pilot's fare and lot not all cakes and ale—Aversion of pilot to long walks and short naps—Blind faith of passengers in him—The pilot as a man of business on the Stock Exchange, etc.—Examiners examined—Weakness and mannerism of elderly pilots—Foreign pilots—A French and Yankee one—Modern pilot's risks and work—The old rule of the road at sea—Pleasures of the starboard tack—Sailing in convoy, etc.

In the days of East Indiamen and sailing-packets, when a Channel pilot dropped into his dinghy alongside, or in rough weather swung himself from the mainyard-arm of an outward-bound ship, down upon his cutter's deck, he was looked upon as the last link, maybe for months, between ship and land; and the big breast-pocket of his oilskin coat was the latest letter-box in which to post farewell letters. The electric wire and steam have greatly changed, not only the character of the pilot himself, but his value as a post-office, and his pockets are now mostly full of sixpenny telegrams, in place of being crammed with those long, old-fashioned, parting letters, so easy to write when a voyage from London to Spithead or Plymouth rarely occupied less than a week or ten days. Still, one often notes, even to-day, as some great ship leaves the dock, or a tender steams away from her in the river, those well-known words of wife or mother, to a husband or son, of " Now, mind and write by the pilot!"

In "Two Years before the Mast," Dana has described the sadness and void that falls upon a ship's crew, after being long at sea, upon the loss of a messmate overboard.* According to my experience, a strange feeling, not quite akin, but rather the complement to this, comes over a ship's company on the first appearance of the man who boards a ship towards the end of a long voyage—the pilot. The captain, perhaps, may have seen him before, or may even be upon sufficiently intimate terms to ask after the health of his missus and family; but to all the rest on board he is a stranger, the one face and figure among us with any novelty about it; and his presence is almost harder to get over for some time than the vacant place of the

---

* Samuel Rogers was so struck with this passage in Dana's delightful book that he had the whole of it by heart, and loved to repeat it, always dwelling upon certain parts, which he said "were to him among the most pathetically touching bits of prose or poetry our language."

man lost at sea. When he speaks, to give his first order, his voice sounds like that of some one from another world. We watch him furtively, and every article of his rig-out has a strange interest about it. Of course the captain and some of the first-cabin people soon get from him the latest news, or the papers he may have brought with him from the still distant port; but the humbler members of our company have to rest content with any scraps of his talk with the captain they may chance to overhear, and these chiefly relate to the weather or other ships and their doings. But though picked up at sea, in the chops of the Channel, there is a certain flavour of the land about a pilot, and the look of a man who has quite recently eaten good fresh beef and spring onions. At any rate, his is the only shore-going hat in sight; and though, like all pilots' hats, it has a character of its own—the brim running in a parallel line round his face like a sea-horizon—still there it is, a regular shore-going bell-topper. Then there is his broad black-satin waistcoat, with a big silver timepiece stowed away in it—the one watch actually keeping shore-time in the ship; while, though the weather may have been rather hot and calm of late, the new-arrival wears a heavy over-coat, oilskin trousers, and a thick woollen comforter about his neck, in which he looks very much as though he had spent the previous night outside a mail-coach.

Indeed, it is likely enough that he did; for in the days I write of, a "through-and-out pilot" was almost as well known upon certain old post-roads as in the wider roadsteads of the Downs and Spithead.

Though a pilot sometimes remained over a week in one ship, he seldom became really at home in her from the day he mounted her side until he and his black-painted canvas bag vanished mysteriously, becoming absorbed among a crowd of other arrivals from the shore as the ship hauled into dock.

In large vessels the pilot mostly dined alone, having something that had been kept hot for him served in a remote corner of the cabin; while many of his earlier or later meals were taken seated upon a deck-stool, the top of a skylight, or some upturned boat, serving him for a table.

Years ago many ships, especially Yankee ones, were sailed upon what were called strictly temperance principles; but "our pilot" has been a master's mate in the Royal Navy of William IV.'s time, and though, as he says, "no doubt water is a great blessing, and a thing we ought to be werry thankful for," yet for the life of him "he never could stand it stark naked." So that, "even in the strictest of teetotal wessels, he feels it a dooty towards his country, himself, and a licensed Trinity pilot, to ask for and be served with a glass of grog, hot or cold, as required, and when wanted, at any hour during the middle watch." On board large passenger-vessels a pilot of course always fared well; while in his own cutter, he suited his taste and victualled his boat at a home port. This was not always his lot, however, when, after knocking about outside the Wight for a day or two, he fell in with and boarded some small inward-bound merchantman, especially if she hailed from a French or Norwegian port. And the appetite of the most experienced of Channel pilots has been known to fail him when, on peeping into the galley of such a craft, he discovered her *chef* busy preparing some stewed cuttle-fish, or, as the pilot called it, "squid," for the cabin *déjeuner*. Then, again, on board Norwegian, Italian, or Spanish ships, pilots often complained of the strong flavour and liberal use of train and other oils in their frying-pans, or the amount of garlic in a ragoût of salt fish and beans. But these small discomforts of a pilot's life on board foreign ships were often greatly counterbalanced by the quantity, and sometimes quality, of the wines or other liquors served in the captain's cabin; and an old pilot, speaking of his fare on board a Spaniard, wound up his yarn almost in the words of Mrs. Gamp, "But the drinks was all good."

From the moment the pilot stepped on board a ship, the captain and his nautical instruments were superseded. The navigation of the ship was now carried on by the stranger—his big silver watch and the palm of his right hand frequently extended before him over the binnacle compass, in the line of distant, misty-looking headlands by day, or glimmering lights at night. As to charts, etc., the pilot's head is not only a regular tide-table, but full of bearings, lights, and buoys, from Gravesend to Plymouth.

Even the tread of a pilot as he paces the deck on cold nights distinguishes him from other officers of the ship, for, being long used to the short deck of his cutter, he rarely takes more than three steps in any direction without a turn, and finds plenty of room for his short promenade athwart-ship between the binnacle and the wheel. His watches below, or times of rest, are most irregular, and are seldom taken unless the ship is brought up in a calm to wait the turn of a tide. But when he does turn in, either on board his own boat or elsewhere, he is, as he says, "rather apt to sleep twice round the clock." This power of the pilot of storing long spells of sleep is not always shared by other seafaring men, some of whom complain that, after keeping "watch and watch" of four hours at a time for months at sea, they find it hard work to stop in bed ashore after eight bells; or not to turn out and keep the morning watch elsewhere.

To passengers, after a voyage of some months, the sight of the pilot-boat is like the arrival of a doctor's carriage at some lone country house where there is a bad illness. Much is expected of both men. However heavy, thick, or calm, the weather may have been, the narrow circle of a pilot's hat is believed to compass power and knowledge that may still the storm, penetrate the fog, or cause a breeze to blow. As he takes his first quick turns across the deck, looking aloft at the helpless sails as they fall to and fro with the roll of the ship, a cheery rub of his hands is regarded as something that should bring a fair wind to help the ship into port. Each time he orders a pull upon a brace here, or clew-line there, the manœuvre is watched with deep interest; and when, other means having failed, he asks the mate, in a low, confidential tone, "to get a cast of the deep-sea lead," passengers watch him, and the result, as people do the doctor when, watch in hand, he counts a patient's pulse. As was said before, steam has much changed the manners and customs of pilots, but there is still about them something of the old style; for the business and good will often descends, as it does among fishermen, from father to son; though, unlike fishermen, retired pilots are seldom badly off; they are indeed among the few men of the sea who are able to keep their wits about them on land. And long after he has left the helm of No. 2 C in the hands of his boys, our Channel pilot is busy dabbling in shares in the ketch *Slippery*, small house property, or even in Turkish, or "Rooshun" bonds, maybe.

The examination of a pilot, especially a local one, must be a delicate matter; for his knowledge is just of that proof-of-the-pudding kind not easily tested by a board of examiners. And one of the oldest and best of local pilots belonging to a large southern port used to tell how he was "let down easy like" at his first and only examination by certain port authorities; his examiners finding, after a question or two, that he was fast changing places with them, though of book-learning he knew little beyond being able to sign his name.

Like some other professional men, as they advance in life, pilots often become mannered and confirmed pessimists respecting weather; and it is related of one well-known Channel pilot that after sixty he never answered a captain's usual greeting of "Well, pilot, what d'ye think of the weather?" in any other form than, "Well, captain, I consider it looks werry inferior —werry inferior indeed."

A well-known formula, always repeated, parrot-like, at the close of his job by an old negro pilot in a South American port, is another instance of this professional mannerism, "Let-go-the-anchor-brail-up-the-spanker-put-four-men-in-a-boat, and-put-pilot-ashore."

In fact, no foreign pilot compares favourably in dignity or bearing with the British article. A French pilot, for instance, will at times board a ship in a rough worsted cap and shirt-sleeves, and on coming on deck handle a rope's-end, or the spokes of the wheel, as though he formed one of the ship's company; which of course at once stamped him in the eye of every one as a person of an inferior class. Then I have known a Yankee pilot board a ship two or three hundred miles east of Sandy Hook in striped kerseymere pants, a black swallow-tailed dress-coat, French patent-leather boots, and an old Panama hat, and the moment he got on the quarter-deck seat himself on a camp-stool, light a cigar, and commence chatting to the skipper as though he had nothing else to do on board.

In these days of steam, the pilot has rather a rough time of it, knocking about in his small sailing-cutter, when on the look-out for some particular vessel, right in the track of all in and outward bound steamers; and it is not surprising that one hears now and then of a pilot-boat being run over and all hands drowned in the narrower parts of the Channel. While, when in charge, steam, though it has entirely changed his mode of handling a ship, has also increased the risks a pilot runs of collision when passing through a fleet of sailing-craft at night, when the lights of such vessels (especially the green or starboard light) are rarely seen until too late to be of much use to him or

French pilot-boat.

any one else. It is at such times that the pilot's own seamanship and constant habit of working under canvas in his cutter is invaluable, and enables him to judge intuitively, so to say, of the position and movements of the many small craft about him.

Before steam, the rule of the road was simple enough. With meeting ships close hauled, or turning to windward, the ship on the starboard tack, *i.e.* with the wind on her right-hand side, held her course. On the port tack, *i.e.* with the wind on her left, a ship had either to 'bout-ship or else port her helm; that is, put her tiller to the left, and pass astern of the other ship, which was the usual thing to do, and probably led to the blind adherence—right or wrong—to the rule of port helm in all cases, among the early masters of steamers. With a fair wind, every vessel had to give way or keep clear of those beating to windward. Thus it came about that in the days of sailing-ships every one, pilot included, on board a ship close hauled on the starboard tack, felt as safe as the driver of a railway train on a single line of rails worked by staff does, when he has the staff, or right of the road, in hand.

Lights were only hoisted when at anchor, unless it were the binnacle-lantern of a vessel lying to, or close hauled in a gale of wind, held up and shown to one running across her track before it. Thick fog and wind rarely occur together, so that half speed or dead slow was, as it should be to-day among steamers, almost compulsory with sailing-ships in foggy weather. It is often said, as an apology for collisions at sea now, that we have so many more vessels afloat. But it must be remembered that during all the long years of war-time, our merchant-ships were seldom under way except in large fleets of a hundred sail or more under convoy of several men-of-war, and that unless scattered by tempest, the whole fleet had to keep together, yet clear of each other as to single ships, day and night, by these simple rules of the road only. The speed of a sailing-ship cannot be regulated in a moment by the turn of a steam-cock, and except by backing his main-yard or letting go an anchor, a pilot had no means of stopping a ship, to say nothing of "full speed astern," a term and resource of to-day quite unknown to old seamen.

CHAPTER XIX.

THE WINGLESS WAR-SHIP OF THE FUTURE, AND THOSE IN CHARGE OF HER.

A seaman's workshop—His tools, etc.—The old definition of seamanship—Soldiers and sailors compared as firemen—Sea-legs required for work upon a modern mastless war-ship—An old one, and how she behaved—How France will always command a good and constant supply of ready-made sailor-men—The naval officer of the future as a protection of our sailing merchantmen —"Lame ducks," or broken-down steamships under canvas— Stokers and firemen as a boat's crew—A prize-master in the hands of his prisoners.

HE is a broad-faced, fair-haired Dutchman, astride on the end of the bowsprit of a large galliot, which has just discharged a cargo of potatoes, and hauled off from the quay to make room for a ship exactly like her to the smallest detail, from the tiny ball of a truck over her vane to the slender flagstaff stepped picturesquely on her heavy carved rudder-head. The bowsprit-end, on which the man sits with the ease of an accomplished rider, overhangs the water about twenty-five feet above it, and just clear of the stern of a collier lying nearly at a right angle to her, over the rail of which a grimy-looking lad is watching him, and chatting partly by signs, and partly in language common to both; for the Dutchman seems to know a little seaport English, and the collier-boy evidently understands some of the other's seaport Dutch.

All the while the man, as he sits, is busy with a marline-spike and some obstinate wire rope, which, with the jib down-haul block, seems to be constantly turning and twisting in his hands; though the man appears rather to feel what to do than to look at it, and might be at work on the jibboom-end after dark, so far as his eyes are concerned. He is really turning in afresh, or re-stropping, the block in his hands, or, maybe, clapping on an extra seizing. But, whatever the work may be, the thing which strikes one is the repose and perfect balance of the man on his narrow-backed wooden horse, which is never quite still; for the galliot, having a clean-swept hold, moves to even the swell of a passing tug, and blows to and fro from the quay in every gust of wind.

But what has all this to do with sailless war-ships? Well, just this. Where and how did this Dutchman get his balance and power of working at his ease in what to most people would be an awkward, if not a dangerous position? Well, simply from much work of the kind at far greater heights, upon spars swaying about at all angles, above a rolling, pitching ship at sea. Very few see him at this work, and those who do would not look twice at him. But here, standing comfortably on the stone quay-side, one is able to watch every turn of his hand and wrist as he tautens each turn of the seizing, and to see that he has about him a knife, a sharp-pointed spike, or pricker, some

Dutch sailor on his narrow-backed horse.

small seizing-stuff, as well as a ball of twine, and some grease. His knife and spike are of course secured by lanyards; but how he contrives to keep all his tools in hand is in itself a marvel. Even the block was evidently all adrift just now to an outsider's eye, though no doubt secured by a yarn in some way. Now, all this man's strange dexterity is included in the old term, "seamanship"—only an A.B., or thorough sailor-man, knowing just what to do, or what could be done, with a bit of new rope or yarn, and how to do it as this Dutchman can, perch him where you will. An ordinary seaman can "hand-reef and steer"—that is, help take in or reef sails—and take his trick at the wheel, which is about all, if not more than all, that some of the crew of a steamer can do now, when all our large sailing-ships are fitted and rigged ready for use, by shore gangs of riggers—usually salts of the old type, who, too old or too cunning to go to sea, make a more comfortable living by such work in dock. All our present men-of-war's men still know something of seamanship; but there must come a time, if sails and rigging are entirely given up in the navy, when even what remains of the "able seaman" about them will be a thing of the past, and they will be no more like sailor-men than a hand on board a penny steamboat or a Thames lighter is: clever fellows in their way, but entirely wanting in the cat-like agility which still marks the English blue-jacket.

Policemen and soldiers are all well drilled and set up; but the smartest dragoon, even the smartest artilleryman, would appear heavy and cart-horse-like in competition with a blue-jacket at a fire,* or about

* Owing to the rapid decrease in the number of real sailor-men

work that demands a steady head and quickness of resource. Owing to the want of the compensating swing of lofty spars, there is nothing so uneasy afloat, unless water-logged, as a mastless vessel in a seaway;* so that all work done on board such craft would at sea be more easily done by men whose limbs and heads had been accustomed to work aloft. While, should we and the French really both decide to abolish sails in war-ships, it must not be forgotten by us that, owing to their system of naval conscription, our *neighbour's* fleets would still be manned by real sailor-men, drawn from their enormous fleet of large sea-going fishing-vessels, etc.

So much for the blue-jacket. But why should the

in our steam merchant-navy, the head of the London Fire Brigade reported a short time ago that he finds more difficulty every year in filling its ranks with men like those he formerly got from the crews of our sailing merchantmen.

* A practical illustration of this occurs in an account in "Anson's Voyage," of the difficulty Captain Saunders had in boarding the "*Tryal* sloop," in a seaway, after she was condemned as unfit for service, and her masts had been removed. He was ordered to scuttle her; but reported that, "having neither masts or sails to steady her, she rolled and pitched so violently that it was impossible for a boat to lay alongside her;" so that though the order to sink her was given him on the 27th of September, it was not until the 4th of October that he was able to carry it out. Seamen in those days were almost in the daily habit of boat-communication between ship and ship, and it must have been no ordinary pitching and rolling that kept one of them dancing attendance for a whole week upon a condemned vessel.

brains and time of young naval officers, already rather overtaxed, be wasted in learning useless sail-drill and details of an almost obsolete seamanship? It has been truly said that, "for a war navy, if sails did not exist, it would be necessary to invent them—practice in handling a ship under sail demanding an amount of attention, *alertness*, and *foresight*, which no other peace occupation ever calls for from an officer."*
Sails and sailing-ships do, however, exist, and among merchant-ships will probably continue to do so for some time; and, so long as this is the case, some knowledge of sail evolutions will be absolutely required of those entrusted with the navigation of even "sail-less war-ships;" if only to enable officers in charge of such craft to judge from the force and direction of the wind, by day or night, what any sailing-ship, brig, or schooner, that may chance to cross his track, is doing or likely to do next, together with her speed, etc.; in order that seeing her rig and the tack she is on by day, or the position of her light, or lights, by night, he may be able to judge of and shape the best course to clear her. This kind of knowledge is already rather on the decrease, and want of it may have helped to swell the number of collisions at sea between steamers

---

* From a letter to the *Times*, signed "Man-of-war's-man," January 14th, 1888.

and sailing-vessels. But imagine some new-fangled young naval officer of the future, educated under steam only, driving H.M.S. *Sheer Hulk* up Channel (at her *measured-mile* speed) on a darkish night, across the tracks of a number of sailing merchant-vessels of varying rigs and speed, which are, say, turning to windward on a flood tide, in a stiff breeze between the Start and Portland. Never having handled a vessel under canvas, it would be unfair to expect *him* to know, by looking at one of these vessels, even in daylight, what her speed was, or even exactly in what direction she was sailing or steering; while, if told that one was in stays, or another just about to haul her head-yards, he would hardly understand the meaning of the terms. Yet this is the state of things that must eventually come to pass if the entire abolition of sails and sail-drill ever takes place in the navy. It may be said that, according to the present rules of the road, it is the business of all vessels under steam to keep out of the way of sailing-ships; or that a young officer even educated under steam has his compass before him, and has only to take the bearings of a sailing-ship's light, and watch it carefully, in order to know what the vessel that carries the light is doing. This may be useful in really clear weather, when a sailing-ship's lights can be seen at some distance (which is just the weather when there ought to be little risk of collision); but in blowing, thick weather the light or lights of sailing-ships (especially the green one) are often only visible a few moments before the ship herself is, and a man at such times had better keep his eye upon the sailing-vessel herself, and act at once upon his knowledge of her speed and course, than stop to take bearings of her, etc. And spite of all rules of the road, positions constantly arise, especially at night in the Channel, in which a good knowledge of sailing seamanship is necessary to a steam captain for the safety both of his own vessel and others; and that such knowledge is still thought important on board merchant steamships, is evident from the fact that all officers in our large companies are required to have served some years in a sailing-ship at sea before beginning their career on board a steamer. This is of course right, and when naval officers, and the men under them, cease to be sailors, they will undoubtedly become the terror, rather than the protectors, of England's sailing merchantmen; numbers of which still exist, happily for us, as schools of seamanship, and, in certain trades, actually pay better than steam. And this reminds me that in describing the two Dutch galliots, I should have mentioned, that, though built on exactly the same old lines, one of them was constructed of iron or steel; her owner evidently being disposed (probably for the sake of economy) to move with the times so far, though still retaining sail as a motive power in place of steam.

I have said nothing of the unseamanlike, selfish character of the idea of exposing men, in case of a breakdown at sea, to the risk and anxiety of finding themselves so utterly helpless, as they would be on board a wingless war-ship reduced to the state of a "lame duck" in bad weather. But a few quite recent extracts from the logs of merchant steamers are sufficient to prove the necessity of giving those who command and man our modern half-tide rock class of war-ships, some reserve form of wing or sail power, and some knowledge of how to make use of it.

"Her Majesty's ship *Orontes* reports that the steamer *Norham Castle* had arrived at St. Helena, with machinery disabled when 417 miles S.E. of that island, to which she sailed without assistance. All well on board; mails transferred, and brought on by the *Orontes*."

"Steamship *Syria*, homeward bound, soon after leaving St. Helena broke main shaft. In consequence of head winds, was seven days before she was able to regain the island under canvas."

"Netherland-American Co.'s steamer *P. Caland*, Captain Bonjer, from Rotterdam to New York, put into Plymouth, having lost three blades of propeller and damaged rudder. In lat. 48° N., long. 38° W., the fourth blade of propeller became loose, and one of the braces of the rudder was carried away, when, finding it impossible to steer and hold way against a heavy sea and head wind, the ship's head was turned east, to the great delight of the passengers, and sail being set, and the engines kept going, the *P. Caland*, before a strong westerly gale, made a good run back to Plymouth, distance about 1800 miles."

These three extracts, taken at random from the shipping news of a month, speak for themselves. But the question also of how, in case of having to abandon a sinking or disabled wingless war-ship in mid-ocean, her boats are to be handled under sail by men trained only on board steam-launches, etc., or how they are to be handled under oars by crews of stokers and firemen, is not without interest; the very largest steam-launch that can be carried on shipboard being sure to prove a poor resource when exposed to a few days' bad weather at sea.

In conclusion, I may remark also here that in war-time a awkward question may arise as to who is to take charge of a sailing prize; the only people on board her really "knowing the ropes" being her own officers and crew, or those least interested in her right navigation after capture.

Skiff of duck-pond.

CHAPTER XX.

AN ALPHABETICALLY-ARRANGED LIST OF SEA-TERMS, SOME OF WHICH, THOUGH OBSOLETE AS TO THEIR MEANING AFLOAT, ARE STILL USED ASHORE.

Aback. The position of a ship when, through neglect of the helmsman, or a sudden shift of wind, her sails lie pressed against the masts and cease to give her headway. "I was taken quite [or, 'all'] aback when I heard it."

Able seaman. One rated as A.B., who could not only hand, that is furl, sails, reef them, and steer by compass, etc., but who was master of all work required in the fitting and repair of rigging: such as knotting, splicing, serving, pointing ropes, mat-making, etc. As a class, he is almost extinct among the younger hands in our *merchant*-service.

"*Aboard main tack.*" An order to draw down one of the lower corners of a mainsail to the chess-tree (*see* Chess-tree).

About. A term usually applied to turning a ship from one tack to another. "He put us about," or,

"We had to go about or get aground." "I was terribly put about."

A Burton. A term for casks stowed athwart-ship. The name also of a small tackle used for many purposes, and sometimes called "a handy billy."

Adze, or *addice*. The tool *par excellence* of the shipwright, and with which our old wooden shipbuilders could "dub" the outside oak planking of a great ship, and leave it almost as smooth as though it had been planed. An adze is considered by shipwrights the most difficult of all tools to handle well. Coopers also make use of the adze. In M. Du Chaillu's book we are told that, when building his large ship, King Olaf employed a special workman or "shipsmith" upon her stern and sternposts, one Thorberg, "scaf-hogg," or "blow-scraper," *i.e.* a man who could trim and smooth heavy timbers with an adze. The Viking ships appear to have been

An adze, or addice.

clench-built, and this part of the work would be just that best done by a man skilled in the use of an adze or "blow-scraper."

Aloof. "Keep aloof," or "Keep your luff." An order to keep the ship nearer the point of the compass the wind blows from. This phrase was oftenest used

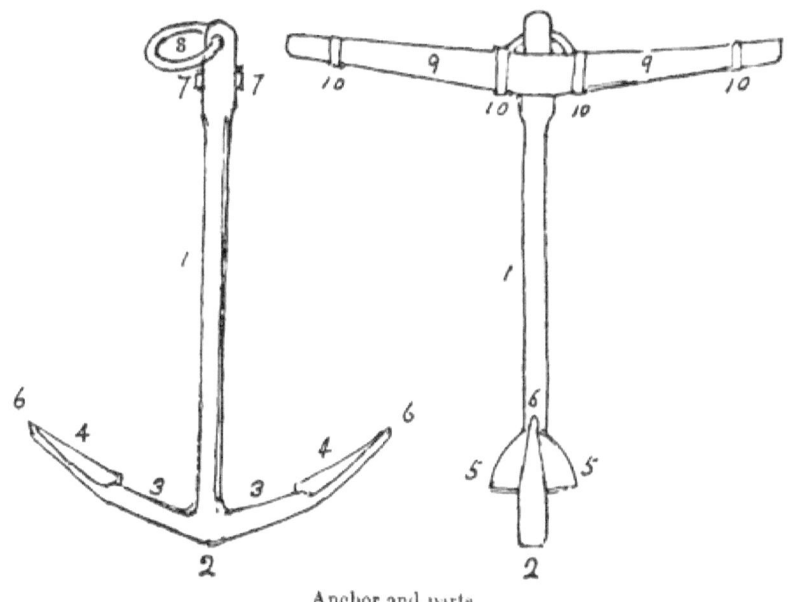

Anchor and parts.

when sailing near a lee shore, from which the pilot ordered the helmsman to keep aloof.

Amain. At once, as "Let go amain."

Anchor. Eighteenth-century anchors of any size varied little in pattern, and, being hand-forged of the finest tough charcoal iron, were light in proportion to their size, strength, and holding powers.

1. The shank. 2. The crown. 3. The arms. 4. The palms. 5. The flukes ("fluke" is an old name for the flounder, either from its resemblance to this part of an anchor or, as flounders were made before anchors, flukes, these named after the fish). 6. The bill. 7. The nuts. 8. The ring. 9. The stock, formed of two pieces of oak clamped together by the hoops, 10. An anchor was "a cock-bill" when it hung from the cat-head ready to let go. "A-peak," when the cable was hove in, so as to bring the ship over it. "A-trip," or "a-weigh," when just out of the ground.

In "Roderick Random," Lieutenant Bowling uses these terms freely in his apostrophe to Roderick's dying grandfather. "What! he's not a-weigh? How fare ye; how fare ye, old gentleman? . . . He minds me no more than a porpoise. Yes, yes, he's going; the land-crabs will have him. I see that his anchor's a-peak, faith!"

The sheet, best, and small bowers differed little in size; the stream and kedge anchors were much smaller. The chief difference between the sheet-anchor and best bowers was the way they were carried; the bower being stowed just abaft the cat-head, in the bows of the ship, while the sheet-anchor was stowed abaft the foremast, near where the rope called the fore-sheet passed into the ship. This anchor was only let go as a resource in case of losing both bowers; in French it was "L'ancre desperance." A steamer's sheet-anchors are her engines. "When things came to the worst, we always relied upon G. as our sheet-anchor."

Apron. A piece of sheet-lead tied over the touch-hole of a gun, to keep the charge dry at sea, or in wet weather. A term also used in ship and boat building for a timber wider than the stem, bolted inside it, and to which the ends of the planking forward were nailed; it was a continuation upward of the knee, or dead-wood, which connected the stem to the fore end of the keel.

A-trip, as applied to sails, meant that they were fully hoisted upon the mast.

Avast. An order to pause in any operation, as "Avast heaving there."

Awning. Any canopy over a ship's deck or boats; but in the old ships that part of the poop-deck which extended penthouse fashion beyond the doors of the poop-cabins, and sheltered the steering-wheel, binnacle, etc., was called "the awning."

Bagpipe the mizzen. A term used when the old lateen-mizzen was laid aback by hauling up the sheet to the mizzen rigging.

Bag-reef. A fourth reef in a topsail used in the navy.

Balance. To contract a sail, mostly applied to the old lateen-mizzen, by lowering the yard, and rolling up about a fifth part of the peak of the sail, and securing it to the yard. A balance-reef was a reef-band crossing a sail diagonally.

Banian days. A seaman's term for days on which no flesh meat was served. The term is derived from "Banian," a sect in India, who, believing in the transmigration of the souls of men into the bodies of animals, eat no animal food.

Bark. A three-masted vessel ship-rigged, but having no square mizzen-topsail. This term was formerly also given to a broad-sterned ship in the coal-trade, without a beak or figure-head.

Barricade. A stout rail extending across the fore end of the quarter-deck, the spaces between the post of which were filled with rope mats, cork, or pieces of old cable, and furnished with a double netting above it to hold hammocks, the whole acting as a breastwork or defence against small-arm fire for those on the quarter-deck.

Bay. A space on either side between-decks forward of the bitts in large men-of-war.

Beak-head. That part of a ship beyond the forecastle. In all the older ships of more than two decks, the forecastle was built square across the bow, from cat-head to cat-head, and the beak-head was fitted with a regular platform of grating with short step-ladders leading up from it to the forecastle, which had also ports and small doors opening upon this platform (*see* chapter on Figure-heads).

Becket. Anything used to confine loose ropes. "Put the tacks and sheets in the beckets," that is, hang up the main and fore sheet and main and fore tack to a small loop, and knot beckets on the main and fore shrouds, to keep them out of water when a ship was sailing close-hauled.

Belfry. The shelter built over the ship's great bell, always in our seventeenth-century ships a richly decorated little structure. The bell itself was usually a fixture, and was struck by a lanyard attached to the clapper.

Bend. That part of a rope which is fastened to another; also the act of fastening one piece of rope to another or any object. Bending a sail, is to attach it to its yard or stay.

Bends. The thickest planks in a ship's side, often called the wales, or wale-streaks.

Binnacle (formerly written "bittacle"). The old binnacle, besides containing the ship's compasses, and a light between them, was used as a place to stow the log-reel, line, and clip, with its half-minute glass, the log-board, and traverse-board, also the charts in immediate use, etc.

Birth, or *berth*. The place or station occupied by

Carved belfry.

a vessel at anchor in a roadstead. "A snug berth," one well sheltered from wind and sea. "He has a snug berth in the War Office." "I did not like the look of him, and gave him a wide berth," etc.

Bitts. Two strong timbers framed together upright

in the fore part of a ship's main deck, round which the cable had a turn when a vessel rode at anchor. Men-of-war usually had two pairs of cable-bitts, and when both were used, the cable was said to be double-bitted. "Bitter" meant one turn of the cable round the bitts, and the "bitter-end" was that part of the cable abaft the bitts, and therefore withinboard when a ship was at anchor; hence the term "To the bitter end." "We veered cable to the bitter-end," etc. "Bitter-end" is also used to-day among rope-makers to denote the fag or ragged end of a coil of new rope. And Mr. Pepys, in his Diary, complains of peculations, or of certain dealings in "bitter-ends," among the dockyard officials of his time. There are also topsail sheet-bitts and carrick-bitts; those that support the windlass; with the pawl-bit, which bears the strain of a short piece of iron, or pawl, working in a rack upon the windlass, and by which it is held from turning the reverse way as the cable is hove in by turning the windlass about by handspikes.

Black-strake. A broad range of planking above the wales, coated with tar and lamp-black to preserve them and form a variety contrasted with the varnished wood above them and the white colour of the ship's bottom below. Oil-paint was rarely used on board ship until the latter part of the eighteenth century, its place being taken by varnished and gilded woodwork, with here and there a bit of bright red varnished paint. And when one considers the many constructive defects so easily covered, after being filled in with putty, by a coat of oil-paint, there appears to be good sense as well as good taste in this love of what seamen call bright work kept well scraped and varnished among the old shipmen.

Boat. The boats of an eighteenth-century man-of-war consisted of the long-boat, launch, barge, pinnaces, cutters, yawls, and jolly-boat. The long-boat was the largest boat in the ship, and was fitted with masts, sails, etc., and armed for cruising; her chief employment, however, was to bring heavy stores, water, provisions, etc., on board, also to go up rivers and creeks for wood or water. The launch was longer and flatter bottomed than the long-boat, and rowed more oars, and was therefore better adapted for landing large parties of men or troops in shallow water. The barge, which would now be termed a gig, was a long narrow boat, used chiefly under oars for the conveyance of the higher officers for short distances. Pinnaces resembled the barge, but were smaller, not rowing more than eight oars; they were used chiefly by the lieutenants. Cutters were broader, deeper, and shorter than the barge or pinnaces, and better suited for sailing; they were all clench-built, or, as it was formerly called, "cutter-built;" they rowed six oars, sometimes more; when short enough to be rowed with four, a cutter was called a jolly-boat. Yawls were like pinnaces, but rowed only six oars. When a vessel had to be careened during a long cruise, far away from dockyard appliances, her larger boats were the only means by which she could be hove down, by tackles from her mast-heads, after the boats had been loaded with a large portion of her heavier stores.

Bolsters. Bags filled with tarred canvas to preserve the stays from the chafe of the masts as a ship pitched in a sea.

Bonnet. An additional piece laced to the lower edge of small vessels' sails in fine weather.

Boot-topping. The act of scraping grass, slime, barnacles, etc., from a ship's bottom, just below the water-line, and daubing or "paying" it over with a mixture of tallow, sulphur, or lime and rosin. The result when newly done was to give the bottom a smooth surface, creamy white in colour.

Bow-grace. Old junk or chain hung over the bow at the water-line to defend it from the cutting, saw-like action of thin drift-ice in a tide-way.

Bowline. A rope used when a ship is close-hauled to keep the leading edge of a squaresail rigidly taut;

hence the term "on a bow-line" for the position of a ship sailing as near the wind as possible. The bowline-knot is the same as that used for the loose end of a bowstring.

Bowline-knot.

Box-hauling. A method of wearing or turning a ship short round before the wind when, owing to a heavy head-sea, tacking was not possible, and when a ship was too near shore to veer her round in the ordinary way. Boxing-off was effected by laying the head-sails aback, when, from neglect of the helmsman, a ship had lost steerage way through being kept too near the wind.

Braces. Ropes by which the yards are turned horizontally about the masts. "Braced sharp up" is the position of the yards when they are as nearly in a line with a ship's keel as the rigging will allow them to go.

Breakers. Originally the name given by seamen to *rocks* near enough to the surface to break the swell of the sea, causing a constant roar; now mostly used for the broken top of a sea or wave.

Bream. To burn off grass and old composition from a ship's bottom. Captain Woodes Rogers, in his journal, mentions the use of a quantity of "Pope's bulls" taken out of the hold of a Spanish prize by him for this purpose.

Brig (short for brigandine). A vessel with two masts rigged like a ship's main and fore mast, except that in the brig the mainsail was attached to a yard or gaff slung fore and aft. This rig was a favourite among sea-rovers, pirates, etc., and is supposed to have taken its name from brigand (*see* Snow).

Broach-to means that when sailing before the wind the ship comes to windward of her course, and lies in the trough of the sea. Both these accidents may occur through bad steering, a very high sea, or from some accident to the rudder or sails.

Broken-backed, or *hogged*. A term for an old wooden ship when, from age, her frame is so loosened as to allow her to droop at either end. It was the custom in the French arsenals to give support, by means of shores resting upon pontoons, to the heavy overhanging sterns of their larger ships when laid up.

Brought by the lee. To fall rapidly to leeward of the proper course when sailing before the wind, so as to throw the sails aback and endanger the loss of a ship or boat by capsizing.

Buccaneers. Originally a name given to certain cannibals of the Caribbee Islands, who cut up their prisoners and spread them on hurdles with fire under them to dry and smoke the flesh, which they called "buccaning." This name was given afterwards to the early French settlers in the island of St. Domingo, who hunted wild cattle, and dried the flesh in the sun. Many of these men turned their attention to the hunting of galleons, and thus "buccaneer" became a name for all the piratical rovers infesting the coasts of Spanish America.

Bucklers. Pieces of wood fitted together to keep the sea out of the hawse-holes, but just having space sufficient between them for the cable to pass.

Bunt. The middle part of a squaresail from top to bottom; hence "buntlines," which led from the lower edge of the bunt to blocks near the middle of the yard, and were used to haul up the bunt of a sail.

Burgoo. Sea-porridge made of oatmeal.

Cable. One which measured twenty inches round contained 1943 yarns.

Cable-tier. The space in a ship's hold where her cables were stowed; used also for the space inside a cable when coiled in the tier.

Cappanus. The worm which, before the use of copper sheathing, destroyed ship's bottoms. Thin wooden sheathing, broad-headed iron nails, and sheet-lead were used to protect the planking of ships before the introduction of copper sheathing.

Capstern, or *capstan*. A, the barrel; B, the whelps (in Spanish "enfanta"); C, the drumhead, which served as reading-desk for the chaplain, etc.; D, the

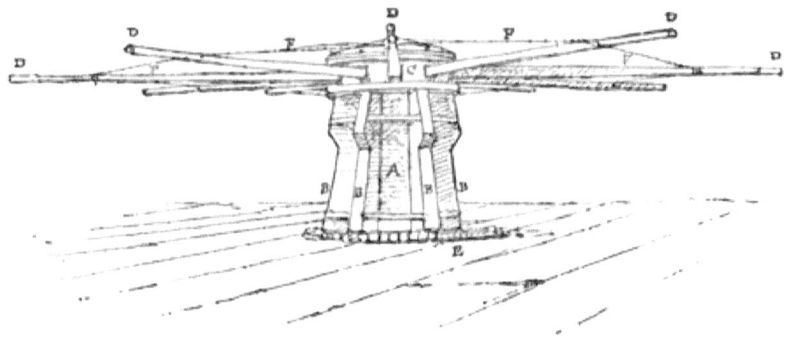

Capstan, with bars, etc.

bars; E, the pawls; and F, the swifters, or lines, connecting the ends of the bars.

Carrick-bend. The real sailor's knot, or "nœud marin" of the French.

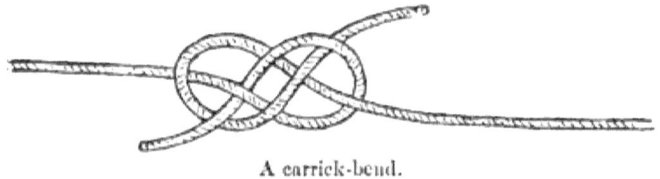

A carrick-bend.

Carrick-bitts. Those which supported a *windlass*; the use of which for heaving up an anchor was formerly confined to ships of the smaller class, or carracks.

Carry on. Often used ashore, as "Don't carry on like that," from the sea-term meaning to carry a great press of sail.

Cartridge-box. A circular wooden box to hold one

cartridge, and preserve it from damp or sparks, made with a lid sliding upon two parts of small rope.

Casting. Just before an anchor was started from the ground, in a sailing-vessel, it was often important to make sure that her head would turn, or cast, in some required direction, which was done by hauling over the sheet of a small headsail to windward at the moment the anchor lost its hold. As on shore, the decision of an equally divided assembly is settled by "a *casting* vote."

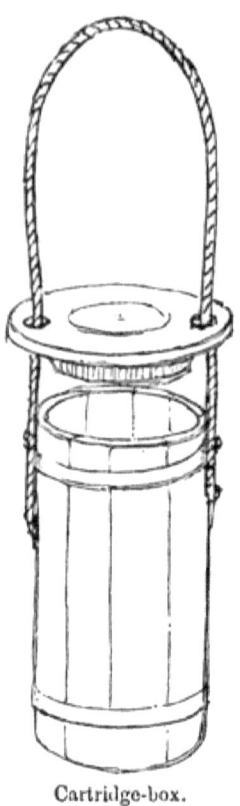

Cartridge-box.

Cat-harpings. An assemblage of ropes and tackles just abaft the lower yards for tightening the shrouds, and to allow the yards to be braced or pointed nearer the wind.

Cat-o'-nine-tails, or *the cat.* Nine pieces of line eighteen inches long, with a stout rope handle; each tail of the cat had three knots in its end. "A thieves' cat" only differed from this instrument in having larger and harder knots in the tails.

Chain-wales, or *channels.* "Wale" seems to have meant any plank on a ship's side projecting beyond the ordinary planking, as the chain-wales which extend the spread of the shrouds did, and through which the ends of the long links of the chains passed to which the shroud deadeyes were secured.

Chappelling. A ship was said to build a chapel when, without headway, she turned completely round in a light or baffling wind.

Chess-tree. A piece of wood bolted on each side of a ship, with a hole in its upper part, through which the rope called the maintack passed, by which the clew of the mainsail was extended to windward.

Choke his luff. Sea-term for "Put a spoke in his wheel." To "choke the luff" of a tackle or running purchase, meaning to stop the action of one of the blocks by jamming a loop or "bight" of the rope of the tackle across and between the other parts and the sheaves of the block. This is often done as a temporary makefast for a small fore-and-after's mainsheet, on account of the facility with which the sheet can be eased by pulling out the loop of rope which chokes the lower sheet tackle-block. The term, however, probably originated among seaman when engaged in what is now known to yachtsmen as "a luffing match;" that is, when of two vessels sailing close hauled the weathermost one is able to luff and get just far enough ahead of the other to take the wind out of her sails, and so stop her way, or "choke her luff" for a time, or as long as she can keep the leeward vessel in this position. The importance, when engaged at close quarters, of choking an enemy's luff, must formerly have been very great, as after his speed was checked in this way, it would be possible to bear away across his bows and pour in a raking broadside.

Club-haul. A method of tacking a ship when dangerously near a lee shore, or when to "miss-stay"

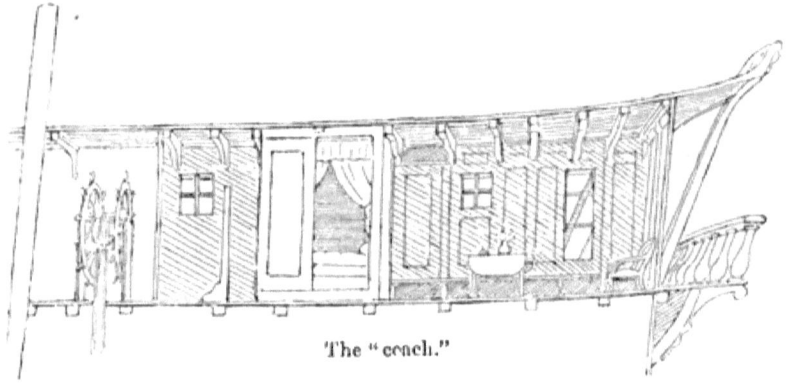

The "coach."

would be fatal to her. It was done by letting go the lee-anchor as soon as the wind was out of her sails, after which, the moment her head-sails were aback, the helm was put amidships, or shifted in case of sternway, the cable cut, and the sails trimmed upon the other tack.

Coach, or *couch.* From the ancient carrosse of the galley, an apartment in our old men-of-war and East Indiamen under the poop-deck, which sometimes contained the fourpost bedstead of the admiral or captain.

Cock-pit. A room near the after-hatch under the lower gun-deck of a man-of-war, where the wounded in action were carried and attended to by the surgeon and his mates. Smollet thus describes this place on board the *Thunder:* " My friend Thompson carried me down to the cock-pit, the place allotted for the habitation of the surgeon and his mates, and when he had shown me their berth, as he called it, I was lost with astonishment and horror. We descended by divers ladders to a space as dark as a dungeon, which was, I understood, several feet below water, being just above the hold. I had no sooner come near this dismal gulf than my nose was saluted with an intolerable stench of putrid cheese and rancid butter, that issued from an apartment at the foot of the ladder like a chandler's shop, where, by the faint glimmer of a candle, I perceived a man with a pale meagre countenance, sitting behind a kind of desk, having spectacles on his nose, and a pen in his hand. This I learned from Thompson was the ship's steward, who sat there to distribute provision to the several messes, and to mark what each received. Thompson here had my name entered in his mess, and, taking a light in his hand, conducted me to the place of his residence, a square of about six feet, surrounded by the medicine-chest, that of the first mate, and his own, and a board by way of table, fastened to the after powder-room; it was also enclosed with canvas, nailed round to the beams of the ship to screen us from cold, as well as from the view of the midshipmen and quartermasters, who lodged within the cable-tiers on each side of us. In this gloomy mansion he entertained me with some cold salt pork, brought from a locker fixed above the table, and calling the boy of the mess, sent for a can of beer, of which he made excellent flip, to crown the repast."

Commander. A large wooden mallet used on board ship.

Counter. An arch or vault terminating above the stern, and below by the wing-transom and buttocks. The second counter was above and parallel to this, but not arched, and extended from the top of the lower counter to the bottom moulding of the cabin or wardroom.

Cross-jack yard (pronounced "crojeck-yard"). The lower square-yard upon the mizzenmast, and only used to extend the mizzen-topsail sheets. The "vergue sec," dry, or barren yard of the French. An old writer speaks of a "crosstree-yard," which stood square just under the mizzen-top, to which it was fastened.

Cut and run. A sea-term meaning to cut the cable, and run off before the wind, to escape an enemy or danger, without waiting to get up the anchor; often used on shore as " He cut away at once, the moment he saw us."

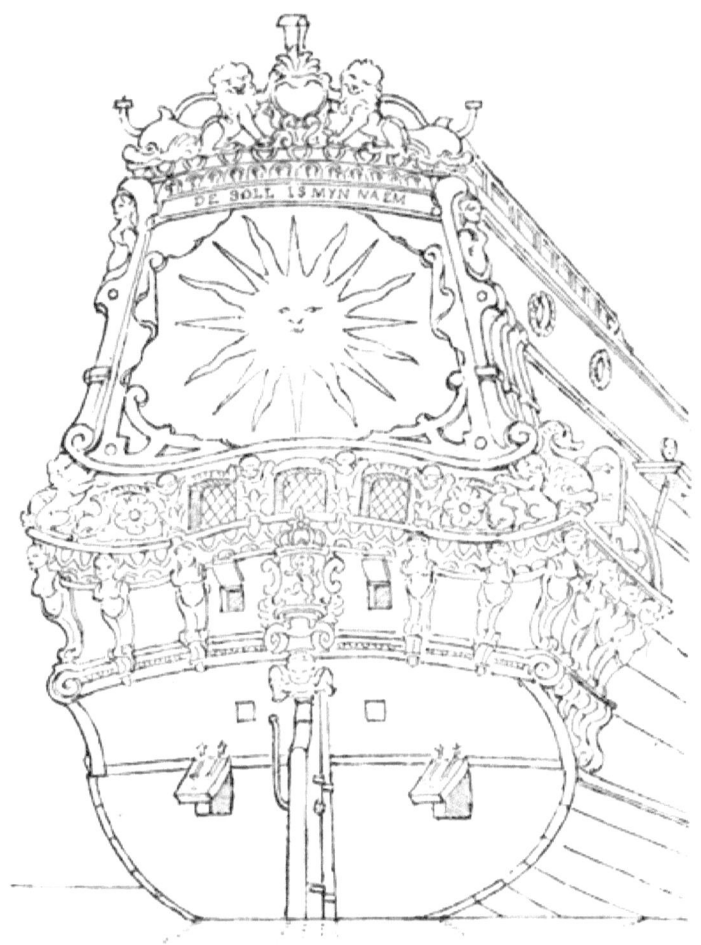

Ship's stern, counter, etc. (Vandervelde).

Cut of his jib (see page 27).

Dame-jeanne. An old French sea-name for a demijohn, a large bottle holding four or five gallons.

Damelopre. A Dutch coaster or sailing-barge, the mast of which can be lowered for passing bridges; a vessel very like our billy-boy—craft manned, as sailors have it, by father, brother, mother, and Uncle Sam.

Deadeyes. The three-holed wooden blocks through which the lanyards that connect the shrouds with the ship's side pass. The word was originally written "Deadmen's eyes," probably from the resemblance they bore to a skull.

Dead-lights. Stout ports to fit into the cabin windows in bad weather, the glass sash-frames being first removed.

Deck. A first-rate had three whole decks, reaching from stem to stern, a forecastle, and quarter-deck; the forecastle extended from the stem aft to the belfry, abaft which, on the upper-deck, between the belfry and the boats on the booms, was a space called "no-man's land," where were stowed blocks, ropes, tackles, etc., likely to be wanted on the forecastle. Over the after part of the quarter-deck was the poop-deck, which in a first-rate formed the roof, the "coach," or chaplain's cabin. The Spaniards called the quarter-deck "alcaza," a palace, castle, or fortress. Under the lower gun-deck was the orlop, where were stowed the cables, sails, etc. Other ships of the line, and some fifty-gun ships, had two gun-decks, an orlop, forecastle, quarter-deck, and poop. Frigates and sloops had one gun-deck, a half-deck, and forecastle, with a spar-deck below to lodge the crew, but no poop. Galley-built ships, brigs, cutters, etc., had no half-deck or forecastle.

Decoying. A way of diverting the attention of an

A dogger.

enemy of superior force at night, by throwing a lighted barrel of tar into the sea, and then changing your ship's course. The same stratagem was also employed by privateers to entice a vessel of inferior force within shot. It was also used sometimes by a single frigate, to induce an enemy's squadron to follow her until within view of the fleet she belonged to.

Dogger. The "dugga" of Iceland. A Dutch fishing-boat, like a ketch, used in the cod-fisheries upon the Dogger Bank.

Dog-vane. The old dog-vane was made of corks with feathers stuck in them, threaded upon a small line and fastened to the staff of a half-pike, stuck upon the weather-rail to steer by when sailing on a wind.

Dolphin. A wreath of plaited cordage round the mast, to support the puddening, and help the jeers to carry the lower yards, in case the chain slings were shot away.

Dolphin striker. (*See* Martingale.)

Double-banked. Oars were called double-banked when two men worked at one oar, or when two opposite oars were worked by two men seated on the same thwart.

Douse. To let down or slacken suddenly. "Douse the glim," to hide a lighted lantern by putting it into an empty bucket.

Drabbler. A piece of sail laced to the bottom of a sloop or schooner's squaresail.

Driver. A large sail, set at times with a free wind on the old-fashioned mizzen-yard. The foot of this sail was extended by a boom far over the taffrail, and was sometimes fitted with a jack-yard to the mizzen-peak; the fore part of the driver was laced to the mizzen-mast.

Duck up. A term used by the steersman when the mainsail, foresail, or spritsail hung in the way of his view of an object ahead; used also by those firing a bow-chase gun when the spritsail obstructed their sight.

Earring. A small rope used to fasten the upper corner of a sail to its yard; each reef in a sail has its earring or reef-earring. When reefing, the man that passed the weather earring held the place of honour.

Ease her. An order to the helmsman to put his helm a little over to leeward when meeting a very heavy sea, in order to deaden the ship's way and meet the sea more bow on.

Edge away. To gradually increase the distance between your ship and the shore, or from another ship.

Edge toward him. To-luff gently toward a ship to windward.

Elbow in the hawse. When a ship moored with two anchors has, for want of proper attention, swung twice the wrong way, and so caused her cables to take half a round turn on each other.

Ensign (originally written "ancient"). The national flag, a very large one in our old men-of-war, hoisted upon the ensign-staff astern.

Entry-port. A port cut down on the middle-deck of a line-of-battle ship as a front door.

Fall off. A ship was said to fall off, or break off so many points, when, owing to the wind heading her, the course had to be changed for the worse. "What a falling off was there."

Fathom. A sea measure of six feet, often roughly estimated by seamen as the distance from thumb to thumb when their arms were fully extended. The fathom formerly varied from six to five feet six, according to the class or size of the vessel it was used in; while, on board small fishing-boats, the "small fathom" of five feet was used.

Fights. The waist-cloths hung round a ship in action to conceal her men.

Filling a ship's bottom. Covering it with flat-headed nails to keep out the worm.

Fish-gig. A harpoon loaded with lead at the end of the staff, which, after a fish was struck, tended to turn it over.

Flag. When the flag was hoisted at the main-top-gallant mast-head, it denoted an admiral's ship; at the fore, a vice-admiral; at the mizzen, a rear-admiral. How is this arranged upon modern mastless war-ships?

Flemish-horse. The outer, or shorter foot-rope near the end of a yard, upon which the man's feet rest who passes the reef-earrings.

Flog the glass. To turn the half-hour glass, by which the ship's time was kept, too soon, or before all the sand was run through, in order to shorten the length of a watch on deck.

Foot-rope. That to which the lower edge of a sail is attached; also ropes below the yards upon which the men stand when furling or reefing sails; these are also called "horses," and pass through eyes in the ends of short ropes attached to the yards, called "stirrups," which help to support and distribute the weight of the men standing upon the horses.

Forecastle. Up to the end of the eighteenth century the forecastle was almost square on top, and fitted with breastworks fore and aft, the forward one commanding the beak-head below it, and the after one the ship's waist-deck; it was also protected on either side by the fore rigging.

Frapping a ship. Passing many turns of a rope hawser round her to strengthen her, as one would a weak box by cording it.

Frigate. This name was first given to a class of long vessels navigated in the Mediterranean under sail and oars. The English were the first to use frigates on the ocean for war or commerce.

Furling (originally written "farthel"). Squaresails are always now furled in the bunt or body of the sail;

formerly this was only done when a long stay in port was contemplated.

Futtock, or *foothook shrouds*. Short ones connecting the lower rigging with the rims of the tops, and by which seamen climb to the topmast-shrouds, without going through the lubbers'-hole in the round-top.

Galleon. Originally a name for all ships of war with three or more gun-decks, afterwards retained by the Spaniards for their larger merchantmen employed in the West India trade, and those ships, large or small, which made a yearly voyage to Vera Cruz.

Galley. One of the last boats of this name with us was an open boat of six or eight oars used by press-gangs and revenue officers on the Thames; the Deal galley and galley-punt are boats of this type. "Galley way" is a term still in use among 'longshore men in the south of England: "Give her good galley way." "Galley" is the name often given to the caboose or cook's cabin on a ship's deck.

Galliot meant formerly a small light-built galley, used for chase, with one sail and sixteen or twenty oars, the crew being all armed.

Gallows-bitts. A strong frame of timber in the form of a gallows, used to support spare topmasts, yards, booms, etc. Yarmouth luggers and many French fishing-boats are fitted with an arrangement

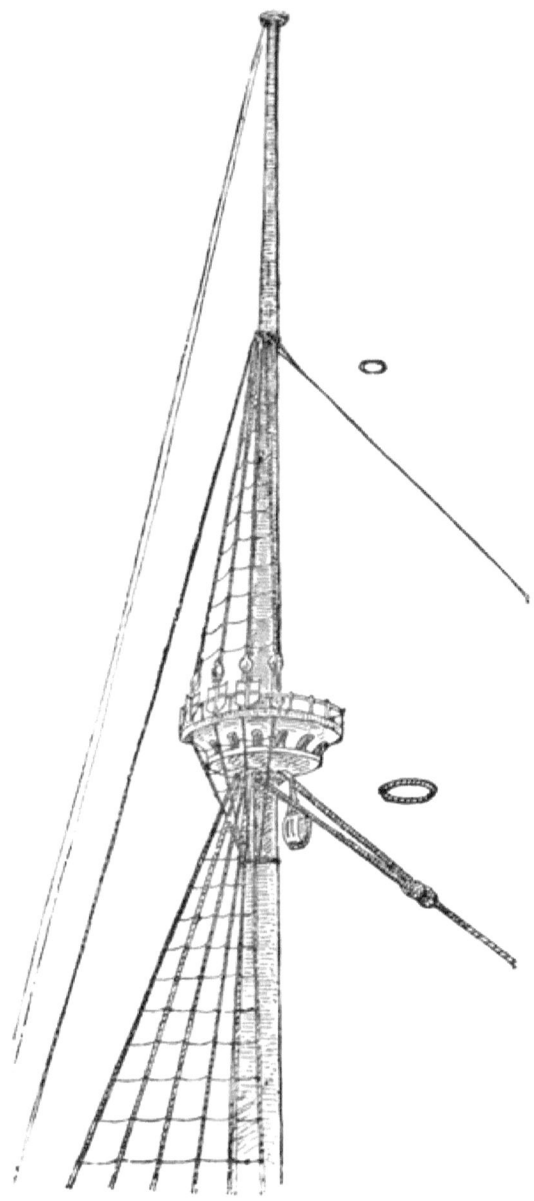

Pole-mast, top, and garlands.

of this sort, upon which the boat's mast rests, when lowered to ease the strain upon the warp, as the boat rides to her nets head to wind.

Gantlope, or *gantlet*. A very old form of sea-punishment, not unlike that sometimes inflicted to-day upon members of Parliament when they meet their constituents. In the sea form of it the offender had to run once or twice up and down a ship's deck between two rows of his own ship's company, each of whom was furnished with a knittle of twisted cord. The criminal was stripped to the waist, and was often tripped up and roughly handled in his passage, according to the character of his offence. From M. Du Chaillu, we learn that this mode of punishment at sea dates back to our Norse ancestors.

Garland. A collar of rope round a mast to support rigging, and keep it from chafing the mast. Round-tops were in use long before striking or movable topmasts were introduced, and topmasts were no doubt so named from being the masts just above the top; but in the old-fashioned pole-masted ship, the only thing that marked or divided the mast above the topmast from it was a rope garland; hence the name for this mast of "top-garland mast," the top-gallant or to-gallan-mast of more modern sailors.

Another use for the word "garland," or "garlands," was for those parts of a ship's top-sides which were pierced for small light cannon by circular ports, and which in all the old ships were decorated outside with a garland or wreath of foliage; hence, I think, the term "top-gallant forecastle," or the deck within, and bounded by the top-garlands forward.

"Garland" also was used for a rack between each

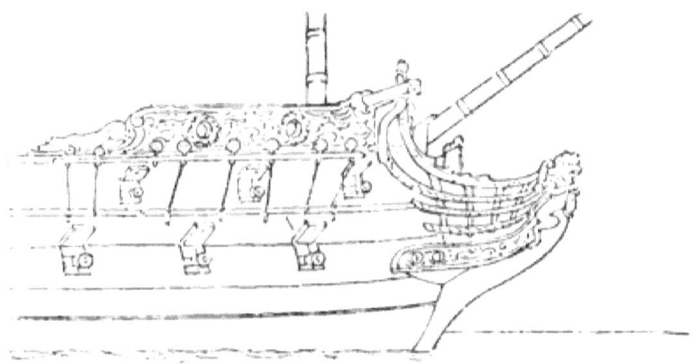

Outside of old top-gallant forecastle.

gun, and round the hatches, furnished with holes to stow shot in, and called the "shot garlands."

A garland also meant a small round net extended by a wooden hoop just big enough to hold a bowl or platter; this was hung to the beam over the table in each berth, and was used by the seamen to stow provisions in, or sometimes a bowl of flip, which swung securely in the garland when the ship was rolling at sea.

Gaskets (formerly written "caskets"). The ropes or plaited cordage bound round a sail when furled.

Goose-wings. The clews or lower corners of a main or fore sail used by old seamen to scud under when, even if reefed, the sail would be too large.

Ground-toes. Rope made of the roughest part or combings of hemp, and only fit for use ashore.

Guess-rope, guest-rope, or *gift-rope.* Any rope thrown to a boat, either to tow by or make her fast.

Ship scudding under goose-winged foresail.

Gunnel, or *gunwale.* The thick strake which bounds the top plank of a ship or boat. The lower edge of each port was also called the gunwale or wale over which a gun projected. "Port-sill" is the common or more modern term for this part of a port.

Handspike. A bar of wood used as a lever.

Hank for hank. The same as tack and tack; meaning two or more ships working their way in company to windward.

Hard up, or *hard-a-weather.* An order to put up the helm to windward, and run the ship off before a squall or gale. "He has hard up," or "He's hard up;" unable to hold his own longer to windward, etc.

Harpings. The fore part of the wales or thick planks round a ship's bows, which are stouter there than amidships (*see* Cat-harpings).

Hawse-bags. Bags of oakum to stuff up the hawse-holes in a seaway.

Horn-pipe. An old Welsh musical instrument consisting of a wooden pipe with holes in it and a horn at each end, one to collect the wind blown into it, the other to carry off the sounds as modulated by the performer; the title also of an English air and dance much used by sailors, and named after this instrument.

Hounds. Those parts of a mast-head which project and support the framework of the round-tops; the upper part of them was called the cheeks of the mast.

Housed. The position of a gun run in upon the middle or lower deck, when the port was closed, with its muzzle resting against the ship's side, above the port, and held there by tackles, muzzle-lashings, and breeching, etc. In officers' cabins a gun was at times housed fore and aft.

Howker, or *hooker*. Originally the name of a one-masted fishing-boat on the south coast of Iceland; now used for any small craft, especially those employed in line-fishing.

Hulluck. A bit of sail cut adrift in a heavy gale, usually a small part of the mizzen, to keep the ship head to sea.

Idler. Any one on board a man-of-war who, being at work all day, does not keep night-watch; but who is nevertheless expected to come on deck at any time when " all hands " is piped.

Jack. A small Union flag set on a staff on the end of the bowsprit, or upon the spritsail-topmast.

Jack in the bread-room. The purser's assistant or steward.

Jears. Tackles by which the lower yards were hoisted, very like those still in use in the lateen-rigged craft of the Mediterranean. The jear-capstan in front of the main jears was the place of punishment by flogging; but a man ordered to the main jears was at times lashed by his extended arms to a bar stuck in this capstan, and left there, with a bag of bullets hung to his neck, until he confessed some crime or mutinous plot.

Jewel-blocks. Two small ones at the extreme ends

of the main and fore topsail-yards, through which the topmast studding-sail halyards were rove; by which, also, mutineers were sometimes slung up to the yardarm.

Jury-mast, or *jury-rig*. Masts and rigging set up by a ship disabled by shot or tempest. The rig of the steamer, etc.

Keckling. Old rope, and sometimes chain, wound round a hemp cable to defend it from a rocky bottom or ice.

Keel-hauling. A Dutch sea-punishment, in which the culprit was suspended from a yardarm with a weight fastened to his legs, and another rope passing under the ship's bottom to a block on the opposite yardarm, and by which the man was let fall several times into the sea on one side of the ship, and hoisted up to the other.

Kevel-heads. The ends of top timbers left standing above the gunwale, and used to belay ropes to, etc.

Knees. Bracket-shaped timbers, cut out of large crooked limbs of oak having the grain of the wood as nearly as possible in the direction of the turn of the knee; they were used principally to connect the beams of a ship with her side timbers and planking. Hanging-knees: those fixed vertically below the ends of the deck-beams, and appearing to support them. Lodging-knees: those placed horizontally, close under the deck, with one arm bolted to a beam, the other to the side timbers. Dagger-knees were those placed somewhat askew to avoid a gun-port. Standard knees were those with one arm bolted to the deck and the other to the ship's side, or to the riding-bitts. Iron knees were used very early in the nineteenth century as a substitute for oak in the French Navy, owing to the scarcity of oak timber; later in the century it was the French who were the first to use iron outside a wooden ship, in the iron armour-plated frigate *Gloire*.

Knot. Usually a term used by seamen for a knob made on the end of a rope by untwisting the strands and interweaving them regularly into each other. It is also used for the various bends, or knots, by which ropes are tied together; such as a carrick-bend, a reef-knot, etc. A single wall-knot, called by French sailors "Le cul de porc," is the simplest form of knot upon a rope's end. A crown knot, the Frenchman's "cul de porc avec tête mort," is a single wall-knot crowned; a double-crowned wall-knot is the French "cul de porc avec tête d'alouëtte;" a granny's knot is the "le nœud de vach" of the French; a jamming knot, "nœud de bois;" and a sheep-shank, "le nœud de jamb de chien."

Langrel, or *langrage*. Bolts, nails, or other scraps

of iron, tied together, and fired at an enemy, to cut her sails and rigging; used chiefly by privateersmen.

Larbowlines. The men of the larboard or port watch.

Lasking. An old term for sailing with the wind free or on the quarter.

Lay. Used by seamen as an order to move from place to place, as "Lay aft," "Lay for'ard," "Lay in off the yard," or "Lay out on the yard," etc.

Lee-fang. An old name for the bar of iron across a deck, and upon which the sheet of a fore-and-aft sail traverses, particularly that of a cutter or schooner's foresail; it is now called a horse.

Lee-way. A ship's drift to leeward of her course, when close hauled under sail. "He will never make up his lee-way," etc.

Lifts. Ropes used to retain the yards in a horizontal position, or to top up either end when required. In the old merchant-vessels the sheets of the top-gallant-sails often formed the only lifts for the topsail-yards, in consequence of which these yards, in shortening sail, etc., fell into various angles with the mast; this is often seen in pictures by W. Vandervelde.

Light. A word often used by sailors in place of "help," or "lift," as "Light along that hawser, or chain."

Light-room. A small room with double-glass windows toward the magazine, for the gunner and his mates to see to fill cartridges by.

Limbers. Holes in the lower part of a ship's floor-timbers near the keel, forming a drain in connection with the pump-well; this channel was protected by short planks over it between each floor-timber, and had a rope or small chain passing the whole length of it, which, being pulled to and fro, loosened any accumulation of filth in it. The health of the crew of an old wooden war-ship, especially a very water-tight one, depended very much upon the state of her limber-ways, just as the healthiness of a house is dependent upon the state of its drains.

Line-of-battle. Under sail, the old line-of-battle was kept as nearly straight as possible, in order to gain and hold the advantage of a windward position, and that all the ships forming it might be on the same tack. The advantages of the weather-gauge were: 1. The ships holding it were soonest clear of smoke, and were thus able to note earlier all signals, etc., than ships obscured, not only by the enemy's smoke, but their own, could. 2. If the weather-line was the stronger one, it could at once detach vessels which, bearing down before the wind upon the rear of the enemy's fleet, would tend to throw it into disorder.

3. The fire-ships of a weather-line could, when ordered, easily bear down upon the enemy. On the other hand, the advantages of the lee-line were: 1. That in case of any ships of the weather-line being disabled, they must drive to leeward, and fall into the enemy's hands. 2. Ships of a lee-line could more readily bear away before the wind, and have their places filled by ships in reserve. 3. Ships of the lee-line could keep the ports which bore toward the enemy open longer in a strong wind and heavy sea, and fight their heavy lower-deck guns long after the ships of a weather-line would have had to shut their lower ports. 4. Those on board the lee-line had the decks, and men upon them, of the weather-line of ships, exposed to the fire of their small-arms, etc.

Lingua Franca. A patois or sea-language composed of Italian, Spanish, Arabian, and French, and used among the Levant traders; understood, also, more or less, by most of the old Mediterranean seamen.

Lintstock. A staff three feet long, with a crotch or fork to hold a lighted slow-match at one end, and having an iron point at the other, by which, when not in use, it could be stuck in the deck.

Loblolly-boy. The man who attended the surgeon and his mates to call the sick, etc. "Loblolly" was one name also for the seafaring dish of porridge, sometimes called "burgoo."

Log-board. Two boards hinged together like a book, and painted black, on which the ship's courses, etc., were written in chalk.

Logger-head. A lump of iron with a long handle, used for melting pitch, by heating it and plunging it into a pitch-pot.

Loop-holes. Slits in the bulkheads of what were called "close-quarters" in armed merchant-ships, and through which small-arms were fired upon an enemy boarding them.

Lubber's-hole. A space between the mast and the inner edge of the top, passing through which, a lubber gained the top without using the futtock-shrouds.

Magazine. A close room in the hold for powder. Large vessels had two of these: the hanging magazine aft, to hold a supply for immediate use, and the principal or fore magazine, both lighted by candles fixed in the light-room.

Mainstay. The chief forward support of the mainmast, and originally, where single, the stoutest rope in a ship's rigging. "He is still the mainstay of his party."

Manger. A space across a ship just within the hawse-holes, and cut off aft by a low bulkhead called the manger-board, which acted as a breakwater in stopping the water that found its way at times through the hawse-holes, from running aft over the main-deck, the water thus stopped being returned to the sea through the manger-scuppers.

Marline. Loosely twisted small line, usually of two strands, for securing rigging, block-strops, etc.

Marline-spike. An iron pin, tapering to a point, for separating the strands of a rope, in order to introduce the ends of another in splicing, knotting, etc.

Maroon. To leave a man ashore upon a desolate or desert island. Selkirk was marooned when left upon Juan Fernandez by Captain Straddling, of the ship *Cinque Ports.*

Martingale. A rope or ropes extended downward from the jibboom-end by a kind of bumpkin below the bowsprit-cap, and called sometimes the dolphin-striker; the martingale acted as a bobstay does to the bowsprit, to keep the jibboom down and resist the upward pull of the jib. The name is evidently taken from the martingale used to prevent a horse tossing up his head.

Match-tub. Tubs made of small casks cut in half, and having scores in the brims to hold lighted slow-matches or port-fires for firing the guns; the bottom of the tub had water in it to extinguish sparks from the port-fires hung round it. In the Naval

Museum at Venice, there is preserved a more elegant form of match-tub of copper, in shape not unlike a small font, standing upon a richly decorated bronze pedestal, the top of which is made to revolve upon the base, and is surmounted by an open-worked copper cover. This elaborate form of match-tub was used on board a seventeenth-century galley.

Messenger. A lighter and more flexible rope than the cable, used to transmit the power of the capstan to it in getting up the anchor (*see* Nippers).

Midship-beam. The longest in the ship, and that from which, as a standard, the lengths of all her spars were taken.

Mizzen, misen, or *misson.* The aftermost sail in a ship, and, in its original lateen form, a far more important sail than the smaller one, now called the spanker, which superseded it. The old form of mizzen could be laid aback, and in this position formed one means by which a ship was able to keep a strain on her cable when swinging round at the turn of a tide, etc. The command, "Change the mizzen," meant shift the yard to the other side the mast. "Peak the mizzen," was to hoist the peak up in a line with the mast, which had to be done before changing it over.

Mouse. A knob or knot worked on a stay to prevent the eye slipping up to the mast-head.

Navel-hood, or *whood*. Thick timbers round the hawse-holes.

Nippers. Pieces of rope, five or six of which were used at once to connect the cable with the messenger or voya, as it was hove in by the capstan; they had to be constantly shifted as the cable came aft, and carried forward again by certain boys of the ship, also called "nippers"—a word still often used by sailors or 'longshore men for boys of a certain age.

No-man's-land. A space just abaft the belfry (*see* Deck).

Off and on. When a ship, in turning to windward, comes in with the land on one tack, and stands out to sea on the other, she is said to stand off and on. "Nothing off," a command not to let a ship fall off her course when sailing by the wind.

Over-rake. A sea "over-raked a ship" when, in riding at anchor, one broke over her bows. The rake of a ship is the curve formed by her upper works, or her rise fore and aft, also called her sheer.

Over-reach. To sail longer upon a tack, in turning to windward, than is necessary in order to "fetch," or reach, a given point. "He has held on too long and over-reached himself; had he tacked sooner he would have done better." Lawyers and stockbrokers do this at times on shore; the latter, for instance, when they hold on too long to some stock.

Outriggers. Strong beams projecting beyond the sides of a ship on the careen, to counteract the strain upon her rigging, masts, etc.

Packet. A vessel appointed by Government to carry mails and expresses in the quickest way.

Palm. The sailmaker's and seaman's thimble; a small round lump of iron securely fixed in thick

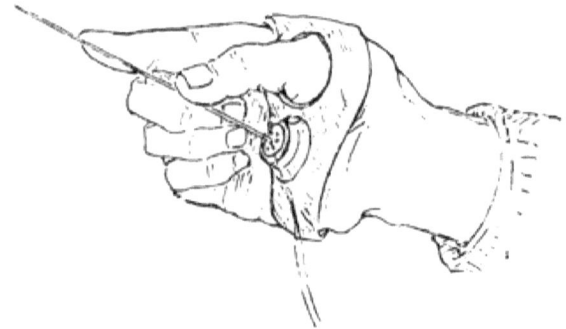

Palm, or sailor's thimble.

leather, made to fit the palm of the hand, and by which a strong roping-needle, about four inches long, can be driven through several thicknesses of canvas and an inch of rope almost as quickly, and quite as regularly, as a lady does her needle through the hem of a cambric handkerchief.

Parliament-heel. Careening a ship sufficiently to clean the upper planks of her bottom, and coat them with fresh composition. Was it a cant sea-term for "eye-service," good enough to please the parliament or people?

Partners. Strong timbers worked round spaces in a deck which receive masts, capstans, etc.; a name also for the spaces.

Passaree. A rope to hold the tacks nearer the ship when running before a light breeze.

Pay. To cover with tar, pitch, tallow, or varnish. "There was the devil to pay, and no pitch hot." The latter part of this phrase is sometimes omitted; but, when complete, the words allude to the fact that, after caulking with oakum, a ship's seams were at once "payed" over with melted pitch, which was always done, if possible, before any water came near them. Of course, with a long length of caulker's work ready, or waiting for pitch, there would be the devil to pay, etc.

Pendants (pronounced "pennants"). Short strong ropes hanging under the tops on either side the masts, with an eye in the end, into which tackles were hooked for hoisting in heavy matters. There were many of these, such as the fish-tackle pendant for fishing or hoisting an anchor to the cat-head, yard-tackle, pendants, etc. Rudder-pendants were strong ropes made fast by chain to the rudder outside the ship, to lift it if required, or prevent its loss if accidentally unshipped.

Pillow. A block of timber supporting the inner end of a bowsprit.

Pink. A narrow or "lute-sterned" vessel; the elliptical stern of modern ship-builders.

Plunder. A name given by the captors to the personal property of the officers, passengers, and crew of a prize.

Plying. Making way by tacking.

Polacca. A vessel whose masts are in one piece. The yards of a polacca are without foot-ropes below them for the men to stand on in reefing or furling, as they come near enough together when lowered for the men to reach the yard above them when standing upon the yard below it.

Pole-axe. A short-handled hatchet, having a sharp point curving downward from the back of the head; called also a boarding-axe.

Pomiglion. A name given by sailors to the cascable or knob at the breech of a gun.

Poop Royal. A short deck above the after part of the poop in large French and Spanish men-of-war, serving as a cabin for the master or pilot. This deck was known among our shipwrights and seamen as the top-gallant poop (*see* Garlands, etc.).

Port-last, or *portoise*, meant the same as "gunwale." "Lower the yards a-port-last," *i.e.* down to the gunwale. "To ride a-portoise," or "a-port-last," that is, with lower yards struck in a gale.

Powder-chests. Small boxes filled with powder, old nails, etc., placed on the decks of merchantmen that had close-quarters, and have a train of powder leading to the quarters below it, so that it could be exploded like a mine among boarders on the upper deck.

Priming-iron. A wire, or long needle, used for piercing the cartridge in a gun through the touch-hole; used also as a rammer to charge the touch-hole with powder.

Pump. The most powerful of the older forms of ship's pumps was the chain-pump, with which two men could discharge a ton of water in fifty-five seconds.

Quarter-cloths. Canvas, usually painted red, extended outside the quarter-nettings from the quarter-galleries to the gangways.

Quarter-master. An inferior officer who helped the mates (navigating lieutenants) in their duties, such as stowing the hold, coiling cables (a most important matter then), attending to the steering and keeping the time by the watch-glasses.

Quoin. The means used to elevate the breech of a gun, consisting of one or more wooden wedges.

Rails. Narrow planks, carved as decorations, and

nailed on parts of a ship's upper works, such as the drift-rails, fife-rails, quarter-rails—these last serving as a fence to the poop and quarter-deck; the sheer-rails and waist-rails formed the fence amidships; the rails of the head, also richly decorated timbers, extended from the bow to the forward end of the beak-head, which they help to strengthen.

Rate. Before the introduction of ironclads, rams, turret-ships, and big guns, men-of-war were all classed or rated according to their number of guns, and men wanted to work them and the ship. Thus, a first-rate included all ships of 100 guns and over, with crews of 850 to 875 men; the second-rate, ships of from 90 to 98 guns, with 700 to 750 men. Third-rates were ships of 80 to 64 guns, with 650 to 500 men. All ships of these three rates were called "ships of the line." Fourth-rates were ships of 60 to 50 guns, with 420 to 380 men. Fifth-rates were ships of 44 guns to frigates of 32 guns, and 300 to 200 men. Sixth-rates included ships of 30 to 20 guns, with 200 to 160 men; this rate, and all above it, ranked as "post-ships," and were commanded by post-captains. Vessels of less than 20 guns were styled commanders and masters; these included all vessels of from 18 to 6 guns, such as corvettes, brigs, schooners, sloops, and cutters. The date of these rates is 1788.

Ratlins. Lines worked across the shrouds as rope-ladders. To "rattle down" was to fix these to the shrouds.

Relieving-tackles were those used to assist in bringing a ship upright after careening, also to prevent her oversetting during the operation.

Repeating-ship. Usually a frigate, which attended a fleet, and repeated each signal made by the admiral, by sailing at once the length of the squadron if the signal was general, or to any particular ship it was intended for, but always returning at once to the admiral.

Rogues-yarn. A rope-yarn differing in colour from the strands of the rope, and twisted in the reverse way, used in the Navy to mark the king's cordage and cables from that of the merchant-service.

Room. This word, which, according to M. Du Chaillu, was used by the Vikings for the space in their ships or boats between each thwart—"Erling Skjalgison had his large skeid, it had thirty rooms, and was well manned"—is in everyday use among fishermen in the west of England in exactly the same sense. "Room and space," is a term also used by naval architects for the distance when set up from timber to timber.

Rope-bands or *robands.* Plaited line by which a sail was tied to its yard.

Rough-tree-rail. A yard or boom placed above the sail amidships as a guard for men passing from the forecastle to the quarter-deck; generally applied to a rough spar with the bark on.

Round-house. A name given in East Indiamen, etc., to any deck-house or cabin, built on the after part of the quarter-deck, and sometimes called the "coach" in men-of-war. But from an old engraving, date 1740, of "the internal parts of a ship of 96 years, having her side cut off to lay her open," it appears that in our larger men-of-war there was an apartment called "the round-house," under the poop-deck and above the main-deck, which was really circular.

Row-ports. Square holes in the bulwarks of small men-of-war between each gun-port, for long oars or sweeps to pass through.

Royal. A sail set upon the pole of the top-gallant-mast, and originally called the "top-gallant-royal."

Saddle. Small cleats upon the lower yardarms, on which the studding-sail boom-ends rest.

Saic. A Grecian ketch without a mizzen-topsail.

Sally-port. A large one in each quarter of a fire-ship, from which her crew escaped in their boats the moment the train was lighted.

Samson's-post. The one close to a hatch with scores in, used as a ladder for those entering or leaving the hold. The name given also to a strong timber placed in a sloping position with one end on the deck, the upper one resting against a beam, and used to make fast a block as a lead for a tackle.

Sciatic-stay. One fixed between the main and fore mast-heads of merchant-ships, for heaving cargo, etc., in and out of the main-hatch.

Scuppers. Holes lined with lead in what are called the waterways, to free a deck from rain or sea-water.

Scuttle. Any square hole in a ship's deck.

Scuttle-butt. A cask with a square hole in it, kept on deck to hold the water in daily use.

Seize. In sea language, to tie up, bind, or make-fast with rope-yarn.

Settee. A Mediterranean craft of two lateen-sails.

Shackles. Irons sliding upon a round bar upon a ship's deck, by which the legs of prisoners were confined to it.

Shallop. A large boat, usually schooner-rigged.

Sheep-shank. A knot by which a rope was shortened temporarily.

Sheep-shank knot.

Sheer. The longitudinal curve of ship's side or deck.

Sheet. A rope attached to one or both lower clews of a sail to extend it in a particular direction. "Three sheets in the wind," not quite drunk or sober; a term applied to a man in this state, when he moves in an uncertain way, as a ship does which has been allowed to come so near the wind that her three chief sails are all shaking. If kept too long in this position, a ship was apt to what sailors term "get in irons," from which she was boxed off by bracing her foreyards aback, etc.

Shoe. An anchor was shod at times by fixing stout triangular boards to each palm to increase its holding power in very soft ground. The name also for a small block of wood fitted to the point of an anchor fluke, to prevent it injuring a ship's bow when being raised or lowered.

Shot of a cable. Two cables spliced together.

Skeet. A long scoop for wetting the sides of a ship in hot weather, or the sails of small craft in light winds, to render them more airtight, etc.

Skiff. A small boat, the skied of the Norseman.

Skin of a sail. That part of it into which the body of it is gathered, and which covers the bunt when furled.

Sky-scraper. Little triangular sails, sometimes set above royals.

Slab-line. A small one used to trice up the lower part of a main or fore sail, when it interfered with the helmsman's view.

Slatch. A period of weather usually applied to the duration of a light passing breeze longer and stronger than a cat's-paw.

Slip. To let the end of a cable run out after buoying it, in order to leave an anchorage quietly and quickly without getting up the anchor; done either to escape an enemy, or when on a lee shore there was not time to get the anchor. "He gave us the slip after all."

Slops. Sailor's clothes, etc., supplied at a certain price by the purser to the crew of a man-of-war.

Smoke-sail. A small one hoisted on the foremast when at anchor head to wind, to keep the smoke from the galley blowing aft.

Snotter. A wreath or gromet upon the mast of a spritsail-rigged craft to support the lower end of the sprit.

Snow. The rig often now called a brig.

Sounding. Finding the depth of water by means of a lead-line. Owing to want of time, not so often used now as formerly. "I sounded him upon that subject."

Sounding-rod. An iron rod, marked in feet and

inches, which, after being well chalked, was lowered down a groove in one of the pumps to ascertain the amount of water in the pump-well. Wooden ships were seldom quite tight; an iron one, of course, should be. Constant use of a sounding-rod in an old leaky ship during a long cruise, has been known to increase the evil for which it was used as a gauge; the iron rod itself having slowly, but surely, pounded a hole through the bottom of the pump-well, and made a leak not easy to detect directly under the pump.

Spanker. A name given to a ship's driver or mizzen.

Splice. Joining two ropes by untwisting the ends and inserting them between the strands of each rope; the first part of this work was called "marrying the ends."

Splice the main-brace. A cant term for a drink all round.

Splinter-netting. Nets nailed up on the inside of a ship to catch and deaden the effect of splinters in action.

Standing-rigging. All that which, like the stays, shrouds, etc., never moves or travels through a block; the part of a rope-tackle made fast to a mast or deck; is also called the standing part, in French "dormant," or sleeping part, as a distinction from the fall, or running part, which is hauled upon.

Standing to, or *from*, an object at sea means the motion of a ship sailing to or from it.

Stay-tackle. One or more upon the mainstay of a man-of-war, for hoisting in boats, etc.

"*Steady the helm!*" Keep the ship as she goes.

Stocks. We still sometimes speak of a ship-builder having "so many vessels on the stocks," though this primitive foundation for a ship or boat has, so far as vessels of any size are meant, been replaced for centuries by blocks of timber laid transversely to the line of a ship's keel. But in the west of England, and no doubt elsewhere, there are boat-builders who still use stout slabs of timber, or "stocks," firmly fixed upright in the ground, in a line a few feet apart, and with spaces cut in the top of each post or stock to receive and hold the keel of a boat. This kind of foundation is now, however, only used for clench work, which requires the keel in the early stages of such work to be firmly cleated or held in place, in order to withstand the force used in bending, shoring, and fitting the planking of the boat's bottom to it. In carvel, or smooth work, the frames or ribs of the ship are all put in place upon the keel before any of the lower planking is nailed to them, and their weight is quite sufficient to hold the keel firmly in place on the *blocks* during the work of planking. Now, as all the remains of Viking ships hitherto found are those of clench-built vessels or boats, it would appear that this term, "on the stocks," must have been left among us by our Norse ancestors; for clench work, as I have said elsewhere, seems to be very much confined to English or Scandinavian boat-builders, and rarely if ever adopted by those of the Latin races.

Stoppers. Short pieces of rope, knotted at one or both ends, used for various purposes. Cable-stoppers, or deck-stoppers, had a large knot and lanyard at one end, and were fastened to a ring-bolt on the deck, and attached by the lanyard to the cable, which they held securely when a ship rode at anchor. A dog-stopper was a stout rope clenched round the mainmast, and used to help these deck-stoppers in bad weather. A wing-stopper was the same thing, but clenched to a timber at the side of a ship.

Stretch. A term used often in the same sense as tack; as, "We made a long stretch out to sea."

Strike. A sea-term for lowering anything from aloft in a ship, as "Strike the topmasts," "He struck his colours." Sailors also speak of striking guns or casks into the hold; etc.

Studding-sails. Light sails extended beyond the

sides of squaresails in steady breezes and fair winds; called also by the old seamen "goose-wings." They have gone out of use lately in many large sailing-vessels.

Swabber. A man appointed to dry the decks with swabs. There were also men called swab-wringers, swabber's-mates, etc.

> "The master, the swabber, the boatswain and I."
> SHAKESPEARE'S *Tempest*.

Swifter. (*See* Capstan.)

Tabling. A broad hem round sails.

Tally-aft. An order to haul aft the main or fore sheets.

Tartan. A small one-masted lateener.

Taunt. In sea-language, high, or tall.

Thus. An order to keep a ship's head as it was when sailing close-hauled.

Timoneer. The helmsman.

Toggle. A short wooden pin tapering toward the ends, used with an eye, in connecting the ends of ropes. In the old men-of-war, toggles were often fixed in the running parts of topsail-sheets and the jears that hoisted the lower yards in such a way that, if the rope was cut by shot, the toggle kept it from running through the blocks, and so kept the yard from falling or the sheets from flying adrift.

Top-lantern. A large one carried in the after part of the top of a ship flying an admiral's flag, or in any leading ship of a fleet or convoy.

Top-armour. A rail three feet high abaft the tops, fitted with nettings for hammocks, the whole in action being covered with red baize or painted canvas.

Touch-and-go. When a ship scrapes over a shoal-ground without actually stopping, she is said to touch and go. "It was touch-and-go with him."

Transom. Beams across the stern-post which support the frame of the stern.

Trice. To hoist up anything quickly; used ashore as a noun, "In a trice."

Trim. The state of a vessel's sails, ballast, etc., upon which her speed and seaworthiness depends. "He appeared in good trim," now rather out of date ashore, the modern land sporting-term "form" having very much superseded it.

Trowsers. It is curious to read in the "Midshipman's, or British Mariner's Vocabulary," of 1801, how these now almost universal coverings for the legs of landsmen were then defined as "a sort of loose long breeches mostly worn by persons on shipboard" (*see* page 201).

Trunk, or *Tabernacle.* Three strong upright timbers or planks, built up from the keelson of a vessel, and for some distance above her deck, to receive the heel of a mast, in such a way that it could be lowered aft on deck if required. Fire-trunks were wooden funnels placed under the shrouds of a fire-ship to carry the flames to the masts and rigging.

Trying. The position, often a very trying one, of a ship endeavouring to hold her own against a head-wind and sea under storm-canvas.

Tuck. That part of a ship where the ends of her bottom planks were gathered together below the stern or counter.

Tye. A stout rope passing through a sheave in a mast-head, and used to transmit the power of a tackle to a yard or gaff. The way in which this tye is "clapped on," *i.e.* attached to the block of the tackle used by our Deal boatmen for hoisting their lugsails, is exactly the same as that used by Spanish fishermen for the tye-block of their heavy lateen-yards.

Vangs. Ropes extending from the mizzen-peak to each quarter. The sprit-mainsail of a Thames barge is provided with a very stout pair of vangs to steady it and keep it from sagging too far over to leeward.

Veer. To turn a ship before the wind.

Viol. Another name for the messenger, probably from its passing through a large block, not unlike a bass-viol in size and shape, which was called a viol-block, and was lashed to the mainmast as a lead for the messenger (*see* Messenger).

Waft. A signal made from the stern of a ship by hoisting the ensign, tied up into a long roll, to the top of the staff or to the mizzen-peak, used especially as a signal of recall for boats.

Waist-cloths. The tarpaulin coverings of the hammocks stowed in the waist-nettings.

Waisters. Men, usually the strongest landsmen, employed on the waist-deck in working ship, having little else to do but pull and haul ropes.

Wales. Thick planks going the whole length of a ship. The "main-wales," those below the line of lower-deck posts. The "channel-wales," or "chain-wales," those between the top of the lower-deck posts and the bottom of those of the upper deck.

Whip. A tackle, or lead, formed of a rope and single stationary block, or of one fixed and another movable block; used mostly for hoisting light bodies quickly. The "whip-staff" was probably so named from a tackle of this kind being used in connection with it and the tiller.

Whip-staff. A piece of wood attached to the helm or tiller, and held by the steersman. Before the introduction of the more modern steering-wheel, about the beginning of the eighteenth century, the connection between a big ship's long tiller, which came in upon her lower deck, was made by means of an upright staff connected with the tiller, and passing up to the steerage or space under the fore-part of the quarter-deck. How this long vertical staff acted upon the tiller in ships of two or more decks, is not very clear, unless it took the form of a Spanish windlass, acting upon the tiller by means of tackles upon the lower deck; the upper end of the staff being then turned about by a smaller cross-bar passing horizontally through it. In many small vessels, like the Thames barge or Dutch galliot, still steered by large tillers, the upright pin or handle which passes through the end of the tiller is evidently a rudimentary form of the old whip-staff.

Winding a call. Piping an order through a boatswain's whistle.

Windlass. This machine for heaving up an anchor was formerly used only in merchant-vessels or carracks, a general name for the smaller single-decked class of old sea-going ships; hence I believe the name carrick-bitts, given to the stout timbers supporting the windlass.

Wingers. Small casks stowed close to the side of a ship's hold where larger ones would raise the tier of casks too high. The hold of a modern ship, being almost flat or level, does not require this arrangement.

Worming. Winding small rope spirally about a cable or rigging so as to fill the interval between the strands in order that what was called the "service" might lie smooth and round over it.

Xebec. A small three-masted vessel of the Mediterranean, which in fine weather, with a fair wind, carried one or two very large squaresails; these, when close-hauled, were replaced by large lateen-sails, which in turn made way for smaller ones in foul weather. Great overhang, both of prow and stern, was a marked feature of the xebec, which usually mounted from sixteen to twenty-four guns, with from three to four hundred and fifty men.

FINIS.

www.ingramcontent.com/pod-product-compliance
Lightning Source LLC
Chambersburg PA
CBHW032047220426
43664CB00008B/896